The Information Revolution
and World Politics

NEW MILLENNIUM BOOKS IN INTERNATIONAL STUDIES

SERIES EDITORS
Eric Selbin, Southwestern University
Vicki Golich, California State University, San Marcos

FOUNDING EDITOR
Deborah J. Gerner, University of Kansas

NEW MILLENNIUM BOOKS issue out of the unique position of the global system at the beginning of a new millennium in which our understandings about war, peace, terrorism, identity, sovereignty, security, and sustainability—whether economic, environmental, or ethical—are likely to be challenged. In the new millennium of international relations, new theories, new actors, and new policies and processes are all bound to be engaged. Books in the series are of three types: compact core texts, supplementary texts, and readers.

EDITORIAL BOARD

Titles in the Series
Global Backlash edited by Robin Broad
Globalization and Belonging by Sheila Croucher
The Global New Deal by William F. Felice
Sword & Salve by Peter J. Hoffman and Thomas G. Weiss
International Law in the 21st Century by Christopher C. Joyner
Elusive Security by Laura Neack
The New Foreign Policy by Laura Neack
Negotiating a Complex World, 2nd ed., Brigid Starkey, Mark A. Boyer, and Jonathan Wilkenfeld
Global Politics as if People Mattered by Mary Ann Tétreault and Ronnie D. Lipschutz
Military-Civilian Interactions, 2nd ed., by Thomas G. Weiss
The Information Revolution and World Politics by Elizabeth C. Hanson

The Information Revolution and World Politics

Elizabeth C. Hanson

ROWMAN & LITTLEFIELD PUBLISHERS, INC.
Lanham • Boulder • New York • Toronto • Plymouth, UK

ROWMAN & LITTLEFIELD PUBLISHERS, INC.

Published in the United States of America
by Rowman & Littlefield Publishers, Inc.
A wholly owned subsidary of The Rowman & Littlefield Publishing Group, Inc.
4501 Forbes Boulevard, Suite 200, Lanham, Maryland 20706
www.rowmanlittlefield.com

Estover Road, Plymouth PL6 7PY, United Kingdom

British Library Cataloguing in Publication Information Available

Library of Congress Cataloging-in-Publication Data
Hanson, Elizabeth C.
 The information revolution and world politics / Elizabeth C. Hanson.
  p. cm.—(New millennium books in international studies)
 Includes bibliographical references and index.
 ISBN-13: 978-0-7425-3852-8 (cloth : alk. paper)
 ISBN-10: 0-7425-3852-4 (cloth : alk. paper)
 ISBN-13: 978-0-7425-3853-5 (pbk. : alk. paper)
 ISBN-10: 0-7425-3853-2 (pbk. : alk. paper)
 1. Communication in politics—Technological innovations. 2. Information
technology—Political aspects. 3. Mass media—Political aspects. 4. World politics—
1989– I. Title.
 JA85.H37 2008
 303.48'33—dc22   2007032569

Printed in the United States of America

∞™ The paper used in this publication meets the minimum requirements of
American National Standard for Information Sciences—Permanence of Paper
for Printed Library Materials, ANSI/NISO Z39.48-1992.

To my mother,
whose simple acts of compassion
made this world a better place

Contents

Preface

New information and communication technologies are transforming the context in which international relations are conducted. More people have access to more diverse sources of information than ever before, as well as a greater capacity to influence national and international agendas. More transcontinental channels of contact are available to more people in the world at far less cost than could have been imagined even a few years ago. The information revolution is a pervasive feature of the world today, yet its effect on world politics is a subject fraught with controversy. What is the impact of the information revolution on diplomacy, foreign policymaking, and the conduct of war? How are these new technologies affecting the structure of the global economy and the distribution of the world's wealth? How and to what extent are they affecting the nation-state's centrality in the international system, its sovereignty, and its relationship to its citizens?

This book examines controversies over the impact of the information revolution on world politics as part of a larger set of debates over globalization and the role of technology in historical change. Considerable attention is given to the origins of the information revolution and to the development of the technologies that have transformed the context of world politics. This historical perspective informs the analysis of controversies over the present and future impact of a radically new information and communications environment. Case studies and evidence from relevant research provide a basis for evaluating the contending arguments. I hope that the focus on these issues will generate both interest and further debate.

Writing about a revolution while it is still in progress is a challenge. Significant technological, economic, political, and social changes have occurred during the time frame in which I struggled to write this book. As a subject, the information revolution is all-encompassing, complex, and dynamic. Many relevant topics and issues have not been included. Some facts and examples will be dated or obsolete by the time the book is in the hands of readers. It would have been easier to focus on a single technology, such as the Internet, or some aspect of the transformation, such as the implications for the global economy. The book does devote considerable attention to the spread of satellite television and the Internet, but it is most concerned with the collective impact of many new technologies and innovations on world politics. The underlying assumption is that an effort to present the "big picture" is valuable, regardless of the compromises that might entail.

I am grateful to Jennifer Knerr, who first encouraged me to write this book, and to Susan McEachern for helping me to bring it to a conclusion. I would like to take this opportunity to pay a special tribute to Deborah (Misty) Gerner, an exemplary scholar, teacher, and human being. As the series editor for the New Millennium Books in International Studies before her untimely death, Misty provided valuable suggestions for the book. I also owe a debt of gratitude to the staff of the Joan Shorenstein Center on the Press, Politics, and Public Policy at the John F. Kennedy School, Harvard University, and to my research assistants there. The intellectual exchange that took place during my fellowship at the center played an important role in the direction of my research. Two Fulbright Awards in India further stimulated my interest in that remarkable country, which is used as a case study several times in this book. I wish to thank all those friends and colleagues in India who continue to inform my work with their knowledge and insights. Finally, I am deeply grateful to my husband, Ken, who took time out from the writing of his book on the Himalayas to help me make sense of this complex topic.

CHAPTER ONE

⌐

The Information Revolution

Technology has an inherent "bias," for it can never be neutral or independent of society's broader social and political biases. At the same time,
however, its potency makes it invariably the site and stake of struggle,
the outcome of which is never preordained.

—Andrew Gillespie and Kevin Robins[1]

On August 11, 2006, a website called Ana al-Muslim carried this message:
"The people of jihad need to carry out a media war that is parallel to the military war and exert all possible efforts to wage it successfully. This is because
we can observe the effect that the media have on nations to make them either support or reject an issue."[2] In fact, an array of new information and
communication technologies (ICTs) is affecting not only the relations of nations in war and peace but also human activity at every level and, indeed, the
nation-state system itself. The impact of these technologies is so profound
and pervasive that it is no exaggeration to claim that an information revolution is taking place.

Although this "revolution" is the product of a long evolutionary process
of innovation and modification, it has certain characteristics that suggest a
sharp break with the past. The most obvious change is simply the abundance
of information available and the variety of sources from which it can be obtained. Equally remarkable is the number and variety of communication
channels and, especially, the reduction in the time and cost for communicating over great distances. The combination of digitization (which converts

1

all signals into 1s and 0s) with satellite technology allows messages, pictures, data, or any other form of information to be transmitted almost instantly to any part of the world that can receive the electronic signals at ground stations. More than two hundred communication satellites now cover most of the earth with their "footprints." These technical innovations, in addition to the advent of small, portable video cameras and mobile satellite hookups for recording and transmitting news from the field, have spurred the growth of what are loosely called the "live global media," which broadcast news of events as they happen in multiple regions of the world.

ICTs have not only proliferated and diffused at an unprecedented rate of speed, but they have also converged. Digital technology enables information to be easily transmitted from one medium to another—from a digital camera, for example, to the Internet or to television—quickly. The former distinctions between the mass media, computers, and telecommunications are eroding as computers—linked together through telephone lines, cable, and satellites—store, process, and transmit information. Newspapers and magazines, the more time-bound media, now publish versions on the Internet with updated news. Television, which typically has given little time to analysis of the news in the past, now supplements on-air broadcasts with information and analysis online. While satellites make possible a global mass audience to witness simultaneously live events, other technologies are customizing the media and fragmenting the audience. Audio and video cassettes, and to an increasing extent computers, provide programs on demand. The development of cable and direct broadcast television by satellite has encouraged the growth of television channels and the shift toward targeted, segmented audiences (narrowcasting). As summarized by Manuel Castells, in his masterful analysis of the information age, "The emergence of an electronic communication system characterized by its global reach, its integration of all communication media, and its potential interactivity is changing and will change forever our culture."[3]

The new technologies affect us as individuals: our ability to accomplish our personal and political objectives, our relationship with government, and the way we perceive and interact with the rest of the world. We can watch wars, famines, coups, and other events unfold as they occur; obtain information on virtually any topic at the touch of a mouse button; read newspapers from countries in remote parts of the world; send and receive messages instantly by a choice of means; and mobilize other individuals to support our worthy causes.

The information revolution also affects governments: their ability to control the information that crosses their borders, the scope of their policy concerns, the speed of decision making, the transparency of their actions, and the way they conduct their relations with other countries. The new technologies have transformed the world's production and distribution processes and have been a major force in the emergence of a global economy. Global networks of communication make transnational activities of all kinds easier and cheaper, creating more opportunities for non–territorially based activities, communities, and identities.

World Politics in a New Media Environment

The technologies that transmit knowledge, wealth, and values across national boundaries have enormous implications for three central concerns of the study of international relations: (1) diplomacy, war, and peace; (2) the structure of the global economy and the distribution of the world's wealth; and (3) national sovereignty, identity, and culture. This book focuses on these concerns.

First, how is the information revolution affecting the way that states conduct their relations with each other—policymaking, diplomacy, and the conduct of war? Do more, faster, better channels of communication increase or decrease the probability of war? Does the capacity to broadcast events as they unfold to a global audience increase the influence of the news media on international affairs? Can the news media affect the outcome of international conflicts in new ways? Are the news media seizing the initiative from policy makers? In particular, do the powerful images of television exert pressures that shape decisions about the commitment of military forces? Does the abundance of information from diverse sources increase the influence of non-state actors, both individuals and groups, over international outcomes? Who is controlling the foreign policy agendas of states in the information age?

Second, how do the new communication technologies affect the conduct of economic relations and the distribution of the world's wealth? Are they increasing economic inequalities among states or reducing them? Are they promoting economic development in some countries and hindering it in others? How have they contributed to the globalization of international business? Do they encourage the concentration of economic power in large conglomerates, or do they improve access to the larger markets for small and medium enterprises? Or do they do both, and if so, what determines the difference?

Third, how are the new communication technologies affecting the international political system of sovereign nation-states? Are they weakening the state as the fundamental unit of the system or strengthening it? Do they reinforce structures of power or undermine them? How do they affect the relationships between citizens and states? Do abundant, diverse sources of information and the ease of communicating and mobilizing across borders empower citizens to

force their agendas on their governments more effectively or even to overthrow them more easily? How does the growth of transnational communities,
created by new forms of communication such as the Internet, and the proliferation of channels to spread "foreign" media products, affect national loyalties
and cultural identities?

Technology, Society, and Historical Change

The controversies over the present and future impact of this radically new information and communications environment on world politics can best be
viewed as part of a larger debate over the role of technology in historical
change. On one side are those who emphasize the importance of technological innovations and their specific properties. This view tends to perceive
sharp breaks with the past with the advent of key new technologies and to
stress the impact they are likely to have on patterns of human behavior. On
the other side are those who emphasize the societal context of technological
innovation and the importance of social forces and structures in determining
the impact of any technology. In their more extreme versions, these divergent perspectives have been labeled "technological determinism" and "societal determinism," respectively. This distinction is analytically useful, as we
shall see, even though most scholarship falls somewhere between the two ex-
tremes. The differences in emphasis, however, underlie very different assessments of the current impact of the new information and communication
technologies at the beginning of the twenty-first century.

Technological determinists may stress the positive or the negative effects
of innovation or the potential for both. What distinguishes this perspective
is that it emphasizes the transformative power of the new technologies' attributes. Ronald J. Deibert, for example, has examined the shift from the medieval world of script to the modern world of print to demonstrate his argument that the intrinsic properties of specific media of communication are
important determinants of social change and that different "media environments" predispose human beings to think, act, interact, and organize themselves in particular ways. Consequently, he maintains, "changes in modes of
communication—the various media by which information is stored and exchanged—have significant implications for the evolution and character of
society and politics at a world level."[4]

Technological optimists stress the possibilities for positive change resulting from the new technologies. The most optimistic are enthusiastic about
the potential for increased empowerment of individuals and other nonstate
actors. The Internet in particular provides a global resource of information to

anyone who has access to a networked computer and knows how to use it. In the words of the World Bank: "The remotest village has the possibility of tapping a global store of knowledge beyond the dreams of anyone living a century ago, and more quickly and cheaply than anyone imagined possible only a few decades ago."[5] The reduced cost and time to communicate over long distances allows those who are stuck on the peripheries to transcend the tyranny of geography and to interact with the rest of the world. This equalizing, leveling effect can help to reduce gaps between rich and poor, urban and rural, and large states and small ones. Enhanced information and communication capacities increase productivity, facilitate international commerce, and foster growth in a global economy. Increased transparency from multiple, globalized media makes authoritarian governments more difficult to maintain and all governments more accountable to their citizens. Electronic networks facilitate the organization and efforts of transnational coalitions to influence the policy agendas of governments and international organizations.

Technological pessimists fear a more negative impact from the new technologies. They argue that the gap between the rich and poor will become greater, not smaller, in the information age. Computer hardware is expensive; the software is complex and requires considerable education and training. Telecommunications infrastructures and network connections require enormous financial investments. Those who are most disadvantaged and most in need of the benefits of the new technologies are the ones who are least likely to have access to them. Social stratification will increase as the world becomes increasingly divided into the information rich and the information poor.

While the optimists see the potential for the democratization of communication in a world of electronic networks, where power becomes more dispersed and less geographically defined, pessimists fear that chaos and insecurity are more likely to result from these systemic changes. For Stephen Kobrin, "neomedievalism" is the best way to describe the postmodern world of "multiple overlapping authorities, sovereign and non-sovereign, territorial and non-territorial."[6] The only thing that is certain, he claims, is that a systemic transition is occurring. The modern nation-state system with its sovereign control over territorial borders is changing. Whether the emerging order will be another Dark Age of rampant crime, walled security communities, and private armies remains to be seen.

In contrast to those who believe that the information revolution is transforming world politics, whether positively or negatively, are those who emphasize the role of society in determining the impact of the new technologies. New technologies are produced and continuously modified in specific social contexts. They emerge in response to some social need or, at least, to someone's perception that the invention will be useful. Governments may encourage the development of a particular technology through policy initiatives and financial support, or alternatively, their policies may hamper its development by legislating restrictions upon its use or further development. In either case, the actions (or inactions) of political authorities significantly influence access to new technologies, the way in which they are used, and the distribution of their costs and benefits.

Economic structures, institutions, and ideologies also shape the access, use, and distributional effects of a technology. The more economic power is centralized in a few large conglomerates or enterprises with a monopoly in a product or service, the greater their influence over the direction the technology takes. The institutions that control the information and communications media determine the costs, the range of choice, and further developments in the technology. The profit motive and the imperatives of competition, which are hallmarks of capitalism, will shape contemporary decisions on these matters. Given the global spread of capitalism and the trends toward privatization and deregulation, many political economists expect increasing centralization of economic power and the dominance of commercial objectives over public interests in the way the technologies are used.

Business decisions are also influenced by millions of individuals—how and when they decide to use the technology. The impact of a technology, then, also depends very significantly upon its social uses. A United Nations Educational, Scientific and Cultural Organization (UNESCO) report makes this point emphatically: "Individuals, groups, enterprises, institutions and organizations do not merely respond to the technology on offer; they also have an effect on configurations and applications. . . . Society is not merely a dumping-ground; it is permeated by its own changes and is a source of action."[7] The customs, values, and other characteristics of a society will significantly influence the way individuals adopt, ignore, or modify a technology.

Some societal determinists emphasize the ways in which existing political, economic, or social structures shape the use and impact of technologies, limiting the extent to which even the most radically new technologies can bring about fundamental change. Robert O. Keohane and Joseph S. Nye have challenged claims that the information revolution will transform the basic political structure of the international system or equalize power among states. They acknowledge that information technology has drastically reduced the costs of transmitting information long distances and that this technology will be the most important power resource in the twenty-first century; but they nevertheless conclude that "geographically based states will continue to structure politics in the information age."[8] Further, the existing distribution of power is likely to persist, as the current world leaders will shape the rules that determine access to information technology and thus maintain their technological lead.

An "Interactivist" Approach to Technological Innovation

The debates that accompany most major innovations—between the technological and the societal determinists and between the optimists and the pessimists—serve a very useful purpose. The controversies help to define the range of possible effects and to provide a basis for policy choices by suggesting conditions and actions that make some outcomes more likely than others. The contending perspectives outlined above suggest that the new technologies have multiple potential effects, indeed some of them contradictory. These technologies may, for example, both increase and decrease the likelihood of war, both exacerbate social and economic inequalities and reduce them, both erode national sovereignty and enhance the power of the state. Drawing upon the contrasting views about the role of technology in historical change, this book maintains that four sets of interacting influences are shaping the impact of the new ICTs, just as they have done with innovations in the past. These are as follows: (1) intrinsic properties of the technologies; (2) political structures, institutions, and policies; (3) economic structures, institutions, and market forces; and (4) social use and adaptation, as conditioned by values, customs, and other characteristics of a society. Although this book focuses on the new media environment that ICTs are creating collectively, it is important to note that the various technologies share some but not all of the same properties and may, therefore, have different effects. This analysis considers the impact of both the new environment and certain specific technologies, especially satellite television and the Internet.

The evolutionary development of the Internet, which will be discussed in greater detail in chapter 3, provides a good introductory illustration of the multiple potential effects of a new technology and how its specific properties; the market and economic institutions; the social uses; and government policies, political institutions, and the larger political environment interact to shape the impact. The Internet is a network that links computers around the world with instant information retrieval and interactive communication capabilities. Inherent in the properties of the medium—global but decentralized, interactive, cheap, fast, and easy to access—is a potentially democratizing and equalizing force. Access to information and communication is available for those who would otherwise be deprived. As a medium of commerce the Internet also fuels economic growth and development. Under the prevailing system of capitalism, however, the imperatives of the marketplace may affect access to the benefits of the Internet, the purposes for which it is used, and the future directions the relevant technologies take. If the information on the Internet should become more proprietary and costly, then simply being connected would not be enough to close the knowledge gap, access would be limited, and the disparities would probably increase. Certain uses of the Internet are more profitable than others; commerce and entertainment could overwhelm the information function and move the Internet further away from its original academic and research origins. The direction the Internet takes also depends to a great extent on the choices of individuals, who decides to use it and how. Lastly, government actions and policies have played a critical role in the development and diffusion of the Internet. Government initiatives and financial support have helped to build the networking infrastructure in most countries and helped to provide facilities for broad public access in some. But in other countries government policies have inhibited the establishment or spread of networks out of political and security concerns regarding the cross-border flows of information.

This brief illustration demonstrates a theme of this book: that the impact of the information revolution is and will be the net result of choices made at many levels—by individuals, groups, enterprises, and states—operating at subnational, national, and transnational levels. These choices affect each other in an infinite series of feedback loops. Technological change consists of a series of major innovations, followed by a progressive refinement and diffusion. There is a push-pull effect in which social changes give rise to new technologies, which produce social change. Equally important are the modifications of technologies that the users inspire. Individuals often use a technology for reasons very different from those anticipated by those who developed it. The Internet, which has become a major form of long-distance, interpersonal communication, was designed originally to link together major research computers in the United States for national security purposes.

The direction that any technology takes and its impact are shaped by choices made deliberately (as in government legislation and the selection of television programs that individuals make), as well as choices made indirectly or not at all. Inaction is as important a choice as any particular action, decision, or policy. The multiple influences and the complexity of their interaction give rise to three dilemmas: the economic, the democratic, and the sovereignty dilemma.

The sovereignty dilemma arises out of the fact that governments possess the authority to make decisions and laws to control the use and development of the new information and communication technologies, but the characteristics of these technologies make it increasingly difficult to do so. Attempting to control the flow of information across a national border may also deprive a government of certain desirable benefits. Governments may, nevertheless, attempt to limit the use of one or more of these technologies in order to maintain domestic order, enhance security, protect domestic economic interests, or preserve cultural values. They may, for example, ban the use of satellite dishes to prevent the circulation of nonofficial views or establish quotas for foreign television programming. The success of these efforts is bound to be limited because of the many diverse modes of communication available to penetrate the most closed of societies. Satellite dishes may proliferate illegally (as in China) and become too numerous to eliminate. Fax machines and Internet connectivity are essential for any nation to survive in the global marketplace, but once established, they expose the state's actions to the rest of the world and encourage its citizens to engage in conversation with a wider community.

The economic dilemma arises from the choices regarding control, access, and purpose of the new technologies. Choices that leave their development and use primarily to the market, with minimal government regulation, will encourage diffusion of the technologies worldwide, spur further innovations, and promote economic growth. Information, messages, and media products such as films, recordings, and television programs will move unhindered across national boundaries. The market distributes benefits unevenly, however, limiting access to those who are able to pay, thus sharpening inequalities within and among societies. In the absence of restrictive government policies, indigenous cultures may be flooded with foreign (especially U.S.) cultural products. An unfettered capitalist approach makes information and communication mere commodities to be exchanged at the highest rate of return that the market will accept. Profit motives dominate any conception of a collective public interest. On the other hand, government intervention in the market to ensure that the technologies serve a broader collective interest may constrain innovation, limit alternatives, and concentrate political power. This is the economic dilemma.

Two democratic dilemmas arise out of the new information environment. One concerns the relationship between the media and government. A major function of the media in every country, regardless of type of political system, is to communicate and explain the policies of the government. How, when, and to what extent should the media question those policies? If multiple sides of the issues are not covered in the media, there is no public debate, which is fundamental to democracy. Do the media serve as watchdogs, a check on government, or lapdogs merely reflecting government policies and "manufacturing consent?"⁹ This is an old question, which takes on new meaning in an environment where alternative interpretations of events to the official ones are more readily available. Further, the pervasiveness and persuasiveness of television, with its enhanced capacity to stir emotion with live images, provides governments with even more effective tools for manipulating public opinion. But those same attributes also make it possible for the media to develop their own policy agendas.

The second democratic dilemma derives from the properties of the new technologies and their convergence. The broad accessibility of the Internet in particular, and its speed, scope, and decentralized structure, enable ordinary people to play a more important role in world politics. By forming transnational networks, individuals and groups can share information, mobilize support, and coordinate action more effectively. Cell phones enhance local coordination activity, and other technologies, such as videos and DVDs, transmit messages to a still broader audience. Digital technologies enable transmission from one medium to another, such as photos from a digital camera to the Internet and television. But the openness, ease of access, and enhanced connectivity of the new ICTs give extremist groups influence out of proportion to their numbers and facilitate the work of transnational drug cartels, criminal organizations, and terrorist networks.

Conclusion

The purpose of this book is to consider how the dramatic changes that have been wrought by the information revolution are affecting the relations between states and societies and the structure of world order. The next chapter begins the exploration with a historical perspective on the new information and communication technologies. How did we get where we are today? This excursion through earlier times identifies certain key developments and demonstrates how four interacting influences, namely, the properties of the technologies, economic forces, the political institutions and policies, and social uses, have shaped the impact and direction in each case. Chapter 3 examines the more recent development of fiber-optic cable, geosynchronous satellites, and the Internet, the globalizing technologies that have transformed the media environment. Chapters 4, 5, and 6 address, respectively, the major questions that have fueled debate in each of the three issue areas that are the focus of this book: (1) diplomacy, war, and peace; (2) the structure of the global economy and the distribution of the world's wealth; and (3) sovereignty, culture, and the nation-state. Each of these core chapters is structured around the controversy over impact in that issue area, which reflects the broader debate about technology, society, and historical change. Opposing views are outlined in order to demonstrate the multiple potential effects in each of these issue areas of world politics. Case studies and evidence from relevant research provide the basis for evaluating the contending arguments and demonstrating the influence of the four factors discussed above.

Notes

1. Andrew Gillespie and Kevin Robins, "Geographical Inequalities: The Spatial Bias of the New Communications Technologies," *Journal of Communication* 39, no. 3 (Summer 1989): 8–9.

2. Reported in a column by Thomas L. Friedman, "Barney and Baghdad," *New York Times*, October 18, 2006, A23.

3. Manuel Castells, *The Rise of the Network Society. The Information Age: Economy, Society, and Culture* (Cambridge, Mass.: Blackwell, 2000), 329. This is volume 1 of a three-volume work on the information age.

4. Ronald J. Deibert, *Parchment, Printing, and Hypermedia: Communication in World Order Transformation* (New York: Columbia University Press, 1997), 2.

5. World Bank, *World Development Report 1998/99: Knowledge for Development* (Washington, D.C.: Author, 1999).

6. Stephen J. Kobrin, "Back to the Future: Neomedievalism and the Postmodern Digital World Economy," *Journal of International Affairs* 51, no. 2 (Spring 1998): 366.

7. Josiane Jouet and Sylvie Coudray, *New Communication Technologies: Research Trends*, Report No. 105 (Paris: UNESCO, 1990), 57.

8. Robert O. Keohane and Joseph S. Nye, "Power and Interdependence in the Information Age," *Foreign Affairs* 77, no. 5 (September/October 1998): 94.

9. The phrase is the title of a book by Edward S. Herman and Noam Chomsky, *Manufacturing Consent: The Political Economy of the Mass Media* (New York: Pantheon, 2002).

CHAPTER TWO

⟿

The Origins of the
Information Revolution

The information revolution is the product of a long, historical evolution of technological innovations and modifications. A quick backward glance suggests that there is a progressive trend toward the expansion of human knowledge, the conquest of time and space, and the democratization of communication. Today more people have access to more information and to more channels of communication than ever before. Only 4 to 5 percent of the European population could read when the first books circulated in the fifteenth century; 82 percent of the world's population above the age of fifteen was literate in 2007, according to the World Bank.[1] Many who cannot read have access in one way or another to news from distant places by way of radio and television. Internet kiosks can be found in isolated villages. At the beginning of the twenty-first century there are few places on earth that are not connected in some way to an emerging global communications system.

Such a sweeping assumption of progress obscures both the unevenness in the distribution of new technologies in today's world and the multiple effects of specific inventions in the past. The dramatic developments of the 1990s aroused new interest in the relationship between changes in communication technologies and social and political change. International relations scholars are just beginning to grapple with the broader implications of large-scale shifts in the means of communication. This chapter explores some of these historical junctures, focusing on the invention and early history of the printing press, the telegraph, the telephone, and broadcasting. In these technologies—and related ones such as photography and motion pictures—are the origins of the information and communication revolution. Each has contributed in a distinct way to the development of the idea of human communication over long distances and to the accumulation of linkages between societies that exists today. The international impact of the telegraph was immediate. Radio, television, and the telephone remained primarily domestic channels of communication until satellites expanded their reach in the 1970s. The printing press played a critical role in the historical transformation from medieval to modern Europe,[2] but that process extended over several centuries. Even at the outset, however, the invention's effects were profound.

The Printing Press: The First Mass Medium

No technological development in any field is credited with a greater social and political impact than the invention of the printing press with movable type by Johann Gutenberg. Until that point, the middle of the fifteenth century, there had been no efficient way to reproduce and store accurately information in large quantities. The difficulty and cost of producing and copying written documents, one at a time, or of making woodblock prints, limited the amount of information in circulation. What was revolutionary about Gutenberg's printing press was how much more could be produced, more quickly and cheaply, than by hand. The replacement of parchment, made from sheepskin, by paper made from rags further reduced the cost of production. About twenty million books were produced in the first fifty years of printing—more than the estimated total for the previous one thousand years.[3] The new medium also made possible the quick, cheap reproduction of pamphlets, flyers, and other materials for widespread distribution.

This capacity to reproduce text quickly and cheaply posed a serious challenge to the Catholic Church. For about seven hundred years monasteries and other establishments of the Catholic Church had essentially monopolized European book production and what a historian of military and communication technologies calls "the medieval society's principal information network."[4] This network consisted of three levels. At the top were the pope and the church's highest authorities, who determined what types of information the network could transmit. At the next level were the monasteries, seminaries, and later universities that stored this information and transmitted it in Latin to the literate elite. On the lowest level were large numbers of churches and priests who transmitted orally to the illiterate majority of the population, in the vernacular (local) language they understood, what the church wanted them to know. Knowledge of Latin was broadly diffused across

Europe but within a very narrow stratum of the population. The vast majority was illiterate and spoke one of hundreds of vernacular languages and dialects that had proliferated after the decline and fall of the Roman Empire.

The invention of the printing press weakened this information monopoly
in two ways. It facilitated the diffusion of dissenting views, most notably
those of Martin Luther and other Protestant reformers. The printing press
also encouraged the shift in Europe away from Latin to the various vernacular languages. Booksellers, driven by the profit motive, wished to reach as
large a market as possible. As the pool of Latin literates was very small, the
"logic of capitalism" dictated that more works be printed in the languages
that people spoke.[5] The increase in the volume and variety of reading materials in the vernacular encouraged the growth of literacy. As the size of the
reading public expanded, so did the booksellers' market.

These commercial interests converged with the interests of Protestant reformers who sought to make their works as widely known and accessible as
possible in order to challenge effectively Catholic doctrine and to win converts to their own. Within two months of the day in 1517 when the German
theologian Martin Luther made public (in Latin) his ninety-five theses crit-
icizing various practices of the church, they were translated into German,
printed, and widely diffused throughout Europe.[6] Flysheets, posters, and
tracts, as well as books, were printed in German and distributed, attacking
church practices and spreading new doctrines. John Calvin, the French theologian, published in French from Geneva his version of Protestantism. Two
French scholars on the impact of printing, Lucien Febvre and Henri-Jean
Martin, consider the effort of the reformers to be the first propaganda campaign in history conducted through the medium of the press.[7] The quick,
cheap reproducibility of print and the explosion of publishing promoted the
circulation of scientific, as well as religious, ideas.

The "logic of print capitalism" helped to consolidate the hundreds of vernacular languages that were used in medieval Europe into a few standardized,
uniform languages, a process that profoundly affected the political structure
of Europe.[8] The search for larger book markets encouraged production in the
language most people spoke, rather than Latin, but there was tremendous linguistic diversity. Which version of French or German, for example, would be
used? In order to reduce costs, expand the market, and maximize profits,
booksellers had to settle on one version and to standardize spelling, vocabu-
lary, and grammar. Certain dialects were closer to the print language than
others, and these eventually became the dominant spoken language across
large territories. By "fixing" and fostering certain dialects for printing, the
new medium encouraged the development of the national languages that

were to become an important basis for differentiating people from people and state from state.[9] The printing press facilitated the communication of ideas and information across large areas, but ironically, it also contributed to the language barriers that would limit communication between nations.

The advent of print and the consolidation of vernacular languages facilitated the rise of the modern state in two important ways. First, larger areas could be administered from a single point more effectively when easily reproducible, standardized documents and uniform laws could be disseminated to a population that understood a common language. This enhanced administrative capacity to make and enforce laws within a large, defined territory aided the process of political consolidation and centralization of power. Second, the development of a single language across a large area created the basis for a psychological connection among the inhabitants and weakened feudal loyalties. This shared sense of group identity gradually evolved into the ideology of nationalism.[10]

Many secular authorities, as well as clergy, viewed the technology with some anxiety, fearing its products would encourage heresy and dissent. One famous example was François I, who in 1535 forbade any book to be printed in the kingdom, on pain of death by hanging.[11] Rulers elsewhere, especially in England, also tried to censor or control what was printed by requiring licenses or granting subservient printers a monopoly. These draconian measures did not succeed in stopping the printers, however, nor did the Catholic Church's Index of Forbidden Books. Printing heretical, illegal works could be dangerous. After the reformers had demonstrated the subversive potential of the press, printers and booksellers were often arrested, and some were burned at the stake. But selling illegal books was also good business, and organized trade networks distributing pamphlets and books defending illegal beliefs sprang up in Germany and France, then throughout Europe. Booksellers' agents, peddlers, played a very important role in spreading the new, illicit ideas during the Reformation.[12]

From its crude beginning the press was an arena of political conflict, revealing its power to challenge authority and influence public opinion. At the end of the eighteenth century, revolutionaries in America and France flooded the streets and countryside with pamphlets of protest, declarations, and calls to action just as Luther and the Protestant reformers had done earlier. With the mechanization of print and the growth of literacy, far more people could be exposed to popular appeals. On the other hand, governments and supporters of the status quo could also use this powerful instrument, and governments possessed the authority to regulate content and distribution.

It was nearly four hundred years before the full potential of Gutenberg's invention as a mass medium was realized, the result of further technological refinements and rising levels of literacy in Europe and America. In the nineteenth century a series of innovations greatly increased the speed of the printing process while reducing the cost—a development that led to the remarkable expansion of journalism, mainly newspapers and magazines. The steam-driven press, first used by the *Times* of London in 1814, for example, contributed to the increase in the circulation of that newspaper from five thousand to fifty thousand by the middle of the century. The advent of Benjamin Day's penny press newspaper, the *New York Sun*, in 1833, represented one of the earliest efforts to expand the number of newspaper readers well beyond anything that had been known in the past. Toward the end of the nineteenth century, the process became further mechanized with the introduction of electricity, which not only sped up the printing but also led to machines that could cut and fold paper and bind newspapers together. Meanwhile, the development of the telegraph and the railroad from the middle of the century further transformed the newspaper industry by speeding up the acquisition of news from distant places and facilitating the distribution of newspapers.

The Electric Telegraph: Conquering Time and Space

Examples of organized message exchange systems, designed to send messages over long distances as fast as possible, are found in the earliest records of human history. In the sixth century BC, for example, the Persian Empire established a highly developed system that covered an area roughly corresponding to what is now Iran, Iraq, Syria, and Turkey. The system consisted of a string of stations at fourteen-mile intervals that were stocked with horses to take royal messengers in relays from one to the next. The Roman system, the *Cursus Publicus*, worked on the basis of a similar principle over an even larger area. At its peak of efficiency a single message might have been able to travel as far as 170 miles in one day and night. An example from a much later time, the fifteenth century, was a carrier pigeon post system established by Venetian merchants in the Mediterranean area.

The electric telegraph was the first mode of communication that could send messages over long distances faster than the most rapid form of transportation. The distance that could be covered was limited only by the extent to which wire could be strung. Samuel B. Morse was not the first to transmit signals electrically, but he is credited with the invention because his simple, low-cost method of signaling made it a success. Messages were sent in a code consisting of dots and dashes (which came to be known as the Morse code) through short pulses of electric current from a battery over a long-distance wire. This device, first tested in 1838, then put into operation in 1844 between Washington and

Baltimore, was the first "user-friendly public-use electric telegraph line in the world."[13] It was the practicality of Morse's version, plus a rising demand for faster communication, that spurred the growth of this invention.

Initially, the telegraph was confined by national borders, as each country used a different system. Messages had to be transcribed, translated, and handed over at frontiers, then retransmitted over the telegraph network of the neighboring country. Countries began to establish arrangements, bilateral, then regional, to facilitate the interconnection of their networks. Eventually, the rapid expansion of networks prompted a group of twenty countries to negotiate the first international telegraph convention in Paris in 1865, which provided a framework of common rules to standardize equipment and operating instructions that would apply to all countries. The convention also established the International Telegraph Union, which would subsequently draw up rules governing telephony, then wireless telephony, and radio.[14] The establishment of the ITU, which continues to exist today as the International Telecommunication Union, demonstrated that only by agreement on rules for usage and an organization to monitor and administer the rules could there be interoperability for rapid, effective international communication.

Besides the political obstacles there was the technical challenge of transcending the water barriers separating continents. Of all the inventions in the nineteenth century, none "contributed to the shrinking of the world quite so obviously as the submarine telegraph cable," claims Daniel R. Headrick, a historian of technology.[15] It took many attempts and many failures to develop a reliable means of laying under large bodies of water sufficiently strong cables with adequate protection to survive. Britain was connected to the European continent in 1851, but the high-cost, high-risk effort to lay a transatlantic cable did not succeed until 1866.

Meanwhile, the colonial empires, especially Britain and France, sought to use the new technology to forge closer links to their colonies. After several failed attempts, Britain and India were successfully joined by cable in 1870, and it became "the spinal cord of the British Empire."[16] This achievement, heavily subsidized by the British government, generated a surge of investment by private cable companies. In 1871 the French government successfully laid the first of several cables to North Africa. Except for these efforts neither the government nor private entrepreneurs in France did much investing in submarine cables in the rest of the world until the end of the nineteenth century. Efforts were directed primarily at laying and operating short cables between French colonies and the British network. The result was that by 1895 British cables linked France to almost all of its colonies except North Africa.[17]

The electric telegraph was the first global communication and information system. The impact on world politics was profound and multifaceted. First, by improving the lines of communication between European countries and their colonies—and between the various administrative centers in each colony—the telegraph provided a tool for more effective colonial administration and control. It enhanced the power of the rulers over the ruled. It strengthened Western dominance in the non-Western world.

Second, the explosion of entrepreneurial activity on the part of British private investors "not only linked together the scattered pieces of the British Empire, but [also] reinforced Britain's position as the foremost naval, commercial and financial power in the world."[18] Britain dominated the submarine cable business up until World War I in every way. Seventy percent of the total number of kilometers of submarine cable circling the globe in 1887 was British owned.[19] Those that were not owned or managed by British companies were often built by them. Having built the first information infrastructure, Britain became the geographic center of the global network of submarine cables. As the dominant power in this new medium, Britain was in a position to make the rules and influence their application.

Third, British information dominance became a source of envy and concern on the part of other major powers, exacerbating their rivalries. This effect ran counter to the expectations of many commentators at the time that a global telegraph network would be a pacific influence on international relations. Hyperbolic predictions were widespread among journalists and telegraph enthusiasts, such as this claim in one of the earliest accounts of the development of the telegraph in 1858: "It is impossible that old prejudices and hostilities should longer exist, while such an instrument has been created for the exchange of thought between all the nations of the earth."[20] There *were* positive effects on the relations between states, particularly in the realm of commerce, but as an instrument of power, the electric telegraph was also bound to generate hostility.

The impact of the telegraph on economic relations between states was profound. The first telegram exchange between North America and Europe quoted the share prices on the New York stock market. By the end of the nineteenth century telegrams between the New York and London stock exchanges could be transmitted in three minutes. The telegraph provided in a timely manner all kinds of information vital to commercial exchange, such as commodity prices, shipping schedules, and accounts of important events. The increase in the speed of communication and the transmission of relevant information made business undertakings more convenient and predictable, and the volume of activity soared. By encouraging transnational economic activities, the telegraph was an important force integrating the economies of the world, a process that technologies in the next century would continue.

Finally, the telegraph gave new meaning to the word "news" and helped to make the news media an important part of the calculations of foreign policy makers. The immediacy of telegraphed news and the amount of information that could be transmitted made newspapers more interesting, expanded circulation, and enhanced the power of the press. In response to the increased demand for up-to-date news, four major international news agencies were founded, setting a pattern that persists to this day. Newspapers that subscribed to the wire services of an agency were able to obtain much more news more cost effectively than was possible by relying on their own resources only. The Associated Press of New York was formed in 1848, just four years after the first public use telegraph cable was laid. Paul Reuter's Telegram Company emerged the same year as the cable between Britain and the continent (1851). Branch offices spread all over Europe and beyond as the international telegraph developed. By 1861 Reuters' agents were located in Asia, South Africa, and Australia, as well as Europe.[21]

Whether using their own reporters or those of news services, newspapers were able to obtain in hours or minutes by telegraph information that had required weeks before to travel by various combinations, including boats, railroads, stagecoaches, and carrier pigeons. The telegraph was the first technology to inform the public as well as leaders about events while they were still occurring. There was less time to make decisions. The press gained influence. Public opinion could be more easily aroused.

The telegraph was the first step in a series of inventions and innovations that eventually made possible instantaneous communication over any distance, but the technology also had serious limitations. Messages were electric impulses communicated in a code of dots and dashes, a method that required considerable skill on the part of the recipient or else intermediaries to translate the message and deliver it to the recipient. Further, the necessity for wires confined the communication channels to fixed land routes and submarine cables. Overland routes required either control of extensive real estate or a patchwork of access agreements with local polities. Submarine cables required landing rights at critical locations for repeater stations. The fact that British companies controlled and monitored most of the submarine cables posed security risks for those countries that had to rely on the cables. Once the idea of rapid, long-distance communication had become an operational reality, the search was on for technologies that could overcome these limitations. One experimental objective was to transmit sounds and the human voice. Another was to eliminate the wires through the use of radio waves to transmit messages.

The Telephone

Although revolutionary in its social impact, the telephone did not become a major medium of international communication until almost a century after its invention by Alexander Graham Bell in 1876. Telephony between most European states was not achieved until the 1920s; and until the 1950s and 1960s the telegraph remained the predominant form of rapid, long-distance communication in Europe.[22] The United States and Europe had no telephone connections until the radio and telephone technologies were combined in 1927 to provide radio telephony, which was subject to fading and interference. Not until 1956, with the first transatlantic telephone cable, was service between the two continents reliable, and only after the U.S. satellite-launching program of the 1960s and 1970s did the telephone become widely affordable for long-distance communication. In sharp contrast, only three decades after Samuel Morse first tested his invention, a permanent transatlantic telegraph line was installed (1866), and by 1872 most of the major cities of the globe were linked with networks of submarine cables and landlines.[23] Why did the telephone spread across the world so much more slowly than the telegraph, and why did the telephone spread across the European continent so much more slowly than the North American?

The telephone began as an urban phenomenon in both Europe and the United States. In the earliest stages of development it was capable of communicating only over very short distances within a city. Intercity communication developed very slowly until the beginning of the twentieth century. The first transcontinental line from New York to San Francisco was completed in 1915, and within ten years toll lines were spread nationwide in the United States. Telephone growth proceeded much more slowly in Europe, and the United States maintained an overwhelming lead in the percentage of the world's telephones until the late 1940s.[24] The slow evolution of the telephone as a medium of international communication is attributable to the combined effect of technological constraints and government policies.

The process of expanding the range, reducing the cost, and increasing the capacity of telephone systems involved a long series of technological innovations. Transmitting voice is a far more complicated technology than transmitting the impulses of a telegraph signal. Voice requires higher frequencies, where attenuation occurs more quickly, that is, the signal fades with distance. Not until the development of vacuum tube amplifiers, which could be placed at regular intervals to boost the signals, was it possible to increase the range over long distances. The New York to San Francisco line in 1915 was the first demonstration of this innovation.

Transmission of telephone signals underwater through cables for intercontinental communication posed even more formidable challenges. It took forty years to develop a successful transoceanic cable technology, using amplifiers or repeaters at regular intervals along the cable. In 1956 the first transatlantic telephone cable was installed, and traffic between Europe and North America increased dramatically, the number of calls tripling over the next five years.[25] Nevertheless, callers still were forced to wait for hours for a free international line to some parts of the world. Only after a series of innovations in the 1960s and 1970s, including fiber-optic cables and satellites, could the telephone begin to aspire to a global reach.

The advance of telephony in Europe was hampered less by technical problems than by government policies and political obstacles to cooperation across national boundaries. France, Germany, and Britain, as well as most other European countries, created postal, telegraph, and telephone administrations (PTTs) to manage their communications. Consequently, the telephone was treated as one part of a combined communications system, and its growth was often sacrificed in the interest of other forms. The telegraph was already entrenched as the rapid, long-distance mode of communication. It was widespread and followed the railroads. Messenger boys on bicycles and later motorcycles provided inexpensive delivery service. Establishing telephone lines and a centralized, interconnected network was an enormous expense. European governments did not make extensive telephone networks a top priority. Financial constraints combined with bureaucratic rivalries to slow expansion.[26] As the countries of Europe were much smaller territorial units, it was technically possible to establish national networks much earlier than in the United States. Instead, Europe lagged far behind the United States even after many of the technical problems had been solved.

In the United States, a private organization, the Bell Telephone Company, took over the commercial development of the telephone, another private company owned the telegraph system (Western Union), and the government ran the post office. In 1885 Bell founded the American Telephone and Telegraph Company (AT&T) to develop long-distance telephone service with a view to creating a single, unified telephone network. When Bell's original patents expired a decade later, a host of new, independent companies began operating in local areas around the country. The new companies' concentration on inexpensive local service greatly increased the distribution of telephones but threatened AT&T's goal of a single network. By concluding agreements with the independent companies to connect with its long-distance lines, AT&T managed to create a national network.

Several factors account for the rapid advance of the telephone in the United States. First, the commercial aspirations of Bell and AT&T provided a strong incentive for the technological innovations that made a nationwide system of telephones possible. Most of the major advances came from Bell's laboratories, which were set up to use some of the company's monopoly profits to achieve the goal of cheaper, long-range service.[27] Second, the period of competition that followed the expiration of Bell's patents allowed new companies to be created at local and regional levels, which expanded services beyond the urban areas and increased the number of users. Third, AT&T's requirement for conformity to its standards and practices as a condition for access to its long-distance lines facilitated the growth of an interconnected network across the country. Finally, government policies influenced the shape and direction of the telephone industry in the United States. Antitrust pressures encouraged AT&T to concentrate on long-distance lines and to conclude access agreements with noncompeting independent companies. Government policies also subsidized local rates from the revenues of long-distance services, thus making the telephone more affordable to a wider segment of the population.[28] Bell's practice of including unlimited local calls (in number and duration) in the monthly fee, charging extra time-based fees for long-distance calls only, increased the usage of the telephone as a routine medium of communication.

In contrast, the pricing policies of European governments discouraged the routine use of telephones and limited their growth beyond the most affluent urban households and businesses. Generally, in Europe, monthly fees were high, relative to those in the United States, and there was an additional charge for each local call.[29] In Germany and France potential subscribers had to raise funds themselves to demonstrate that there was enough demand for the government to provide lines.[30] Even businesses continued far longer than their American counterparts to rely heavily on the telegraph for rapid long-distance communication. Although most countries in Europe had developed centralized telephone systems by 1920, they were less extensive and more expensive than the U.S. system because the European governments did not make the expansion of telephone networks a top priority.[31]

Europe remained a "messy patchwork of national systems with poor intercommunication" until the 1970s.[32] By 1915, with the invention of the vacuum tube amplifier, the technology was available for the establishment of continent-wide telephone service in Europe, and the feasibility of long-distance service over such a wide area was demonstrated by the completion of the New York–San Francisco line that same year. Satisfactory telephone service across national boundaries, however, required some centralizing impetus and an international organization to establish uniform standards. By the early 1920s the European business community began to see the value in cross-polity telephony, and the International Chamber of Commerce eventually played an important role in pushing for Europe-wide service. In 1924 the French Telephone Administration called an international meeting, which established the Comité Consultatif International des Communications Téléphoniques à Grande Distance (CCI). The CCI did manage to establish some uniform standards and to facilitate long-distance service in Europe, but the delays and high cost involved in these calls contributed to the persistence of telegraphy as the dominant form of long-distance communication in Europe until after World War II.

The Strange Career of Wireless Telegraphy

The effort to develop a wireless form of long-distance communication that effectively overcame the limitations of the telegraph and the telephone began in earnest when Guglielmo Marconi successfully transmitted a radio signal across the Atlantic in 1901. Over the first quarter of the twentieth century Marconi's wireless telegraph, transmitting Morse code point to point (one sender to one receiver), evolved into "the most ubiquitous mass medium ever known," the radio.[33] A series of innovations that improved wireless telegraphy also moved the technology in other directions, developing its capacity to serve multiple purposes. Somewhere between 1906 and 1912 the term "radio" began to be used interchangeably with the term wireless, to cover both wireless telegraphy (dots and dashes) and wireless telephony (voice and music transmissions).[34] The term "broadcasting" came into use when radio stations began to appear in Europe and the United States in the early 1920s. Originally an agricultural term, meaning to "scatter seed over a broad area rather than sowing it in designated places,"[35] it was used to convey the idea of transmitting a radio program to a wide audience.

Wireless telegraphy, then radio, raised new issues regarding the use and control of communication channels that remain contentious today. Whereas telegraph wires were tangible pieces of property that required prior agreement on ownership and rules for usage, wireless telegraphy traveled through the "ether" or airwaves.[36] Are the airwaves a common property resource? Who decides on access, for what purposes, and according to what criteria? Can a private company be allowed to determine who can use the airwaves? These questions arose as soon as the technology of wireless telegraphy was applied.

As wireless technologies were developed and applied for different purposes, the fundamental question of who should have access to the airwaves and for what purpose became even more contentious. The military in most countries sought a privileged status for the use of the wireless telegraph on grounds of national security. Navies in particular viewed this medium of communication as ideally suited for transmitting messages between ships at sea and from ships to shore stations. By the time the wireless came into use, most European countries had nationalized their domestic telegraph companies, typically combining the telegraph with the post and telephone to form a single bureaucratic entity. Commercial long-distance wireless companies were allowed to operate, however, with the result that a great deal of competition ensued at the international level, and the use of the airwaves dramatically increased.

The invention of the Audion vacuum tube by Lee De Forest in 1907 greatly improved the quality of sound transmission and encouraged a surge of experimentation from a wide variety of enthusiasts—from teenage boys to seasoned inventors—to improve the technology for transmitting voice and music. The development of simple, inexpensive crystal sets democratized the wireless, as hundreds of young amateur experimenters ("hams") began building their own wireless sets.[37] High-powered amateur stations proliferated, transmitting and receiving chatter and music, as well as Morse code messages. By 1910 there were hundreds of high-power amateur stations in the United States, far surpassing the number of naval and commercial stations, which comprised only 15 or 20 percent of the total.[38] For the ham operators the wireless technology was a hobby. For the commercial wireless telegraph companies, it was a business. For the military, wireless communication was the backbone of national security, and the increased presence of amateurs was regarded as a serious threat to the security of military communications. Even more alarming than interference was the frequency with which naval communications were deliberately intercepted by ham operators. The lack of secrecy in wireless communication, which so distressed the navy, was what made the radio most interesting for the amateurs.

In the absence of rules or regulations, interference increased as the message traffic expanded. Recognizing the need for an international effort to regulate the use of the airwaves, thirty nations met in 1906 and managed to draft a treaty for that purpose. The treaty contained an agreement on the allocation of wavelengths, which restricted the longer, more useful waves (at that point) for the use of governments. In Europe, the scene was not quite as chaotic as in the United States because most of the countries quickly ratified the 1906 convention. The U.S. delegation to that conference, consisting largely of military men, played an important role in shaping the treaty. Navy officials pushed very hard thereafter for its ratification and for regulation that would avoid interference with official messages. Many officers, especially the Secretary of the Navy under Woodrow Wilson, Josephus Daniels, saw communication as a government function. They forcefully advocated government control of wireless telegraphy in America, with the U.S. Navy in charge, and used the danger of the amateur's interference with official, especially emergency messages as a supporting argument. That position made no headway against the powerful democratic rhetoric of amateur operators and the wireless companies, who insisted the air was free and the property of the people.[39] Their successful lobbying against any regulation succeeded in paralyzing action in Congress until 1912.

Nothing less than the sinking of the *Titanic* in 1912 and the loss of 1,500 lives was necessary to persuade Congress to legislate regulation for the use of the wireless. The magnitude of the death toll was attributed in large part to communication failures—messages were not received by ships that could have come to the rescue most quickly. Congress passed the stringent Radio Act four months later. The act was a watershed in the development of radio in the United States. It established the principle of government control over access to the airwaves. It required all operators to be licensed and restricted all stations to the wave allocations assigned in the 1906 treaty. Amateurs were relegated to the shortwave end of the spectrum, which at that time was considered useless, while commercial stations were allocated the medium wave range. The longer waves were reserved for government use. In time of war or disaster the president was empowered to close private wireless stations or to authorize an agency of the government to take them over.

The advent of wireless telegraphy did not result in a massive shift away from the electric telegraph. Both forms of communication continued to be used with radio more as a supplement because of its security implications until the late 1920s. Radio telephony was potentially more useful, but transmitting voice over long distances was far more challenging than sending dots and dashes through electrical impulses. The signal of voice messages is subject to attenuation, that is, it fades with distance. As with the telephone, it took a long series of technological innovations to develop the capacity to transmit voice messages over long distances by radio waves. As noted earlier, it was not until the two technologies were combined in 1927 that voice messages, subject to fading and interference, could be sent across the Atlantic.

Only after the "shortwave revolution," initiated by none other that the inventor of wireless telegraphy himself, was there a significant shift from cable to radio in long-distance point-to-point traffic. In 1924 Marconi discovered a system for high-frequency, shortwave radio transmissions that was faster, simpler, and cheaper than any system using long waves. New shortwave stations immediately sprang up around the world in the late 1920s and early 1930s, and by 1927 the telegraph cable companies had lost half of their traffic to shortwave.[40] The rapid spread of this technology was aided by patent-sharing arrangements among the four major wireless companies. This new technology significantly changed the environment for long-distance communication in the 1920s. By 1929, radio telephony provided daily telephone service to more than twenty-six countries, although the cost was high at seventy-five dollars for a three-minute call and twenty-five dollars for each minute thereafter.[41] By 1937 international wireless circuits almost equaled the amount of the globe covered by the submarine cable network, and radio reached many places that could not be served by cable.

Radio telegraphy and radio telephony had a somewhat less dramatic impact on international relations than did the electric telegraph. It *was* a remarkable achievement to be able to communicate by radio with areas that could not be served by cable, such as ships at sea. It did provide an alternative to the British-dominated cable network. The development of wireless communication also affected the conduct of war. As the technology advanced, it improved command and control capabilities. The downside was the vulnerability of this form of communication to interception because radio scatters its signals in many directions. This property of radio mandated greater efforts to protect one's own communications through codes but also provided opportunities to tap into enemy lines. From World War I onward interception and code breaking of enemy communications was an important element of military strategy and tactics.

Radio telegraphy and radio telephony essentially enhanced the impact of the electric telegraph on international relations with one important difference. Whereas British control of the cable networks had reinforced British power, the development of shortwave radio telephony undermined this hegemony. This different impact is attributable in large part to the particular properties of shortwave, high-frequency technology and to corporate choices. The characteristics of the technology limited the possibilities for monopoly control. To lay a cable or to build any wireless system using long waves (lower frequencies) was complex and capital intensive. In contrast, shortwave (high-frequency) systems were relatively simple to install and required far less power than other wireless systems. The agreement among the four major international wireless companies to share patents further ensured that no one company or country would gain a monopoly, as Marconi and Britain had done with the electric telegraph. Consequently, on the eve of World War II no one country controlled international wireless telecommunications.

Long-distance wireless, point-to-point communication took a quarter of a century of experimentation to develop. Corporate competition, national rivalries, conflicting domestic interests, and the ambitions of a remarkable collection of inventors interacted to shape the evolution of this technology. One direction it took was also influenced by thousands of ordinary people whose curiosity and imagination found a way to apply the technology that diverged sharply from Marconi's original vision. What was designed to be an improved method of sending messages in Morse code from one sender to one distant receiver became a method for distributing information and entertainment to a mass audience—an entirely new idea.

The evolution of the wireless telegraph to broadcast radio is a remarkable example of technological advances and social adaptation shaping a technology through a process of mutual feedback. The discovery of ways to transmit voice and music generated widespread interest in the wireless, which encouraged further experimentation to increase the capacity of the technology for that purpose. Amateur operators ("hams"), with their homemade wireless sets, played an important role in developing and popularizing broadcast radio. In their eagerness to explore the possibilities of wireless communication, the amateur experimenters helped to advance the technology, extending its range and performance.[42] They began to send out music and other programming for anyone able to tune in. By increasing the demand for this equipment, the amateurs helped to turn the manufacturing of radio receivers into a big business. Their enthusiasm for communicating information and entertainment by radio, and the proliferation of amateur stations, popularized the idea of radio broadcasting even before the term came into use.

The Invention of Broadcasting

The Diffusion of Radio

In 1920 the first radio stations with regular broadcasting began to appear in the United States and in Europe. During the next two decades the radio became a medium of mass communication, accessible to larger and larger audiences in more and more countries. In the United States, for example, one-third of all homes had radio by 1930, and five years later the proportion had increased to two-thirds.[43] As broadcasters increasingly competed with other users of the airwaves, the specter of chaotic interference prompted the governments who were members of the International Telegraph Union to agree in 1927 upon an allocation of frequency bands for the various broad categories of radio services in use at the time, such as maritime communication, broadcasting, and amateur operators. For similar reasons of practicality and efficiency, governments everywhere assumed the regulatory authority to license stations and to determine who could broadcast on what frequencies for what purposes within their respective territorial boundaries. Beyond these basic regulatory powers, governments had to decide just how much and in what manner to shape the structure and substance of broadcasting.

Radio broadcasting in the United States developed very differently from the pattern in most European countries. In the United States there was minimal government regulation. Involvement was limited primarily to assigning licenses and allocating wavelengths. The Radio Corporation of America (RCA) established a network, the National Broadcasting Corporation (NBC), as a subsidiary in 1926; it was soon joined by another network, the Columbia Broadcasting System (CBS). Advertising and sponsorship of programs became a major feature of American radio, with the market as the major influence on programming. The prevailing view of those who most significantly influenced the shape and direction of American broadcasting can be illustrated in the commitment expressed by the president of the CBS network, William S. Paley, in a speech to an industry group in 1946: "First of all we have an obligation to give most of the people what they want most of the time."[44]

Government regulatory policies in the United States consistently favored the interests of commercial stations from the beginning of broadcasting. In 1923 President Herbert Hoover sought to relieve congestion of the airwaves by dividing radio stations into three classes, high power, medium power, and low power, and assigned specific wavelengths to each. The least crowded and most desirable wavelengths were assigned to the most powerful stations (owned by AT&T, General Electric [GE], and Westinghouse), while the low power stations (operated by universities, churches, and labor unions) were confined to the most crowded wavelengths.[45] Many of the first radio stations had been founded by colleges and universities. When the Federal Communications Commission (FCC), which the Communications Act of 1934 created as the regulatory authority over all telecommunications, began allocating frequencies, no specific reservations were made for noncommercial stations. Eventually, in 1945 the FCC reserved a small portion of the frequency modulation (FM) band for noncommercial use, but there were few radios in circulation at the time that could receive FM broadcasts.

The combination of government decisions and a strong personality in the early stages of British broadcasting produced a very different model, which came to be known as public service broadcasting. This model prevailed in Western Europe with organizational variations. In contrast to the U.S. approach, the British government placed all broadcasting under the unified control of a public corporation, the British Broadcasting Corporation (BBC), and financed the operations from license fees levied on set owners. The BBC operated under a royal charter that made it independent of the government. The first general manager, John Charles Walsham Reith (subsequently Lord Reith), remained in that position for sixteen years and significantly influenced the development of a public broadcasting tradition. Reith envisioned the BBC as an independent broadcaster, free from both political interference and commercial pressure, with a mission to educate, inform, and entertain the whole nation. He believed that the BBC had "a high moral responsibility" to "carry into the greatest possible number of homes everything that is best in every department of human endeavor and achievement."[46]

Public broadcasting remained a minor player in the U.S. media arena, in contrast to the strong presence of counterparts in Western Europe, Australia, Japan, and Canada. The laissez-faire, free market tradition in the United States provides much of the explanation for these divergent trajectories. As one scholar of public broadcasting has suggested, "The assumption remained that there was such considerable identity between private and public interests in broadcasting that . . . the best public services would emerge in a largely unfettered private enterprise."[47] Any kind of government role in broadcasting, other than the minimal regulatory functions, tended to be regarded as the slippery slope to "state broadcasting." Commercial broadcasters reinforced this polarized view of the options in their defense of advertisement-based programming, as illustrated by another quote from CBS president Paley's 1946 speech: "The advertiser buys freedom for the listener at the same time he buys time and talent. For it is an historic fact that the only other kind of radio is government radio."[48] The idea of government radio or television was particularly distasteful to Americans in the Cold War environment, when the United States was waging an ideological battle on behalf of free enterprise values against the Soviet Union's state-controlled economy and society. Capitalist ideology combined with superpower rivalry to stifle the development of the strong philosophical underpinnings necessary for public broadcasting to become a more influential force in American culture.

The International Impact of Shortwave Radio

Initially radio had little international impact because most broadcasting stations transmitted signals on medium-wave channels, which limited reception to local areas, unless repeated by relays or boosted with enormous power. Amateur operators, who were confined to the "useless" shortwave bandwith after 1912, discovered that their messages could sometimes travel vast distances but that reception was erratic and unpredictable. The development of beam technology in 1924, which improved point-to-point transmissions, made shortwave broadcasting feasible.

The advent of shortwave broadcasting affected international relations in two ways. First, it helped to make radio an international news medium, a source of timely, on-the-spot information about world events. Shortwave relays were used to insert foreign messages into domestic broadcasts, providing an international audience for such prominent personalities of the 1930s as Mohandas Gandhi, Benito Mussolini, Adolf Hitler, and Franklin D. Roosevelt.[49] Major U.S. broadcasting systems established bureaus in Europe and sent correspondents there to gather news and send back reports to be aired on their networks. Most notably, CBS sent Edward R. Murrow to head its European Bureau in 1937. His dramatic eyewitness reportage of the German occupation of Austria and the Munich Conference in 1938, the German takeover of Czechoslovakia in 1939, and later the Battle of Britain during World War II brought the turbulence of Europe into American homes and established a standard for radio journalism. Radio joined the press as an influence on domestic public opinion.

Second, and more directly, shortwave radio affected the conduct of international relations by introducing a new tool of foreign policy, international radio broadcasting for the purpose of influencing opinion in other countries. Although Morse-coded messages had been transmitted during World War I for that purpose, the potential for voice messages, recognized almost immediately, was obviously much greater. The first regular international broadcasting services were established by European governments in their colonies to keep their administrators in touch with the homeland and to infuse colonial elites with the culture of their rulers.[50] The Netherlands was the first, in 1927, to establish continuing service to its citizens in colonial territories, especially the Dutch East Indies. In that same year Britain inaugurated an experimental "Empire Service" with a Christmas message by George V, although regular service did not begin until 1932. France, Germany, and several other European countries also established services to their colonies about the same time, as did Japan in some Asian countries.

The Soviet Union was the first country to establish an international broadcasting service with the explicit purpose of influencing international opinion. Radio Moscow went on the air in 1929 with broadcasts in German, English, and French. Initially, the tone was positive with emphasis on domestic achievements and the benefits of communism, but with the coming into power of the National Socialist Party in Germany, much airtime was devoted to warning the rest of Europe against the dangers of fascism. Meanwhile, a state-of-the-art international broadcasting service from Hitler's Germany concentrated its hostile attacks on the Soviet Union and Bolshevism.

Mussolini's designs for expansion in North Africa provided the impetus for the Italian government to establish in 1934 the first international radio service in a non-Western language, Arabic. There were few radio sets in the Middle East at that time, and the electricity to run them was rarely available. The Italians distributed some sets and developed very attractive programming that was not at first very political but later included vitriolic attacks on British Middle Eastern policy. To counter what threatened to be a challenge to British influence, the BBC Empire Service began an Arabic service in 1938, its first foreign-language endeavor. Shortly thereafter, Germany, France, and the Soviet Union also began transmitting Arabic programming.[51]

International radio broadcasting expanded further during World War II as all belligerents sought to rally allies and to counter enemy broadcasts. In Germany's sweep through Europe, the capture of radio stations was one of the first steps in the occupation of conquered countries. By end of summer 1940 Germany possessed the largest broadcasting network in the world after seizing control of most major broadcasting stations in Europe.[52] The prize was Radio Luxembourg, a commercial high-powered station that could be heard in Britain and throughout Western Europe. From there the elegant speaking "Lord Haw Haw" broadcast to Britain discouraging war news to demoralize the British public. A colorful innovation of the Axis powers was the use of attractive personalities, such as Axis Sally in Europe and Tokyo Rose in the Pacific, to combine popular programming interspersed with propaganda designed to influence Allied troops. The effectiveness of these tactics is questionable, but they inspired countermeasures.

When the United States entered the war in December 1941, it possessed neither the facilities nor the capabilities for international broadcasting. Within a year the Office of War Information (OWI) had enlisted the services of the six networks and had cobbled together a few transmitters for shortwave broadcasting to present news from the Allied point of view to listeners in Europe, Latin America, and the Pacific. This was the beginning of the Voice of America. From this point onward the United States was a key player in international broadcasting. The United States also established a network of stations to provide programming to troops stationed abroad in order to boost their morale, incidentally spreading a little American culture along the way. Listeners in many countries acquired a taste for American comedy by tuning in to the armed forces network.[53] This form of cultural spillover persisted after the war, when U.S. troops were stationed in Europe under the North Atlantic Treaty Organization, and the network remained in place.

At the end of World War II the BBC was the leading international broadcaster, transmitting more hours of programming (over five hundred) in more languages (thirty-nine) than any of the other twenty-six countries with international services.[54] The reputation of the BBC for reliability and objectivity and the quality of its reporting created a worldwide audience of loyal listeners and provided a model that others have attempted to emulate. In countries where state monopolies or censorship significantly restricted the amount of news, many people came to regard the BBC as an alternative Home Service.[55] The United Kingdom lost its dominant position in quantitative terms in the1950s.

International radio broadcasting expanded further after World War II, encouraged by a variety of motivations. Most important was the strategic use of external broadcasting as a weapon in the Cold War. The political and ideological rivalry between the two superpowers gave a new lease on life to the Voice of America, which had been created as a wartime expedient. Although the official objective was to make available to people behind the "iron curtain" and elsewhere a source of balanced news and information that they would not otherwise have, it remained unclear and controversial just how hard the programming should also push American values and policies. This ambivalence produced, in the eyes of one observer, "spasms of objectivity" alternating with "high pressure selling of freedom and democracy."[56] In addition to the Voice of America, which broadcast programs about the United States and general news from the U.S. perspective, Radio Free Europe and Radio Liberty were created to provide an alternative domestic service for the people in Eastern Europe and the Soviet Union respectively. The USSR attempted to counter these efforts with its own broadcasts from Radio Moscow, which promoted the virtues of socialism, portrayed the USSR as a benign military and economic power, explained Soviet foreign policies, and attacked the evils of capitalism and imperialism.

New broadcasters emerged out of this rivalry, as the USSR helped the countries of Eastern Europe to establish international stations, and the United States encouraged West Germany and Japan to resume international broadcasts.[57] Following its Communist revolution the new government of the People's Republic of China significantly expanded its external broadcasting, and by 1960 China had become the third largest international broadcaster in the world. Although the main target audience was in Asia, a considerable part of the output was directed at the Soviet Union after 1962, when relations between the two Communist countries deteriorated.[58]

Egypt began international broadcasting in the early 1950s with revolutionary goals of a different kind, namely, to advocate radical social change and Arab unity throughout the Middle East. After leading a coup against King Farouk, Gamal Abdel Nasser established a high-powered broadcasting system, including the "Voice of the Arabs," as a key weapon in his revolution. He was one of the first leaders in the region to understand the power of radio as a medium for mobilizing opinion among lower-income and illiterate segments of the population. In the late 1950s relatively inexpensive transistor radios became available. This technological revolution coincided with political movements in North Africa and Iraq that overthrew royal families or gained independence from colonial powers.[59]

Other developing countries established international broadcasting services during this same period, when they gained independence. Radio Ghana broadcast strongly nationalistic and anticolonial programming, for example. All-India Radio's external service was aimed primarily at Indians living abroad and to promote the Indian position vis-à-vis Pakistan. By the early 1970s approximately one hundred governments in the world had at least a rudimentary international foreign-language radio service, almost double the number that existed in 1945.[60] Some governments were more interested in enhancing their prestige; others actively sought to influence foreign opinion or otherwise promote certain national interests; and still others were more concerned with cultivating cultural ties. Most government-supported services aimed to serve multiple objectives, a fact that often complicated the task of programming.

Other types of international radio broadcasting also developed rapidly after World War II. In the late 1940s and early 1950s religious stations, generally sponsored by Protestant groups, spread particularly in Africa and Asia, for the purpose of proselytizing. In the next two decades Islamic international stations were established, aimed at strengthening the faith of believers.[61] Commercial stations also proliferated after the war. Entertainment fare and advertising dominated the programming of these stations. Both religious and commercial international shortwave broadcasting is widespread today. Clandestine stations with political purposes played an active role in the Cold War; they continue to crop up in civil conflicts and where incoming information is restricted. Typically, an insurgent group will establish a clandestine station in a neighboring state in order to rouse the population to overthrow the government. Finally, all these external broadcasters shared the high-frequency band with amateur radio operators transmitting two-way, noncommercial radio communications. Their growth in numbers surged after World War II. Although amateur radio is primarily a hobby, operators often provide a communication link during emergencies, disasters, and political turmoil, when no other alternative is available.

In spite of the efforts that went into international broadcasting, radio served primarily domestic audiences. From the earliest days, however, even domestic programming had implications for the conduct of international relations. Newscasts helped to shape images of other countries and interpretations of international events, providing a potential influence on individual opinions about foreign policy and conceptions about world politics. Developments in sound recording, especially the tape recorder, made it easier for reports to be made in the field, then inserted into domestic newscasts. Hearing sounds and voices from distant places gave an immediacy that made the reports more compelling. After the development of the transistor in the 1950s, radios became smaller, cheaper, more portable, and more widely distributed. Although television displaced radio as the dominant mass medium in many countries about the same time, radio has continued to be the most ubiquitous and widespread global medium.

Television

Whereas the major impetus for the development of radio came from thousands of amateur operators, the technology of television was developed largely within the radio industry, depending from the beginning on research grants from governments and from large companies.[62] Early experimental telecasts in Britain and the United States in the late 1920s and for most of the next decade generated little public interest. This lack of demand was attributable in part to the popularity of radio at the time, the Great Depression, the poor quality of the initial images, and the high cost of television sets. The world's first regular television service was begun in Germany in 1935, but it was discontinued within the year. The quality of pictures was poor, programming was sporadic, and no television sets were ever sold. More successful was the London Television Service, which opened the following year and transmitted regular, varied programming with high-quality pictures. On September 30, 1938, the service even managed to broadcast "live" the arrival of the British prime minister Neville Chamberlain from Munich, proclaiming that his meeting with Hitler had produced "peace in our time." This was the first broadcast of a major news event as it occurred.[63] Television sets were just beginning to sell in large numbers in Britain when World War II began.

The growth of sales in Britain inspired David Sarnoff of RCA to make the development of television in the United States a top priority. The revenues from RCA's manufacture of radios and from its radio network, NBC, provided the finances for this endeavor. Further, RCA controlled many relevant patents as the result of the navy's efforts in 1919 to keep them out of Marconi's hands. Television service began in the United States on April 30, 1939, when President Franklin D. Roosevelt opened the RCA exhibit at the New York World's Fair. Sets went on sale, but the quality of the service was low, and few were sold. World War II suspended the development of television broadcasting, but the spin-offs from weapons research in the electronics industry significantly improved the quality of television transmission. When regular television broadcasting resumed after the war with these improvements, the American public was far more receptive. According to the U.S. statistical abstracts, the number of households with televisions increased from 8,000 to 3,875,000 between 1946 and 1950, then by 1955 swelled to 30,700,000 households.

The early regulatory decisions for television in the United States were no more favorable to noncommercial television than the ones for radio. The FCC decision to locate television service in the very high frequency (VHF) portion of the electromagnetic spectrum restricted the total number of channels to twelve nationwide and only three stations in most cities. Most channels were licensed to commercial operators. When, after much lobbying on the part of educational organizations, the FCC decided in 1952 to reserve channels for noncommercial broadcasters, two-thirds were in the ultrahigh frequency band (UHF), which could be accessed by only 7 percent of the television sets in use at that time.[64] Further, the higher the frequency, the smaller the range of a transmitter. With unfavorable channel allocations, no interconnected national network, and no reliable sources of funding, noncommercial TV and radio had little impact until pressures for change culminated in the Public Broadcasting Act of 1967. This legislation created National Public Radio and established some basis for federal funding for public radio and television. Even then, federal support depended on annual appropriations in Congress. The remaining financial support came from varied and diverse sources, including state and local governments, educational institutions, foundations, corporations, and individual contributions.

Although television grew much more rapidly in the United States than elsewhere in the 1950s, it began to spread widely not only in industrial countries but also in the developing world. By the end of the decade eighteen Latin American countries had some form of television, and by the middle of the 1960s eighteen Asian countries were broadcasting television. By the end of the 1960s half of the countries of the world had launched television services, including fifteen African countries.[65] U.S. commercial interests encouraged some of this expansion, especially through their investments in television stations in Latin America. Beyond Latin America, the U.S. government sponsored television exhibits at international trade shows. U.S. television equipment manufacturers aggressively promoted their products and helped to establish television systems. For example, RCA provided a complete television service for Egypt, which went on the air in 1960, and the beginnings of a service for Syria.[66] Another impetus for the introduction of television was the demonstration effect of U.S. television stations abroad that were located on military bases, notably in the Philippines and South Korea, and the camps of American oil companies in some of the Gulf states.

In Africa, the initiative for the development of television services came in many cases from the departing colonial powers.[67] In Asian countries such as China, India, Indonesia, Taiwan, Singapore, and Hong Kong, the introduction of television was part of development and modernization policies. The governments of many new nations took a special interest in the potential for radio and television to unify and integrate the various ethnic groups, which the boundaries of the colonial masters had left behind, and to encourage the growth of a national consciousness. In addition, there was great interest in the media's potential for national development by promoting literacy and health, improving agriculture, and encouraging limits on family size.

India was the leading experimenter with "development TV." In the first decade of television the government focused attention on educational experiments in the villages. Most notable was the Satellite Instructional Television Experiment (SITE), a pilot project in 1975–1976 to test the feasibility of satellite broadcasting to rural areas. The SITE project used a satellite from the U.S. National Aeronautics and Space Administration (NASA) to broadcast special programs to several million people in 2,400 villages, where 8,000 community television sets were installed. Subsequently, India developed its own satellite system for radio and television broadcasting. India also pioneered the world's first long-running prodevelopment television soap opera, "Hum Log," a series that ran for seventeen months from 1984 to 1985. It began as a family planning soap opera, but this theme was later toned down to emphasize family harmony and the status of women. The series was extremely popular and inspired other developing countries to launch programs following the same pattern.[68]

It was this popularity, however, that demonstrated to the government how lucrative the revenues from advertising could be for the state-owned monopoly, Doordarshan, and convinced potential advertisers of the tremendous benefits to be gained by sponsoring programs. The sponsor of "Hum Log," a hitherto unknown instant noodle product, became a middle-class household staple overnight. Commercial sponsorship became a more significant feature on Indian television thereafter, and the air soon filled with song and dance numbers from Indian musical films. Although development objectives continued to be reflected in Doordarshan's programming, the move toward commercialization contributed to the shift in the focus from the villages to the urban middle class. Political objectives, such as education, national integration, and political mobilization, did continue to influence programming, but to a lesser extent. The arrival of satellite television in Asia would move India and other developing countries further toward commercialization.

Whether a government adopted the U.S. marketplace model or the public service monopoly model, the public-private sector issue persisted, leading over time to modifications that have resulted in a mixed public-private system in most countries. Government policies in Britain and the United States, pioneers in the development of radio and television, led to two different broadcasting traditions, but each eventually made adjustments in the direction of the other. The development of public broadcasting in the United States indicated that the market alone could not guarantee that certain kinds of valuable programming would be available. Ironically, in the same year that the first not-for-profit television station went on the air in the United States, 1954, the British government authorized a commercial system to operate alongside the BBC.[69] Pressures to move in this direction came not only from industrial and financial interests but also from those who found Lord Reith's high-minded programming boring and longed for more lively fare. The British move toward a mixed public and commercial system was replicated in dozens of other countries over the next two decades. Even in some countries where the government monopoly was retained, advertising was permitted as a source of revenue and as a means of accommodating commercial pressures.[70] In sum, a diversity of broadcasting structures have evolved with varying degrees of emphasis on the public or the commercial purposes. As the next chapter will indicate, television in most countries has become increasingly dependent upon advertising revenue.

Conclusion

This survey of the introduction and early development of the printing press, the telegraph, the telephone, and broadcasting provides historical background for assessing the impact of the communication and information technologies that transformed the world in the last quarter of the twentieth century. The narrative is instructive regarding the influences that shape the direction and impact of new communication technologies more generally, and it indicates how these particular technologies laid the foundations for today's information revolution.

This historical analysis illustrates many characteristics of the innovation process. One innovation often leads to another, as each encourages experimentation to address its predecessor's limitations. The push-pull effect between technology and social change is well exemplified in the above cases, particularly the printing press and the wireless telegraph. Gutenberg's press was a response to the growing demand from groups that had interests in the wider dissemination of information for quicker, easier reproduction of manuscripts. The invention was both a response to an increase in the size of the reading public and an impetus to greater expansion, which in turn encouraged the proliferation of printing presses.

The electric telegraph popularized the idea of rapid, long-distance, point-to-point communication, but the cost and difficulty of stringing wires across borders and British dominance of the submarine networks stimulated the search for wireless alternatives. National security concerns, corporate rivalries, and the curiosity of amateur hobbyists propelled experimentation in several different directions, one of which was broadcast radio. Like the Internet a half century later, the role of the users was crucial in moving the technology in a direction quite different from the objectives of the original designers. In its earliest stages of development, radio was a democratizing medium in the sense that cheap crystal sets allowed millions of amateurs to transmit messages from a single point to multiple audiences at minimal cost. But heavy usage of the airwaves for many different purposes—military, commercial, and amateur experimentation—led to government regulation to avoid chaos. Government policies, reflecting different cultural and political preferences and responding to economic pressures, gave each broadcasting system its distinctive character by defining who would have access to the new medium for what purposes. The trajectory that began with the wireless telegraph dramatically illustrates the indeterminate character of technological innovations, the way in which the properties of a technology, political institutions and policies, economic forces, and social uses interact to shape its direction and impact.

Each invention discussed in this chapter has contributed to the expansion of access to information and to the development of the idea of human communication over long distances. Collectively these inventions have vastly increased information flows across national borders and multiplied the channels of communication between societies.

The spread of mechanized printing in Europe encouraged the spirit of scientific inquiry, expanded the body of knowledge, and facilitated the exchange of information and ideas across space and time. The increased availability of reading materials in vernacular languages also encouraged the growth of literacy. It was four centuries before books, newspapers, and magazines were read by such large segments of the population that they could be considered mass media, but Gutenberg's invention began the process.

The electric telegraph was the first communication technology to establish a worldwide network that spanned the continents and the oceans to transmit information quickly over almost any distance. It was the first form of communication to convey messages faster than the fastest form of transportation. It connected not only the urban, economic centers of Europe and North America but also places quite remote from those centers. This multicontinental network of telegraph cables made possible regular interactions among political and business elites and helped them to be more informed more quickly about distant events. In an indirect way it also affected the daily lives of a broader segment of the population by giving newspapers access to news as it happened. The newswire services emerged contemporaneously with the spread of the telegraph, establishing patterns of news gathering and distribution that persist today.

The telephone introduced the first truly interactive medium and the idea of two-way conversations across distances. Technical problems associated with the transmission of voice over distance and the absence of European initiatives to devise uniform standards across the various national systems delayed the development of the telephone as a major medium of international communication. Only in the last quarter of the twentieth century did new technologies—especially orbiting telecommunication satellites and intercontinental cables—and a different political environment bring to fruition the potential of this personal form of communication to connect societies as well as governments and other elites.

Broadcast radio was the first medium to bring distant events—elections, coronations, and wars—into the living rooms of ordinary people. Radio has the potential to inform much larger audiences than the newspaper-reading publics and to present news about the world with more immediacy. As regular newscasts became a standard fare on radio in most countries, the potential expanded for the medium to shape individual interpretations of international events and the images that people of different countries had of each other. Governments quickly recognized the potential of the medium to influence popular attitudes and opinions. In a variety of ways even those governments that did not directly control the institutional apparatus used it to mobilize domestic support for their foreign policies. Many governments even established international shortwave broadcasting services that aimed to influence the opinions of populations beyond their own borders. Although the quality of information varied considerably, international broadcasts did provide a window on the world, an alternative perspective to domestic programming. The BBC in particular has served as a kind of alternative service in countries where the radio is primarily a mouthpiece for a dictatorship, illustrating radio's capacity to challenge as well as strengthen existing political authority. The significance of radio lies in its affordability and portability, which make it accessible to a broader portion of the world's population than any other medium of communication.

Television brought not only the sounds of distant people and events into the home but also the pictures, adding new dimensions of realism, immediacy, and persuasiveness to broadcasting. As photographers and filmmakers had already demonstrated, images convey simple messages with an economy of words—or none at all—and they can generate a range of intense emotions. To see the dying soldier, the starving child, the royal wedding, or the president's funeral cortege is to experience the event directly and personally, yet in the company of millions. Television connects members of the mass audience together in the shared experience of watching the same programs, especially those occasions that celebrate the collective identity. Film newsreels had performed these functions, but with television the events were brought into the home. From the earliest flickering, snowy images it was clear that television had the capacity to serve many different, even contradictory, purposes. It was a potential instrument of social and political mobilization. Leaders could explain their policies face-to-face with their citizens. Educational and entertainment programs could inculcate cultural values. Television could convey information and expand viewers' knowledge of the world beyond the living room—from the local community to the most distant and unfamiliar places.

And, of course, television could entertain. It was this attribute that has made television such a lucrative business and has moved most systems—however different at the outset—toward the U.S. commercial model. Once a system became even partially dependent on advertising, the lure of entertainment fare with the widest audience appeal became irresistible to programmers. This trajectory for television was set when the dominant economic power, following its free-market tradition, relegated all but the most minimal regulatory control over broadcasting to the private sector, and the pattern of commercial sponsorship quickly took hold. The aim of the sponsor was to sell products. In search of greater revenues, the newly created national networks established distribution systems to promote and export films and tapes of their programs abroad. It was soon clear that these exports, and other popular programs that were domestically produced, could provide substantial revenues for the corporations or the governments that controlled and financed broadcasting in each country.

The development of the press and broadcasting marks the emergence of what came to be known as the "mass media." The potential of the printing press to become a mass medium was not fully realized until the nineteenth century with increases in the level of literacy and technological innovations that accelerated the production process while reducing costs.

Radio and television made news and information accessible to even larger numbers of people. As literacy was not necessary, even the poorest and least educated individuals could learn from these media.

The capacity of radio, television, and the press to transmit ideas, information, and entertainment to vast numbers of people put tremendous power in the hands of those who control the media and the purposes for which they are used. That control has been a contested issue with ongoing tensions between the private and the public sector. State control over content as well as infrastructure presents an officially sanctioned picture of reality that reinforces existing political authority. A minimally regulated broadcasting system under private control might produce many more channels, but content for all will be determined by the same market imperatives that favor certain types of programming over others. Political, social, and cultural factors further limit the boundaries of discussion and orient interpretation of events. The media systems of the most democratic states, as well as the most authoritarian regimes, are obliged to report the actions and statements of officials. Prevailing norms, values, and concerns of the population also operate in subtle ways to influence content. In short, the press, radio, and television significantly affect the way in which people and societies know, perceive, and understand the world, but the picture of reality the mass media present is limited because the media are inherently selective. The technological developments discussed in this chapter are the vanguard of the information revolution. They have led to enormous increases in the magnitude, density, and scope of communication channels across national boundaries. They began a process of informing and connecting humankind that rapidly accelerated in the last quarter of the twentieth century.

Notes

1. World Bank, *World Bank Report, 2006: Equity and Development* (Washington, D.C.: World Bank Publications, 2005), 293.

2. This is the theme of Ronald J. Deibert's *Parchment, Printing, and Hypermedia: Communication in World Order Transformation* (New York: Columbia University Press, 1997).

3. Stephen Saxby, *The Age of Information: The Past Development and Future Significance of Computing and Communications* (London: Macmillan, 1990), 45, as quoted in Deibert, *Parchment, Printing, and Hypermedia*, 65.

4. Leonard M. Dudley, *The Word and the Sword: How Techniques of Information and Violence Have Shaped Our World* (Cambridge, Mass.: Blackwell, 1991), 146.

5. This phrase comes from Benedict Anderson's *Imagined Communities: Reflections on the Origins and Spread of Nationalism* (New York: Verso, 1991), 39, an excellent analysis

of the role of the printing press in the development of the modern state and national consciousness.

6. Elizabeth Eisenstein, *The Printing Press as Agent of Change: Communications and Cultural Transformations in Early Modern Europe* (New York: Cambridge University Press, 1979), 1:307.

7. Lucien Febvre and Henri-Jean Martin, *The Coming of the Book: The Impact of Printing, 1450–1800*, trans. David Gerard (Atlantic Highlands, N.J.: Humanities Press, 1976), 288.

8. Anderson, *Imagined Communities*, 39.

9. Anderson, *Imagined Communities*, 107.

10. For a discussion of these ideas see Anderson, *Imagined Communities*, chap. 3, and Deibert, *Parchment, Printing, and Hypermedia*, chap. 4.

11. Febvre and Martin, *The Coming of the Book*, 310.

12. Febvre and Martin, *The Coming of the Book*, 237–38.

13. Peter J. Hugill, *Global Communications since 1844: Geopolitics and Technology* (Baltimore: Johns Hopkins University Press, 1999), 2.

14. International Telecommunication Union (ITU), "History," at www.itu.int/aboutitu/overview/history.html (accessed July 9, 2007).

15. Daniel R. Headrick, *The Tentacles of Progress: Technology Transfer in the Age of Imperialism, 1850–1940* (New York: Oxford University Press, 1988), 98.

16. Headrick, *The Tentacles of Progress*, 101. In addition to Headrick, a good discussion of the cable to India can be found in J. M. Adams, "Development of the Anglo-Indian Telegraph," *Engineering and Science Education Journal* (August 1997): 140–48.

17. Headrick, *The Tentacles of Progress*, 117–19.

18. Headrick, *The Tentacles of Progress*, 101, 104. Except where otherwise indicated, most information about submarine cables comes from Headrick.

19. Headrick, *The Tentacles of Progress*, 106.

20. Charles Briggs and Augustus Maverick, quoted in Tom Standage, *The Victorian Internet* (New York: Walker and Company, 1998), 83. He provides a collection of similar statements.

21. Kuldip R. Rampal, "The Collection and Flow of World News," in *Global Journalism: Survey of International Communication*, ed. John C. Merrill, 3rd ed. (White Plains, N.Y.: Longman, 1995), 36–39.

22. Hugill, *Global Communications*, 53.

23. J. C. Nyiri, "Cyberspace: A Planetary Network of People and Ideas," *UNESCO Courier* 50 (June 1997): 25.

24. Eric Barnouw, ed., *International Encyclopedia of Communications* (New York: Oxford University Press, 1989), 212.

25. *Encyclopaedia Britannica Online*, "Telephone and Telephone System," at www.britannica.com/eb/article-9110260/telephone-and-telephone-system (accessed August 12, 1999).

26. Barnouw, *International Encyclopedia*, 213. Information in the next two paragraphs comes from this source.

27. Barnouw, *International Encyclopedia*, 53.

28. Barnouw, *International Encyclopedia*, 213–14.

29. Hugill, *Global Communications*, 77.

30. Barnouw, *International Encyclopedia*, 213.

31. Barnouw, *International Encyclopedia*, 214.

32. Hugill, *Global Communications*, 80. The information in the following paragraph on European telephony comes from Hugill, *Global Communications*, 77–80.

33. Barnouw, *International Encyclopedia*, 417.

34. Susan J. Douglas, *Inventing American Broadcasting: 1899–1922* (Baltimore: Johns Hopkins University Press, 1987), xviii–xxix. This excellent account of the transition from wireless to radio provides the basis for the discussion of that topic here.

35. Barnouw, *International Encyclopedia*, 418.

36. This is a major theme in Douglas, *Inventing American Broadcasting*.

37. Douglas, *Inventing American Broadcasting*, 198.

38. Douglas, *Inventing American Broadcasting*, 207.

39. Douglas, *Inventing American Broadcasting*, 214–15.

40. Daniel Headrick, *The Invisible Weapon: Telecommunications and International Politics, 1851–1945* (New York: Oxford University Press, 1991), 203–6.

41. Hugill, *Global Communications*, 137.

42. Douglas, *Inventing American Broadcasting*, 198. This book, especially chap. 6, provides an excellent discussion of the role of amateur operators.

43. Douglas, *Inventing American Broadcasting*, 420.

44. William Boddy, "The Beginnings of American Television," in *Television: An International History*, ed. Anthony Smith (New York: Oxford University Press, 1995), 38.

45. Douglas, *Inventing American Broadcasting*, 316.

46. Robert K. Avery, *Public Service Broadcasting in a Multichannel Environment* (New York: Longman, 1993), 2.

47. Avery, *Public Service Broadcasting*, 158.

48. Quoted in Boddy, "The Beginnings of American Television," 38.

49. Barnouw, *International Encyclopedia*, 419.

50. See James Wood, *History of International Broadcasting* (London: Peter Peregrinus, 1992), especially chaps. 6 and 8; Gary D. Rawnsley, *Radio Diplomacy and Propaganda: The BBC and VOA in International Politics, 1956–64* (New York: St. Martin's Press, 1996), chap. 1.

51. Douglas Boyd, *Broadcasting in the Arab World: A Survey of the Electronic Media in the Middle East*, 2nd ed. (Ames: Iowa State University Press, 1993), 284–87; Wood, *History of International Broadcasting*, 38–40.

52. Wood, *History of International Broadcasting*, 69.

53. Barnouw, *International Encyclopedia*, 421.

54. Julian Hale, *Radio Power: Propaganda and International Broadcasting* (Philadelphia: Temple University Press, 1975), 53.

55. Hale, *Radio Power*, 97.

56. The objective of the Voice of America is stated in a speech by the director, San-ford Unger, to the Overseas Press Club of America, December 13, 1999. The quoted description of the Voice of America (VOA) comes from Hale, *Radio Power*, 164.

57. Barnouw, *International Encyclopedia*, 424.

58. Hale, *Radio Power*, 27.

59. Boyd, *Broadcasting in the Arab World*, 4, 28–29.

60. Hale, *Radio Power*, xii.

61. Barnouw, *International Encyclopedia*, 424.

62. Barnouw, *International Encyclopedia*, 418; Anthony Smith, "Television: A Pub-lic Service Medium," in *Television: An International History*, ed. Anthony Smith (New York: Oxford University Press, 1995), 63–64.

63. Albert Abramson, "The Invention of Television," in *Television: An Interna-tional History*, ed. Anthony Smith (New York: Oxford University Press, 1995), 30.

64. Boddy, "The Beginnings of American Television," 56.

65. Barnouw, *International Encyclopedia*, 221.

66. Boyd, *Broadcasting in the Arab World*, 38.

67. Dietrich Berwanger, "The Third World," in *Television: An International His-tory*, ed. Anthony Smith (New York: Oxford University Press, 1995), 310–11.

68. Arvind Singhal and Everett M. Rogers, *India's Information Revolution* (New-bury Park, Calif.: Sage, 1989), 62–67.

69. Barnouw, *International Encyclopedia*, 221.

70. Barnouw, *International Encyclopedia*, 222.

CHAPTER THREE

⌁

The Globalization
of Communication

Today, after more than a century of electronic technology, we have extended our central nervous system itself in a global embrace, abolishing
both space and time as far as our planet is concerned. As electronically
contracted, the globe is no more than a village.

—Marshall McLuhan[1]

We now have at hand the technological breakthroughs and economic
means to bring all the communities of the world together. We now can
at last create a planetary information network that transmits messages
and images with the speed of light from the largest city to the smallest
village on every continent.

—Former Vice President Al Gore[2]

High in the Himalayas, not far from Mount Everest, sits the Namche Cyber
Café, where trekkers from many nations can report on their progress to the
folks back home and receive messages with news about the family, the business, or the world. It is this improbable kind of connectivity that inspires the
metaphors that permeate the discourse on the developments in communication at the beginning of the twenty-first century. It is not merely the "World
Wide Web" that is connecting distant parts of the world. A whole array of
technologies has extended the reach of the telephone, radio, and television;
channels for transmitting information, messages, and ideas across vast distances are proliferating.

Globalizing Technologies

In order to consider the impact of the information revolution on world poli-tics, it is necessary to identify some of the key technological developments that have contributed to it. Some have merely improved and extended the reach of earlier inventions. Others have created entirely new means of com-municating, accessing, and diffusing information. Most significant in their po-tential to create global communication networks are fiber-optic cables, geo-synchronous satellites, and a combination of innovations that produced the computer and the Internet. One way to understand these changes is to view their impact on the three major branches of communications: telecommuni-cations (telephone, cable, and satellite transmission); audiovisual products (television, radio, and the press); and computer-mediated communication.

Fiber-Optic Cable

As indicated in chapter 2, the electric telegraph was the first global commu-nication and information system. By the beginning of the twentieth century a network of submarine cables, with the capacity to transmit telegraph mes-sages instantaneously, connected the continents. Technically, the transmis-sion of the human voice over long distances by wire is far more complex than sending dots and dashes. To maintain a high-quality voice signal over a long distance requires amplification at close intervals, which in turn demands tremendous amounts of power. The challenge of developing a submarine ca-ble that met those requirements and was sufficiently protected against the hazards of the ocean was formidable. It was not until 1956 that the first tele-phone cable was installed across the Atlantic (TAT-1), using two coaxial ca-bles, one for each direction.

There had been transatlantic telephone service by radio since 1927, but it suffered from poor speech quality and low capacity. TAT-1 was a major im-provement, but long delays and distortions continued to impair telephone service between Europe and the United States. The cable had only thirty-six circuits, which meant that only thirty-six simultaneous conversations could be transmitted between the two continents. Walter Wriston, the former chairman of Citibank, describes in his book on the information revolution the difficulties of getting a telephone connection between Brazil and the bank's headquarters in New York during the 1950s and 1960s. It could take a day or more just to get a circuit and then, "once the connection was made, people in the branch would stay on the phone reading books and newspapers all day just to keep the line open until it was needed."[3]

A succession of transatlantic cables followed TAT-1, advancing the technology and expanding capacity. However, the most significant undersea cable breakthrough did not come until 1988, when the first fiber-optic cable across the Atlantic went into service, providing far more capacity than all the coaxial cables combined. Using pulses of laser light to transmit voice and data over thin glass strands, it could transmit forty thousand calls at one time. It was a joint venture of twenty-nine telephone companies from Europe and North America, including AT&T, ITT World Communications, MCI, British Telecom, France Telecom, and Western Union. AT&T installed and operated the cable.[4]

Spurred by the demand for high-speed communication networks for the Internet, investment in fiber-optic cables to traverse oceans as well as continents soared in the 1990s. In the last two years of the twentieth century alone, one hundred million miles of optical fiber were laid around the world—"enough to reach the sun."[5] But this added capacity far exceeded the demand, and in 2004 only 11 percent of available undersea bandwidth globally was being used.[6] One reason for all the excess capacity was the number of companies that were established with ambitious plans for building intercontinental fiber-optic networks. A second reason was that technological innovations continually increased the capacity of fiber-optic cable, so that capacity continued to outpace demand, even when demand increased. Yet a third reason was a shortage of high-speed local access connections, which limited growth in demand for high-speed, long-haul information pipelines. All that excess capacity sent the prices on leased lines plummeting and dried up future investment funds. By the year 2000, the bubble had burst for the undersea cable industry, and nearly every company involved had been restructured or had gone bankrupt.

Meanwhile, Internet use was taking off in Asia and the Middle East, where many countries had little access to global undersea cable networks. Entrepreneurial enthusiasm resurfaced, and ambitious new projects were developed for cables under the Indian Ocean, the Persian Gulf, and the Mediterranean Sea to connect Asia, the Middle East, and Europe. There is and will undoubtedly be a growth in demand for high-speed Internet data and telephone transmission in these underserved areas, and five years into the new century general demand once again accelerated. This instability in the fiber-optic industry illustrates the interconnectedness of the properties of the technology (high capacity), market forces, government policies (that affect the distribution and use of the Internet), and the choices of individuals and companies to use the Internet.

Geosynchronous Satellites

Meanwhile, during this period when transoceanic cables were being installed, the technology for satellite transmission also was developing. Satellites are orbiting space stations that are used to relay signals from one point
on earth to another (or to many other points). The first artificial satellite,
Sputnik, was launched by the Soviet Union in 1957. Although it was very
primitive and could do nothing more than send continual beeps to earth, this
demonstration of technical prowess on the part of its Cold War rival
prompted increased U.S. government support for scientific research in general and satellites in particular. The first experimental satellites in the latter
part of the 1950s and early 1960s had minute footprints, that is, the area from
which they could receive signals was very small, and they had a very limited
capacity. They were "passive," merely reflecting radio signals back to earth.
They required expensive ground stations, which had to be able to track the
constantly moving satellite. The first communications satellite was Telstar I,
launched in 1962, an "active" satellite, capable of receiving signals from
earth, then amplifying and retransmitting them back to earth. Telstar I was
the first satellite to transmit live television signals and telephone conversations across the Atlantic Ocean.

A defining moment in the development of satellite communication was
the launching of Syncom 2 in 1963 into a geosynchronous orbit. Because a
satellite orbiting the earth at approximately 22,300 miles above the equator
rotates around the earth in twenty-four hours, it moves exactly in synchro-
nization with the earth's rotation on its axis and appears to have a fixed location in relation to any particular spot on earth. Geosynchronous (or geostationary) satellites operated with cheaper and, eventually, much smaller
ground stations. Syncom 3, which was launched in 1964, relayed the first sustained transpacific television pictures—the Tokyo Olympic games.

Research and development for communications satellites was conducted in
the context of U.S.-Soviet rivalry, projecting it into space. Scientific and military interest in rocketry led to the development of the rockets necessary to
launch satellites, and the very first satellites were launched by the military.
One outcome of the Sputnik shock was the creation by President Dwight D.
Eisenhower in 1958 of the National Aeronautics and Space Administration
(NASA) as the civilian vehicle for space research and development and as
the coordinating mechanism for the activities of government and industry.
President Eisenhower made the establishment of a commercial satellite system
a national objective, and he strongly encouraged private-sector leadership in
U.S. space initiatives.[7] By 1960, the major communication and aviation com-
panies were conducting research and competing for NASA contracts.

President John F. Kennedy continued his predecessor's efforts to develop an operational satellite system as soon as possible, both for commercial gain and for the prestige that leadership in this technology would bring to the United States. He was reluctant, however, to turn operational control entirely over to the private sector because he viewed U.S. leadership in developing a global satellite system as an important tenet of his administration's foreign policy. Official speeches for both domestic and international audiences were replete with references to the need for cooperation in outer space and to the potential benefits to all humankind of a global system of communication satellites. Illustrative of this policy was a proposal to the United Nations by the U.S. ambassador, Adlai Stevenson, which resulted in a General Assembly resolution stating that "communications by means of satellite should be available to the nations of the world as soon as practicable on a global and nondiscriminatory basis."[8]

The development of communication satellites raised a host of complex policy issues regarding further research and development, as well as the ownership and operation of increasingly more powerful and sophisticated satellites. To make maximum use of the technology's benefits, a global satellite system was necessary. What should be the institutional framework of this system? What should be the role of the private sector, and how open should the system be? What form should U.S. leadership take? How should they ensure that the benefits were widely distributed, even to developing countries? There was no consensus on these issues within the U.S. administration or Congress. The outcome of lengthy deliberations in Congress was the formation of the Communications Satellite Corporation (Comsat), a unique compromise on the public-private issue—modified private enterprise.[9] Half of Comsat was owned by corporations and half by the public through shares. The board consisted of representatives of the corporations, the public stockholders, and the government.

Comsat was authorized to participate in the establishment and operation of an international satellite system. A series of negotiations with European countries resulted in a treaty in 1964 that created the International Telecommunications Satellite Organization (Intelsat), an international consortium with a mandate to develop, own, and manage a global satellite system. The charter members were nineteen industrialized countries of Western Europe and North America, plus Japan and Australia, but the membership ballooned to 144 by the end of the century. Intelsat operated as a commercial cooperative and wholesale provider of satellite communication services. Ownership and investment (measured in shares) was distributed among the members of the organization according to their respective use of the services, and investment shares determined each member's total contribution (and its voting power). The revenue from services provided was redistributed to members in proportion to their shares.

The global satellite system that developed in the two decades following the formation of Intelsat both reflected and enhanced U.S. leadership in satellite communication. It was the Kennedy administration's eagerness to see an international commercial satellite system in place as soon as possible that provided the impetus for its creation. The United States always had the largest ownership share and, consequently, the loudest voice. U.S. corporations provided most of the technology and equipment for the satellites launched by Intelsat.

Intelsat maintained a near monopoly as a global satellite telecommunications network until the 1990s. The Soviet Union and other Communist countries did not join Intelsat but established in 1971 a separate consortium, the International Organization of Space Communications (Intersputnik), to provide international satellite telecommunications services among its allies. The International Maritime Satellite Organization (Inmarsat) was established in 1979 to provide worldwide maritime communications. Although many nations depend upon Intelsat telecommunications for their domestic telecommunications, in the 1980s a number of governments and regional organizations began to establish their own satellite systems. Regional satellite systems include Eutelsat, AsiaSat, Arabsat, and Palapa (Southeast Asia). In 1989 Pan American Satellite Inc. began operations, the first organization to operate global satellite services in competition with Intelsat. Since that time many other private firms have intensified the competition.

In order to meet this competition more effectively, Intelsat became a private company in 2001 after thirty-seven years as an intergovernmental organization, and in 2006 it merged with PanAmSat holding corporation.[10]

At the beginning of the twenty-first century there were over two hundred active communications satellites in orbit, creating a global network with the capability of connecting any two points on earth. The first commercial communication satellite, Intelsat I (Earlybird), which was launched in 1965, provided only 240 telephone circuits and one television circuit for transmission across the Atlantic. Successive generations of satellites, benefiting from a conjunction of technologies, have vastly increased the capacity, power, versatility, and scope of communications satellites.

In the 1970s and 1980s the capacity of satellites grew far faster than that of undersea cables, and about two-thirds of all international telephony was routed through satellite channels during those decades. With the proliferation of fiber-optic cable systems in the 1990s, the pattern shifted in the other direction. By the end of the century undersea fiber-optic cables handled about 80 percent of all cross-continent telephone and data traffic. One reason for this shift is the difference in capacity—a single fiber-optic cable can handle a thousand times more capacity than a single satellite.[11] Fiber-optic systems are cheaper to deploy, more economical to operate, require less maintenance than satellites, and have a longer life. They have a shorter lag time, or delay in signal transmission, than geosynchronous satellites. For that reason they are preferable for point-to-point voice transmissions.

Satellites can broadcast signals over the entire area of the satellite footprint, which can be as large as one-third of the world. Satellites are best for point-to-multipoint services, that is, transmissions from a central point to large numbers of sites. Consequently, television broadcasting is one of the heaviest uses of satellites. Only satellites can transmit information and telephone services to landlocked and remote places, connecting them with other networks. Earth stations placed anywhere in the satellite's beam are linked with each other through the satellite, and they can be placed wherever they are needed. Because they do not require an extensive infrastructure of wire, cable, or microwave facilities and can serve any remote area with an earth station, satellites provide the potential for access to global communication systems that would otherwise be unavailable to developing countries. Many have leased capacity from Intelsat to expand and improve domestic telecommunications services, and some, such as India, Brazil, and Mexico, have launched their own satellites.

As successive generations of satellites have become larger and more powerful, earth stations could be smaller, cheaper, and even transportable. This technological advance is important for developing countries but also has other profound implications, such as the growth of direct broadcast satellite television services. On the production side of television, the availability of small, portable earth stations makes possible reporting and transmission instantly from the field. Mobile telephony, networks that link cellular phones and other mobile services, is another fast-developing satellite sector.

Together, undersea fiber-optic cables and geostationary communication satellites provide the infrastructure that makes global connectivity possible today. Their development and deployment are central features of the information and communication revolution. They compete with each other for business, and the flow of traffic has shifted with technological developments. They also supplement each other, and they complement as well as connect the ground-based cable and microwave systems to globalize communication.

Computers

Computers globalize communication in at least two important ways. They route and manage traffic through the worldwide system of satellite, cable, and microwave networks, optimizing the volume and speed of the flow. They also provide, through the Internet, a medium for communication and dissemination of information that is worldwide in scope. Initially expensive, room-sized machines used primarily for calculations, then data processing, computers became a new medium of international communication when two technological streams converged: the development of the personal computer and the combination of inventions and innovations that produced network computing and the Internet.

The earliest computers were the culmination of a long search for a tool to make laborious calculations quicker, easier, and more accurate. The first functional electronic computer, called ENIAC (Electrical Numerical Integrator and Calculator), was completed in 1946 by two young scientists at the University of Pennsylvania, John Mauchly and J. Presper Eckert. The U.S. Army, in search of a machine that could be used to calculate the trajectory of artillery fire, provided four hundred thousand dollars in the early days of World War II to support the idea. ENIAC, a huge machine weighing thirty tons, was not completed until after the war. Its eighteen thousand vacuum tubes gave off enormous heat and frequently burned out. It had no memory. Instructions had to be entered into the machine by throwing a large number of switches, one by one, each time a computation was made. A new, improved machine, EDVAC, became operational in 1951 after the Hungarian-born mathematical physicist, John von Neumann, joined the research effort. It accepted instructions and input data from punch cards and was able to store programs for future use.

Eckert and Mauchly founded the first computer company, which made the first electronic digital computer constructed for commercial purposes, UNIVAC. Sperry Rand soon bought out the company and took over the patents for all of the two inventors' machines, including ENIAC. An antitrust suit resulted in a court decision to invalidate the patents, an action that in effect severed Eckert and Mauchly's names from the invention. This tragedy for the inventors was a boon to young computer innovators in the 1970s and 1980s, who were able to build upon these earlier prototypes.[12]

The commercial possibilities for computers were extremely limited until the second generation of computers replaced vacuum tubes with transistors in the latter 1950s and early 1960s. The early room-sized machines were built one at a time and were extremely costly to purchase and maintain. The computer industry was supported primarily by the government and universities, which provided most of the research and accounted for most of the sales. During this period, the height of the Cold War, military-funded research was critical to the development of the transistor and other electronic advances.[13]

Invented in 1948, transistors made the computer a more practical reality because they used less power and were more reliable than vacuum tubes. In 1963 the first minicomputers began to be mass-produced, primarily for scientific laboratories and business. The computers were a scaled-down version of the huge mainframes but were still costly and cumbersome. The market potential for computers and the possibility of their wider usage changed radically with the introduction by Intel of the integrated electronic circuit in 1969. Informally known as the chip, the "microprocessor" integrated multiple transistors and all the components needed for central processing on a single piece of semiconductor material. This was a crucial step in the development of small, faster, cheaper computers.

Personal Computers

The next logical step, in retrospect, was a desktop or personal computer (PC), which would be cheaper, be more accessible, and serve a broader market. The major computer companies ignored this opportunity for almost two decades after the advent of integrated circuits created this possibility. There were instances in which specific designs proposed by their engineers were rejected. The real inspiration for the PC came from electronics hobbyists and engineers who wanted easier access to computers.[14] The San Francisco Bay area, where the microprocessor made its debut, was a hotbed of hobbyists, who were organizing clubs to discuss how to build their own computers. When a small company called Micro Instrumentation Telemetry Systems (MITS) started selling a do-it-yourself kit with all the components for a computer in 1974, the product (the Altair) was a big hit among these groups and an impetus to further experimentation. Because it required many hours of assembly, its commercial appeal was limited.

History was made in 1976 when Stephen G. Wozniak presented his design for a PC to the Homebrew Computer Club, a design that Hewlett-Packard, where he was an intern, had declined to build. Steven P. Jobs, another participant in the meeting of hobbyists, suggested a partnership with Wozniak to produce a preassembled personal computer. When Apple Computer Inc. began to mass produce the Apple II in 1977, the personal computer industry was launched—from a garage.

Other companies also introduced personal computers, but the world's dominant computer maker, the IBM corporation, did not enter the market until 1981. It soon came to dominate the PC market, and its operating system, which was based on the Microsoft Corporation's MS-DOS system, became the industry standard. Other manufacturing companies brought out "IBM clones" at cheaper prices. Apple continued to win converts and to produce innovations. The most notable innovation was the graphical user interface (GUI), introduced by Apple in 1983 and incorporated into a new model, the Macintosh, the following year. This now familiar format allowed the user to "point and click" with a mouse to give instructions to the computer, instead of typing in commands. In 1985 Microsoft introduced Windows, a GUI, which soon became the dominant operating environment for personal computers. These improvements in software and operating systems, making computers easier to use, combined with the vigorous marketing efforts of the manufacturers to boost computer sales to individuals, educational institutions, and businesses.

The popularity of PCs also increased as other improvements made them more powerful and capable of performing more functions. Progressive advances in microprocessors dramatically increased the speed and memory capacity in each new model. One of the pioneers of the industry, Gordon Moore, estimated that chips were becoming twice as powerful and twice as cheap approximately every eighteen months, a trend that he predicted would continue. What came to be known as "Moore's Law" has proven so accurate that by the beginning of the twenty-first century the average personal computer was comparable in capacity and speed to government-funded supercomputers of the past. It was the combination of technologies that produced the Internet and made the computer a tool of communication that gave the strongest impetus to the growth of personal computers.

Digital Technology

With the progress of computers came the application of their system of processing information to the transmission of information by physical support systems, such as optical fibers and satellites. Computers use a binary system in which information is coded into a string of binary digits (1s and 0s) representing a pulse or no pulse of electrical current. Any type of information—numbers, words, images, or sounds—can be converted into a particular binary sequence of digits that defines that information. Digital systems have certain advantages over analog systems. Digitized information can be preserved, manipulated, and regenerated almost perfectly by computer. This capability is essential for satellite transmission and useful for many other purposes. Satellites have transponders to receive signals, change the frequency if necessary or more efficient, then transmit them back to earth. The reliability of the transmission of digital signals over long distances is greater because computers can recognize and reproduce digital signals more accurately. Second, digitized information can now be compressed (digital compression) to enable more information to be transmitted through any given channel more quickly. Third, digital transmission is also more flexible. Data, music, voice, and video can all be converted into digital signals and sent through the same channels. Progress in digitation has significantly affected all three branches of communication—telecommunications, audiovisual industries, and computer-mediated communication. Telephones have been employing digital technology for some time. Radio, television, and film are moving in that direction. And digital technology makes the World Wide Web a conduit for all forms of communication.

The Evolution of the Internet

The origins of the Internet are often described as the outgrowth of military research to design a computer network (ARPANET) that could survive a nuclear attack. The Department of Defense did provide the institutional and financial support that made the development of the Internet possible, and the high level of support was available because it was justified in terms of national security. The real impetus for the development of the Internet, however, came from the aspirations and vision of a remarkable collection of individuals who happened to become involved. These were not Cold War scientists but rather unorthodox computer programmers and electrical engineers who wanted to redesign the way that computers worked. Howard Rheingold writes in his historical account of the Internet, "The essential elements of what became the Net were created by people who believed in, wanted, and therefore invented ways of using computers to amplify human thinking and communication."[15]

The origins of the computer networking concept, according to a memoir by nine of the major participants, are to be found in a series of memos written in 1962 by J. C. R. Licklider, a psychologist at MIT. Claiming that computers could enhance human intellect and transform scientific thinking, he proposed the idea of a "Galactic Network," a globally interconnected set of computers through which data and programs could be accessed quickly from any site.[16] This visionary academic became the first head of the computer research program in the Advanced Projects Research Agency (ARPA) of the Department of Defense.

ARPA, like NASA, was created in 1958 in response to the Soviet launching of the first artificial satellite into space. Sputnik was perceived by U.S. leadership and portrayed by the media as a double threat. It demonstrated the potential capability for the Soviet Union to send an intercontinental ballistic missile to the United States, and it suggested that the technological superiority of the United States was declining. This defining moment allowed advocates of basic scientific research to link research support to national security. President Eisenhower, sympathetic to this linkage, selected as secretary of defense Neil McElroy, who, as president of Procter & Gamble, had created a large laboratory for basic research, where scientists were given a great deal of autonomy.

It was in this context that ARPA was created with a broad mandate to fund cutting-edge research, both basic and applied. It reported directly to the secretary of defense and was designed to be independent of pressures from the individual services for specific projects. The head, Jack Ruina, appointed Licklider to direct the computer research projects because he believed that exploring new ways of using the computer could benefit scientific research in general, as well as weapons research. Licklider knew there was "a whole subculture of unorthodox programming geniuses" around the country eager to "reinvent computing."[17] Throughout the 1960s groups at various universities and research centers were funded to work on different aspects of interactive computing and networking.

Initially, the research focused on building computers that enabled individuals to interact with a computer through terminals instead of enduring the tedious process of waiting in line to submit data on punched cards to a computer operator. The next step was to figure out how to connect computers in different geographical locations so that they could share resources and collaborate. This possibility was demonstrated in 1965 by connecting a computer in Massachusetts to one in California. The weak part in the scheme was the telephone network, which encountered traffic jams when confronted with large blocks of data.

The concept of packet switching proved to be the solution. The network that ARPA eventually built was based on a system for distributing messages by breaking them up into addressed packets, which could follow independent routes to the destination, where they are put back together again. There is no central control. Routers make sure the addressed packets flow around saturated channels. Besides improved efficiency, an important advantage of this technology is that it provides a more secure system of communication. If one node goes down, the network routes around it.

Packet switching was an idea that was developed independently by two different researchers, whose work was shaped by different priorities.[18] Paul Baran at the Rand Corporation developed the idea of packet switching as part of a study to devise a communications system that could survive a nuclear war or other disaster. Rand was a nonprofit corporation for military research, which was funded primarily by air force contracts. Baran published his research and specific plans for a networked "distributed communications" system in 1964, but his proposed project was never funded by ARPA.

Meanwhile, Donald Davies, with a team at the National Physical Laboratory in England, developed the idea of a packet-switching network as a means of increasing the economic efficiency of data communication across the United Kingdom and making the country more competitive with the United States. He failed to convince the appropriate decision makers of his project's commercial benefits, and it also was never funded.[19]

The ideas of both innovators were widely circulated, and both contributed informally to the design of ARPANET that linked together the major universities and research centers that were funded by the agency. Packet switching was an unproven technology, and the idea of a nationwide network based on that principle was a high-risk project indeed. Two conditions made the funding possible. The first was the generous budget for the project from the Department of Defense, a product of the Cold War. The second was ARPA's basic research orientation, which did not require projects to have immediate and direct military relevance.

ARPANET was launched in 1969, and by the end of the year there were four host computers connecting about one thousand researchers. Two years later twenty-three host computers were linked into the network, and more were quickly added. Although a major purpose of ARPANET had originally been to allow expensive resources to be shared among the funded centers, the electronic connections were soon used more for sending messages than for anything else. In 1972 the first electronic mail program was written, launching a revolution in communication.

Because of ARPA's basic research orientation, the operational branches of the military paid little attention to the networking project until after ARPANET passed through the early experimental stages and became a working system. In 1975 the operational management of ARPANET was transferred to the agency in the Department of Defense that provided communications for the armed forces, the Defense Communications Agency. Thereafter, the military began to use ARPANET more extensively for communication, and research was oriented more toward military applications, especially for computerized command and control systems. The new military managers imposed more stringent controls to prevent unauthorized access to the network. As pressures for greater access increased, a decision was made in 1982 to split ARPANET into two networks. MILNET became an operational military network under tight security. ARPANET reverted back to its original purpose of connecting ARPA-funded researchers.

The computer-related research projects funded by ARPA helped to define and develop the discipline of computer science, and by the late 1970s departments were expanding rapidly in American universities. Very few of these departments could avail themselves of the benefits of ARPANET. Of the 120 academic computer science departments in the United States in 1979, only fifteen were ARPANET sites. At the initiative of computer scientists at several universities, CSNET (Computer Science Network) was built in 1981 with seed money from the National Science Foundation (NSF) to provide networking services to computer scientists in universities, industry, and government who had no access to ARPANET. Two years later more than seventy sites were online.[20]

As knowledge spread regarding the benefits of computer networking for communication and collaboration, potential users began to create their own networks and to devise ingenious means of networking computers. Many were modest, experimental efforts. In 1979 two students at Duke University set up a news exchange system between Duke and the University of North Carolina using dial-up connections. Word spread about this inexpensive network communication, which was described by its founders as "a poor man's ARPANET," for those who had no other access.[21] As more people at other universities joined, an informal network was created that came to be known as USENET. In 1981 a computer scientist at City University of New York and another at Yale obtained funding from IBM for an experimental connection between the two schools, which became the basis for a network for IBM users called BITNET. Both networks expanded far beyond their original sites and eventually served thousands of host computers in the Americas, Europe, Australia, Asia, and Africa.[22] Local area networks (LANs) began to appear, especially in universities, in the late 1970s after the introduction of Ethernet technology. The spread of personal computers in the mid-1980s vastly expanded the number of users connected to these local networks and spurred the further development of LANs. Universities with ARPANET connections began to attach their LANs to it, thereby multiplying the number of users connected to ARPANET.

In 1986, the NSF embarked upon an ambitious and inclusive nationwide network project, designed to serve the entire higher education community. It was a two-tiered system. Individual universities could be linked to regional networks connected to NSFNET, the "backbone" that was created by the linkage of five supercomputers scattered around the United States. The NSF encouraged the building of regional networks with funding. Any computer on NSFNET could communicate with any other through a series of links.[23] Eventually, all ARPA sites were connected to these regional networks, and ARPANET ceased to exist in 1990.

What made this transition relatively simple and, incidentally, what laid the basis for the Internet as we know it today was the development by ARPA researchers of a set of rules for transferring information that enabled different kinds of computers, operating systems, and networks to communicate with each other. The Transmission Control Protocol/Internet Protocol (TCP/IP) was developed to provide a common language for a Defense Data Network, which would connect the various military networks, and to achieve interoperability among the very different systems using ARPANET. All ARPANET sites were required to use this protocol, and its adoption by the widely used NSFNET helped to spread the use of TCP/IP. The fact that the protocol was an open design with software and documentation freely available also contributed to the growth of its usage. The Internet became the network of networks using this protocol.

The NSF encouraged the regional networks to seek commercial customers as a way of encouraging the private sector to begin building their own long-haul networks. Commercial network services providers did, in fact, proliferate, and a competitive market in high-speed nationwide networking services emerged—all using the TCP/IP protocol. This development was part of the NSF's privatization policy, and in 1995 the NSF backbone was dismantled. The Internet was no longer under the control of the U.S. government and was open to all users who could pay.

Privatization of the Internet in the United States also accelerated the growth and expansion of linkages with computer networks abroad. The worldwide expansion of the Internet was not simply a matter of spreading from the United States, where it originated, to the rest of the world. State-run networks were established in a number of countries by the mid-1970s, but U.S. ownership of the Internet was an obstacle to linkages with networks abroad. On the U.S. side, the ARPA managers worried that the American public would see these connections as sharing tax-supported resources with foreigners. On the European side, there was the possibility that citizens would view the expansion of U.S. networks as imperialism. What did spread were networks connecting to the user-supported networks, such as BITNET and USENET, which had no connection with the U.S. government. For example, in Europe, EUNET was created to provide e-mail and USENET services, originally between the Netherlands, Denmark, Sweden, and the UK. In addition to the political obstacles, a technical reason that Internet linkages abroad were limited until the latter 1980s was that different protocols produced incompatibilities. Few of the national networks abroad used the TCP/IP protocol until so many private network builders outside the United States began adopting the protocol that the trend gradually shifted in that direction. When the NSF stopped operating the Internet in 1995, the number

of foreign networks that were part of the Internet had increased to twenty-
two thousand, more than 40 percent of the total number.[24]

Although the Internet spread rapidly and internationally in the latter
1980s, it was still text based and difficult to use for all but experienced computer experts. At the beginning of the next decade a series of innovations literally changed the face of the Internet, making it easier to use, as well as
more useful to more people for more purposes. The most important enabling
technology for these improvements was the World Wide Web, which was developed by Tim Berners-Lee and his group at the European Center for Nuclear Research (CERN) in Switzerland and introduced to the public in 1991.
The World Wide Web introduced a new concept called hypertext, which allows the Internet user to click on a highlighted word (hyperlink) and go directly to that information. The now familiar method of accessing information, which allows the user to jump from one link to another rather than
follow some predetermined format, came to be known as "browsing."

New browser programs, which greatly simplified access to the World Wide
Web, were developed to run on the user's computer. The popularity of the
Web began to soar as soon as a browser program called Mosaic began to circulate among American universities in 1993. More than forty thousand
copies were downloaded the first month after it was officially released.[25] Developed by Marc Andreessen at the University of Illinois, Mosaic became
commercially available the following year in a faster, simpler version as
Netscape. It remained the dominant Internet browser until 1997, when Microsoft began to bundle its new browser, Internet Explorer, into Windows,
the operating system on most of the world's computers.

Browsers not only made the Web more "user-friendly," but they also paved
the way for other innovations that gave the Web new capabilities and functions. The Web became more entertaining, as hypertextual links were integrated with multimedia so that users could hear sounds and see color pictures,
as well as read text. Users could also become producers of Web content, as
new applications facilitated the creation of Web pages. As the Web's popularity increased, its commercial potential became more obvious. The Web, in
conjunction with browsers, produced an exponential growth in the Internet—in long-haul networks, local Internet service providers, hosts, users, and
new services. Among other functions, the Web serves as a postal service, a radio and television station, a shopping mall, a "chat room," a support group, a
political mobilizer, a conference room, a classroom, and a worldwide library.

From a research tool for a small band of computer specialists to a worldwide mass medium, the evolutionary development of the Internet provides a
dramatic illustration of the four sets of interacting influences that shape the

direction and impact of new technologies: government policies, political institutions, and the larger political environment; social uses; economic structures; and the specific properties of the technology.

Government actions and policies have played a critical role in the development and diffusion of the Internet. Without the sustained investment and commitment to research of the U.S. government, the ideas of computer scientists probably would never have been transformed into the Internet as we know it. The international political environment of the Cold War provided the motivation for this commitment. The basic research orientation and informal management style of ARPA, the agency in the Department of Defense that laid the foundations for the Internet's development, was also important. Projects were allocated to scientists who were thinking way ahead of their time, and they were given a great deal of autonomy along with their funding to pursue their ideas. In most other countries government initiatives and financial support have also helped to build the networking infrastructure. Conversely, government policies in a few countries have inhibited the establishment or spread of networks, inspired by political and security concerns regarding the cross-border flows of information from the Internet.

Government support was only part of the story. The users of the Internet at every stage in its development shaped its trajectory. Researchers working on the original networking project found the network that they had designed for sharing scarce computer resources to be more useful for communication and collaboration, so they improved its capacity to meet those needs. As the benefits of computer networking became known, aspiring users exerted pressure on government agencies and corporations to support the building of networks serving other segments of the population. User-supported experimental networks helped to advance both the idea and the technology of networking, especially in the cases of BITNET and USENET, which expanded abroad. And once the user-friendly browsers were introduced it was "the spontaneous decisions of thousands of independent users" that popularized the Internet.[26]

The popularity of the Internet generated tremendous interest throughout the business world. It was a boon to the personal computer and related hardware industries, providing more reasons for more people to purchase their products. New software applications proliferated. New services providing databases and information retrieval were created. Governmental, intergovernmental, and nongovernmental agencies went online to provide information and an electronic alternative for interacting with their publics. E-commerce was born. The phasing out of U.S. government support for NSFNET shifted its clients to commercial providers, a policy that spurred the growth of long-haul networks and Internet service providers. The competition among hardware and software vendors, as well as Internet service providers, impelled heavy advertising campaigns, which attracted a multitude of new users.

Although the Internet was not a single invention of any one individual or group, and its identity and functions changed over time, certain characteristic were built into ARPANET in the early stages that persisted and influenced the trajectory. Two technologies were particularly important in establishing the basic characteristics of the Internet as it evolved. Packet switching made rapid interactive communication across distances possible and made the Internet a decentralized system, rather than one that operates from a central point. The TCP/IP protocols, which were designed for interoperability across diverse computer and networking systems, facilitated worldwide spread of the Internet.

The New Media Environment

Fiber-optic cables, geosynchronous satellites, and interconnected computers—in conjunction with digital, microwave, and other technologies—provide an infrastructure that has vastly increased the technical capacity of human beings to act and interact across great distances and to do so on a regularized, sustained basis. One authority on telecommunications refers to the evolving global electronic network as the "meganet," a "patchwork of networks, big and small, local and global, primitive and high tech, that fit together because they use compatible technologies."[27]

This network has been evolving since the middle of the nineteenth century, when the telegraph began to link continents, but in the latter part of the twentieth century the concomitant development of new technologies multiplied the channels of communication, improved the efficiency as well as the quality of transmission, and drastically reduced the cost of international communication. The first transatlantic fiber-optic cable in 1988 provided more capacity than all the existing coaxial cables combined. The development of satellite networks increased global capacity, provided alternative means for transmission, and made communication possible in places that do not have well-developed telecommunications infrastructure. As fiber-optic cables and satellites proliferate, the computers that manage the transmission of information grow faster and more powerful. Digital technology and digital compression further increase the transmission speed and capacity of cables, satellites, and computers, while decreasing the cost. For example, a three-minute telephone call between New York and London, which cost $245 in 1930, could be made for only $3 by 1990.[28]

These technological developments created new opportunities that encouraged widespread shifts in the way governments managed their telecommunications and broadcasting systems. Traditionally, telecommunication services were territorially organized as monopolies either owned or protected as such by the government to serve a national market. This model was based on the assumption that the telecommunications sector was a "natural monopoly," given the need for technical compatibility and for economies of scale to pay for high costs involved in establishing and maintaining the services. The government monopoly had a political as well as technical justification. It was generally assumed in most countries that telecommunications services were "a government responsibility, not a market commodity."[29] Government agencies known as PTTs (for postal, telegraph, and telephone) controlled these services. The U.S. model was different in that only the post was run by the government, but American Telephone and Telegraph (AT&T) was a government-protected private monopoly.

Radio and television also developed everywhere as a collection of national systems serving primarily domestic audiences. The broadcasting systems of most countries were government owned or regulated monopolies. They served, for the most part, domestic audiences, the main exceptions being international shortwave broadcasting and the trade in taped television programs.

In the 1980s a change in the political climate moved many governments to end protection of the monopolies, to encourage (or at least permit) private firms to operate in telecommunications and in broadcasting, and generally to reduce the amount of regulation that governed these sectors. The trend toward liberalization of international trade has opened up many national markets to foreign entrepreneurs. The combination of expansive new technologies, market pressures, and political choices has spurred the growth of a privatized global communication infrastructure and the commercialization of services.

Telecommunications

The breakup of the AT&T monopoly in the United States in 1984 and the introduction of competition in the long-distance market played a critical role in this fundamental shift in the control and operation of telecommunication services. The next year Margaret Thatcher's government moved toward privatization of telecommunications in the United Kingdom, allowing up to 51 percent of British Telecom (the telecommunications arms of the PTT) to be privatized.[30] In 1991 the British government made the decision to privatize the telephone system entirely.

The actions of the United States and the United Kingdom to reduce the role of government in telecommunications generated pressures for change in the rest of Europe, most notably from European business leaders and officials of the European Community (later European Union). The former, particularly European businesses that operated transnationally, were eager for a more extensive, reliable, and affordable network of communications. British and American telecommunications companies were eager to establish a foothold in Europe. European Community officials began to view telecommunications reform as essential to support further regional integration, to develop a strong regional economy, and to make European telecommunications industries competitive in global markets. A series of proposals and initiatives on the part of the European Union provided the impetus for member countries to restructure their telecommunications industries and services. Initially, ordinary telephone services remained protected government monopolies, while private competition was allowed only in "value-added services" such as data networking and in the mobile communications industry. By the end of the 1990s the government monopolies for most of the fifteen members of the European Union had been eliminated, and private sector services were operating across national borders.

The policy shifts of the United States, the United Kingdom, and other European countries generated pressures on governments elsewhere to open up their telecommunications systems to both domestic and international competition. These pressures came from not only aspiring competitors but also multinational corporations seeking the more extensive, reliable, and affordable networks of communications; local businesses; and ordinary people wanting a workable telephone.

Direct pressures for change in the structure of telecommunications also came from international negotiations to reduce barriers to trade at the global level under the auspices of the General Agreement on Tariffs and Trade and its successor, the World Trade Organization (WTO). As successive rounds of negotiations reduced tariffs on manufactured goods, the United States pressed for the liberalization of trade in services, its most important export sector. The United States was particularly interested in opening markets to its telecommunications industries and was the moving force behind the major international agreement to achieve that objective. With the help of brinkmanship diplomacy and bilateral arm-twisting on the part of the United States, seventy governments, representing 82 percent of the world's telephone main lines, signed the WTO Agreement on Basic Telecommunications in 1997.[31] The agreement obliged the signatories not only to make their domestic markets more competitive but also to permit international corporations access to these markets on the basis of equal treatment.

These moves toward privatization and liberalization have transformed the telecommunications industry—intensifying competition, expanding the world's network of telephones, and increasing the flow of international traffic. By the end of the twentieth century, eighty-eight countries had privatized their telecommunications networks to some extent.[32] A total of forty-nine countries allowed at least limited competition in international telecommunications services, a dramatic change from six just a decade earlier. The number of licensed international carriers (providers of communications transmission services) grew by more than 40 percent.[33]

Over the decade of the 1990s the number of main telephone lines doubled from 546 million to one billion in 2001.[34] Increased competition in international telecommunications services plus the dramatic increase in capacity from the expansion of fiber-optic undersea networks drastically reduced the cost of international telephony. In the last two years of the decade, call prices from Western Europe to many international destinations fell by 90 percent.[35] This growth in telephone networks and the reduction in the cost of international telephone calls increased the volume of international telephone traffic from 38 billion minutes in 1991 to 145 billion minutes in 2004.[36]

Despite these impressive statistics, vast differences in access to telecommunications services throughout the world persist. A 1997 study by the International Telecommunication Union (ITU) indicated that one-quarter of member states (that is, forty-seven) had less than one main telephone line per one hundred individuals, or a "teledensity" of less than one.[37] At the end of the century the average for the entire world was sixteen main lines per one hundred people, and five years later the number had risen to only nineteen.[38] Development of telecommunications infrastructure is painfully slow. The 1997 ITU study estimated that, after reaching the threshold of a teledensity of one, it can take from twenty to fifty years to reach fifty, an indicator of high telecommunication development.[39]

The invention of the handheld, mobile cellular telephone (cell phone) offers the possibility for much more rapid progress, enabling a country to "leapfrog" over such intermediate stages as copper wires and analog telephones. Evolving from Guglielmo Marconi's idea of wireless telegraphy, mobile telephones communicate through radio waves with a cellular network of base stations containing transmitters and receivers, which are connected to antennas on high towers. Although radio telephony had been in use much earlier, it was not until the 1990s that advances in microprocessor chip technology and the miniaturization of components made it possible to produce handheld mobile telephones.

Building cellular networks requires a significant financial investment, but the cost is far less than installing a system of telephone landlines. This relative cost, in addition to the convenience of mobility, explains the explosive growth of cellular telephones globally, even in some of the poorest parts of the world. They can be found in the most unexpected places. It is now possible to make a cell phone call from the top of Mount Everest, thanks to China Telecom, which set up a tower at the base camp on the north side of the mountain.[40] By 2002 there were more cell phone than landline subscribers. By 2005, 63 percent of all telephone subscriptions were for cell phones, for a total of 2.2 billion, a number equivalent to one-third of the world's population.[41] The advantages of cell phones for developing countries are apparent in teledensity statistics for Africa, where surprising growth has occurred, and where 83 percent of all telephone subscriptions are for cell phones. By 2005, the number of cell phones per one hundred people for the whole continent was fifteen, whereas the number of landlines had increased only slightly, from 2.5 to 3, over the preceding five years.[42]

The Transformation of the Mass Media

Prior to the 1990s broadcasting was limited by both state regulation and the technical scarcity of electromagnetic frequencies. As chapter 2 has indicated, technical limitations forced governments to make choices about who should have access to the airwaves and for what purposes. Different political preferences and cultural values created a variety of structures for broadcasting, but even the most laissez-faire systems were regulated. For example, in the United States there were limits on cross-media ownership. This combination of technical constraints and government policies limited the reach and expansion of broadcasting, which remained essentially a national medium. The television and radio media were dominated by broadcasting monopolies in Europe and much of the rest of the world and by three commercial networks in the United States.

New technologies for transmitting television and radio signals transformed broadcasting from a medium of scarce supply to a medium of abundance. First the spread of cable systems, then the falling cost of launching communication satellites and the development of smaller, cheaper equipment to receive their signals opened the way for an ever-expanding number of channels. These technological developments occurred at the same time that many governments were implementing broad policies of deregulation and privatization, and the two trends were mutually reinforcing. In Western Europe, the number of terrestrial commercial television channels increased from three in 1980 to fifty-nine in 1997.[43] Cable and satellite channels also proliferated, further eroding the public service monopolies in Western Europe, in Eastern Europe after the end of Communist-party rule there, and elsewhere.

Alliances and mergers proliferated in response to the changes in regulatory policies in the 1980s and 1990s. In the United States policies of deregulation, especially the Telecommunications Act of 1996, removed or relaxed some of the limitations on ownership, including, significantly, cross-media ownership. The subsequent wave of mergers and alliances created conglomerates that not only control production and distribution within a single medium (vertical integration) but also across different media, notably film, television, and Internet companies (horizontal integration), and across national markets. The largest media companies in the world are now major players in multiple sectors of the media industry, operating in many countries.[44] A few examples illustrate the scope and complexity of these new structures.

In January 2001 the merger of AOL and Time Warner created the world's largest media company at that time. The new entity was described in triumphant words by *Time* magazine, one of its subsidiaries, as "a vast empire of broadcasting, music, movies and publishing assets, complemented by AOL's dominant Internet presence, all fed to consumers through Time Warner's cable network."[45] With the acquisition of the Turner Broadcasting System in 1995, Time Warner had already gained an international television presence with the Cable News Network (CNN). This spectacular merger lasted only two years, but the two companies continue as separate entities to be important.

The Walt Disney Company achieved its ranking by merging its Magic Kingdom theme parks, film studios, and television channels with one of the major television networks in the United States, ABC. The company also owns the Entertainment and Sports Network (ESPN), which broadcasts to over 165 countries. The merger in 1999 of Viacom and CBS, another major television network in the United States, produced another giant media conglomerate. The holdings of Viacom/CBS included MTV, the most widely distributed cable network in the world, reaching over three hundred million households in eighty-three countries, and Nickelodeon, one of the world's largest producers of children's programming, distributed in over one hundred countries.[46] Like AOL-Time Warner, the anticipated synergies did not materialize, and in 2005 the giant company split into two smaller conglomerates.

Rupert Murdoch's News Corporation has newspaper, television, film, and Internet operations spread across five continents with a firm foothold in both the developed and developing world. The conglomerate includes Twentieth Century Fox film production studios; HarperCollins, a major book publishing company; four major newspapers in the United Kingdom, more than one hundred national and local newspapers in Australia, and fifty-five in New

Zealand; the Fox news channel plus ownership of twenty-two television stations; and a majority interest in the Satellite Television for the Asian Region (STAR) network. The STAR satellite television network pioneered satellite television in Asia and has significantly altered the media environment in that region. In 2006 it was broadcasting sixty services in nine languages, reaching three hundred million viewers in fifty-three countries in Asia.[47]

Not all of the media giants are American. Vivendi Universal, which began as a French water and sewage-treatment utility, through a series of acquisitions, including film (Universal Studios and theme parks), music, two mobile phone companies, Europe's biggest pay-TV operator (Canal Plus), and books (Houghton Mifflin), edged out the Walt Disney Company in the number 2 spot in 2002. This ranking was short lived, although it remains in the top ten, list of media companies. In a case of imperial overstretch, the company became heavily indebted and was soon forced to begin selling off some of its assets. Bertelsmann AG is another European conglomerate in the top ten, with operations in fifty-one countries. Ownership of multiple publishing houses (including U.S.-based Random House), magazines, and newspapers makes it the world's largest book and publishing company. It is also one of Europe's leading broadcasting and production companies, operating twenty-four television and fourteen radio stations. Bertelsmann's website claims that it is "the world's most international media company."[48]

Although there is considerable stability in the composition of the top ten media companies, the specific holdings and rankings shift along with their fortunes, as they seek "synergies" from other acquisitions and mergers and reduce debt with sales of assets. This trend toward consolidation and vertical integration follows market logic, providing multiple opportunities for cross-promotion and for recycling of material produced for one channel or one medium in another. As a survey on television in the *Economist* noted, "Once the cost of producing the material is met, every extra viewer adds directly to your profit margin."[49] This search for economies of scale also propels television and other audiovisual companies to seek creative ways to expand the audience or user base internationally, a goal made more feasible by the new technologies and policies.

As a result, the transnational flow of media products is increasing in volume and expanding in scope in a global marketplace. Satellites, cables, microwave relays, and computers make it possible to transmit instantly to distant parts of the globe vast quantities of information, news, and entertainment. The miniaturization and reduced costs of satellite dishes have increased the numbers of people who can receive these distant signals. Digital technology allows images, sounds, and data to be transferred easily from one medium to another and vastly increases the number of channels for transmission. Video and audiocassette recorders further expand the potential size and geographic scope of the audience. Radio signals are available in some of the most remote areas, and transistor radios are widely distributed.

The global media conglomerates dominate the production and distribution of media products, concentrating economic power in the audiovisual industries and expanding the potential for Western, especially American, cultural influence. But the same technologies and policies that have contributed to this globalizing trend have also generated enormous entrepreneurial activity at the regional, national, and even local levels. Regional channels, broadcasters, networks, production centers, and news exchange agencies have multiplied, significantly changing the media landscape, especially in the developing world. Private channels aimed at domestic audiences have proliferated but so have transnational satellite networks, which extend the areas of reception beyond national borders even to distant continents. The multiplicity of channels makes it possible to target particular segments of the population within a single country, as well as transnational audiences catering to specific interests (such as business, sports, or music) or to linguistic and cultural affinities. Particularly important for world politics are the transnational satellite networks that cover "geolinguistic regions."[50] A brief analysis of the new media environment in Asia, the Middle East, and Latin America suggests some of the issues raised by these changes, which will receive further attention in chapter 6.

Internationalization and Regionalization of Television in Asia

No region illustrates better than Asia the complementary trends apparent in the new global media environment: "Powerful internationalization of the television market and increasing regionalization."[51] These trends apply to both ownership and program content. With approximately 60 percent of the world's population, this region is an irresistible attraction to the international media companies, such as CNN, BBC, MTV, ESPN, and especially the News Corporation. At the same time entrepreneurs at the regional and local levels have profoundly changed the media landscape in Asia.

The critical step in this transformation came from within the region itself. In 1990 a reconditioned U.S.-made satellite, owned by a Hong Kong–based consortium, AsiaSat, was launched into orbit with a Chinese rocket from a military base in the center of China. Li Kashing, a Hong Kong billionaire whose conglomerate, Hutchinson Whampoa, held part ownership of AsiaSat, decided to enter the broadcast business by creating the first Pan-Asian satellite television service, STAR TV. AsiaSat's footprint covered an enormous area from the Far East to Europe. When AsiaSat 2 was launched in 1995, that area was extended even further to cover fifty-three countries—about two-thirds of the world's population. Initially STAR TV had five television channels offering a mixture of entertainment, movies, sports, music, and news—all in English.

In 1993 Rupert Murdoch acquired 64 percent of the equity in the STAR group of channels, which later became a wholly owned subsidiary. His plans for a panregional satellite channel were soon abandoned in favor of country-specific channels that catered to local tastes. After limited success with all-Western programming, the network was restructured with channels broadcasting programs in other languages, most prominently Hindi and Chinese, and with more locally produced content. He further improved his position in Asia by establishing partnerships with national media firms. His extensive interests in India and China gave him a prominent position in the media of the world's two largest consumer markets.

As indicated in the previous chapter, many developing countries traditionally regarded the broadcasting media as instruments for education, development, and strengthening national unity. Government-owned and -directed monopolies restricted the number of channels and the content of programming. In 1992 the region averaged 2.4 television channels per country.[52] The launching of AsiaSat with the STAR TV service, along with the development of smaller, more affordable satellite dishes, undermined these monopolies and served as a catalyst for explosive growth in the media industry throughout the region. With the launching of other satellites and channels that followed, there are now thousands of television channels in the region. The shift toward more liberal economic policies that was taking place concurrently in many countries—more supportive of both domestic and foreign investment—was also an important, indeed essential, condition for this growth.

The Case of India

India is a useful case for viewing the changes in the media environment in Asia. In no other country have so many new television channels been made available to so many people so quickly. Before the Gulf War in 1991 the sight of a satellite dish was rare in any Indian city. When CNN began international coverage of the war, hotels began to install the large dish antennae that were required at that time for adequate reception of satellite signals, and the Indian English-speaking elite flocked to the hotels to watch. STAR TV with its array of programs was launched a few months later, further stimulating popular demand for access to satellite television.

To meet this demand, thousands of small entrepreneurs began to buy locally made satellite dishes to receive international channels. These "cable wallahs" then proceeded to cable apartment blocks in the major cities and to provide access to these channels to individual households for a small fee. This cottage industry vastly increased access to cable networks, which had been growing slowly, unregulated, since the mid-1980s.

The speed with which these activities occurred caught the government off guard and unable to agree on a policy, which meant that there was no policy. The only relevant piece of legislation was the Indian Telegraph Act of 1885, which prohibited digging up a road to lay a cable without the permission of the Telecommunications Commission. To circumvent this law, cable TV operators ran their lines over rather than under the streets—"flinging cables over tree branches and attaching them to streetlamps."[53] From the large metropolitan areas satellite TV expanded to smaller towns, with TV similarly delivered via unauthorized cable. By the time a Cable TV Act was passed in 1995, an estimated sixty thousand cable operators existed in India with subscriber bases from only fifty to several thousand.[54] Thereafter, there was some consolidation among cable operators as larger, better-financed operators, who were able to invest in the equipment for more channels and better reception, started buying up local networks or franchising local feeds. The current number is estimated at about thirty thousand, some of which are very large operators. Meanwhile, the "cable-wallahs" had played a very important role in "transforming satellite television from a private facility for wealthy homes to a mass entertainment and communication phenomenon."[55]

The introduction of foreign television programming by satellite was a catalyst for phenomenal growth in Indian media industries. Only a year after STAR TV began broadcasting Western television programming in English, an Indian entrepreneur, Subhash Chandra, bought a channel on AsiaSat and launched Zee TV, the first private Hindi-language satellite channel. It was a general entertainment channel providing an array of programs produced in India, including soap operas, music, and films. It became so popular that it was making a profit within the first year. Its success inspired other initiatives, and private channels proliferated, both domestic and foreign.

A particularly important development was the growth of satellite services in the various Indian regional languages. The earliest and most notable developments occurred in the Tamil-speaking south, where Hindi was least likely to be understood. Satellites gave southern entrepreneurs the opportunity to provide regional alternatives to both domestic and foreign channels, where the Hindi language was dominant. Although the markets are smaller than those in the Hindi-speaking northern belt, the southern channels, particularly Sun TV, gained commercial success in part because they met the advertising needs of small businesses, and they spoke more directly to the rural areas and small towns.[56] In 1999 Zee TV launched twenty-four-hour regional channels in the Marathi, Gujarati, Punjabi, and Bengali languages. In response, Doordarshan, the state broadcaster, expanded the number of its regional channels.

The growth of private channels, both foreign and domestic, posed a serious challenge to the erstwhile state monopoly broadcaster, Doordarshan, which attempted to meet the competition through emulation. By the year 2000 the state broadcaster had expanded from two channels to nineteen, including several regional language channels. Prior to 1991 Indian viewers had access to only the two channels provided by Doordarshan. Ten years later there were over ninety channels broadcasting around the country—a hodge-podge of private, public, domestic, and foreign channels, broadcasting from seventeen satellites.[57] As indicated in the previous chapter, the Indian government had already discovered the benefits of advertising in the latter part of the 1980s, even before Doordarshan's monopoly was broken. With the arrival of satellite television, Doordarshan became more market oriented and focused less on the earlier political objectives of development and national unity.

Fierce competition for advertising has led to an emphasis on entertainment programming and to a hybridization of form and content for both public and private broadcasters. The new channels transmitted by AsiaSat brought the novelty of Western programs to India, but their appeal was limited by their use of the English language, which is spoken by about 10 percent of the population. Almost immediately Subhash Chandra, an Indian businessman with no media experience, recognized these limitations but saw the tremendous potential for a mass market for satellite television. His Hindi-language entertainment channel, Zee TV, was designed to attract that market with a basic fare of Indian films but also with a novel form of programming that adapted Western formats to the Indian context. Game shows, quiz shows, a twenty-four-hour Hindi news channel, and an Indian version of MTV, the Music Asia channel, are examples of this kind of cultural fusion. Zee TV's most popular programs have generally been those that had a more distinctive Indian flavor.[58]

Foreign media companies, eyeing the enormous potential mass market in India and the success of Zee TV, were also forced by market pressures to "indigenize" their Western programs. Murdoch led the way when his STAR group of channels began to broadcast in Hindi as well as English. He dropped one channel, MTV, with its Western popular music, and launched a new "Channel V," with more Indian popular music and VJs (video jockeys). In response to the dramatic growth of Murdoch's new "Indianized" music channel, MTV relaunched itself on another satellite in 1996 and adopted a more Indian profile with a new programming strategy that allotted 70 percent of its content to Indian popular music, mostly from Indian films.[59]

Most foreign media companies have sooner or later adopted some form of a localization business strategy. The least accommodation is the provision of subtitles or dubbing in Hindi. Other channels have adapted Western programs or formats to the Indian context. This approach involves arrangements with local producers of media products, providing a stimulus to Indian media industries. The scope for creativity varies, however. Some formats, such as "Who Wants to Be a Millionaire?" are highly scripted, with three hundred pages of precise rules from the British production company about the set, music, lighting, and timing. The response to these cultural hybrids also varies. "Who Will Become a Ten-Millionaire" has been wildly popular, even in such places as the slums of Mumbai, shattering ratings and spawning Indian imitation game shows. The reality genre has been a less successful adaptation, because, as Peter Mukerjea, the chief executive of STAR TV India, explained, "For the average Indian citizen, day-to-day existence is hard enough."[60]

Local positioning, involving strategic alliances with Indian companies, is another form of localization. Murdoch has pursued this strategy from the very beginning of his foray into Indian television. For six years he was engaged in joint ventures, including a cable network, with Zee Telefilms, the parent company of his biggest rival, Zee TV. When Subhash Chandra bought out Murdoch's shares of this venture, STAR TV bought 26 percent of India's third largest cable system. Alliances were also established with production companies. For example, Murdoch launched a twenty-four-hour all-news channel in Hindi with an emphasis on regional news, in partnership with a New Delhi Television (NDTV) production company. In 2001, soon after the Indian government decided to license private FM radio stations, STAR launched the country's first private FM radio stations in partnership with an Indian company.

News Corporation was not the only foreign media company to pursue a localization strategy, but it has undoubtedly been the most successful. Although earlier Zee TV dominated the ratings, in 2003 STAR TV became the market leader in India with forty-five of the programs on its Hindi entertainment channel rating in the top fifty. The weekly news magazine, *India Today*, headlined one of its critical articles "Boss of the World."[61] Responding to this criticism and to political pressures, in March 2003 the Indian government established a 26 percent foreign direct investment cap on news channels uplinked via satellite.

Although the case of satellite television in India is unique in many ways, it also illustrates some of the contradictory effects of new media technologies and the issues that have concerned policy makers and scholars about their impact. The entry of international satellite television and advertising companies into India brought in foreign programs that often challenged traditional values and threatened to dominate the market. But it also spurred a phenomenal growth in the Indian media industries—new channels, new production centers, and a chaotic but widespread network of cables for distribution.

The competitive advantage of programs with Indian content in the Hindi language over Western programs broadcast in English illustrates a phenomenon that has been observed elsewhere, namely, a preference for programs that resonate with the local identity. But often, as the case of India demonstrates, local content is an adaptation of Western genres to local languages and culture, a cultural hybrid. In any case, for many, especially in India, "local" identity is at the subnational level. The satellite media market initially reinforced the dominant position of Hindi in the national media, but later, on the initiative of southern entrepreneurs, satellites created new possibilities for regional channels to broadcast in other languages with regionally generated content.

Finally, the case of India illustrates the economic dilemma inherent in the question of who controls the media for what purpose. The shift from state-centric to market-oriented broadcasting stimulated dynamic growth in the Indian media-related industries and greatly expanded the choice of programs for viewers. The competition from the private channels forced the former state monopoly broadcaster, Doordarshan, to increase its channels and to make its programs more attractive. As the lure of advertising revenues became more compelling, and the competition with the private channels—domestic and foreign—more intense, Doordarshan's programming became more oriented toward entertainment with less attention to the former objectives of education, development, and national integration.

The Middle East and Pan-Arabic Television

The growth of Pan-Arabic television has transformed the media environment in the Middle East and beyond. Prior to the 1990s the media in the Arab world were under the direct control of the governments of the respective states, with content heavily censored in most. Thereafter, private, as well as state-owned satellite networks began to emerge, transmitting programs in Arabic across the region and to Arabic speakers in Europe and North America. Improvements in satellite technology reduced the costs of both transmission and reception, making Direct to Home Broadcasting

(DTH) more feasible and affordable and government control more difficult. The global coverage of the 1991 Gulf War by the U.S.-based Cable News Network International (CNNI) proved to be a catalyst for these developments, as it demonstrated the power of television as a medium for international broadcasting at a time when the region was a focus of the news. The war and its coverage also gave impetus to the idea that there was a need for international media with an Arab perspective on the news.

The first private Pan-Arab satellite network, the Middle East Broadcasting Centre (MBC), was launched in 1991. It is owned and operated by a Saudi Arabian consortium (ARA Group International) based in London. It began broadcasting a mixture of news, information, and entertainment from London to Europe and North Africa via Eutelsat II and to the Middle East via Arabsat.[62] Ten years later MBC moved to Dubai because, in the opinion of the director general, both the technical facilities and the political environment in the Middle East had changed sufficiently to accommodate a Pan-Arab channel. "In Dubai we believe that we can enjoy the same freedom and technical provision that we enjoyed in London," he noted in an interview with TBS Journal. Another major consideration, he claimed, was a desire to be "closer to our audience . . . to meet at least a significant number of one's audience in cafes, restaurants, or at universities."[63] Shortly after this move, in February 2003, MBC launched a twenty-four-hour news channel in Arabic, called Al Arabiya, a joint venture with investors from Lebanon, Saudi Arabia, Kuwait, and the United Arab Emirates. This move was an ambitious effort to compete with the first twenty-four-hour, all-news Arabic-language satellite channel—Al Jazeera, which was established in 1996.

Al Jazeera emerged from the failed effort of the British Broadcasting Corporation (BBC) to run an Arabic news service on contract with a Saudi-owned pay-TV network. The venture was short lived—from 1994 to 1996—because the Saudi Arabian government objected to the network's frank reporting of Saudi affairs. The emir of Qatar decided that he could enhance his tiny country's visibility on the world stage by taking up this initiative, providing a home and funding for an Arab news network committed to independent programming. Almost all of the news executives and correspondents have come from Arab states other than Qatar. Many of them have honed their skills at the BBC in London, some as part of the earlier effort.[64] Al Jazeera's motto, literally translated from the Arabic as "the opinion and the other opinion," has inspired program formats and content that are a radical departure from the norm in the Middle East. These include talk shows in which opposing sides battle it out while members of the audience phone in comments, tough interviews with officials, and investigative journalism, as well as well a steady stream of news with live reports from the field, using the latest technology. Quotes from one side of a conflict are often balanced by quotes from the other side. Not surprisingly, the channel frequently steps on toes and has infuriated both Middle Eastern and U.S. governments at one time or another.

Al Jazeera first gained international visibility—notoriety in the United States—when it broadcast and sold to other media videos of Osama bin Laden's pronouncements after September 11, 2001. It broadcast gruesome images of civilian deaths during the war in Afghanistan and of dead American soldiers in the war in Iraq. To American protests Al Jazeera's managers have responded, "What we are doing is just showing the reality," and "We learned independence from the United States, and now the American officials want us to give up what we learned from them."[65]

The case of Al Jazeera illustrates two dilemmas inherent in the contemporary media and world politics. One, as described above, is the democratic dilemma. More democracy, in terms of less censorship and more openness in the media and more responsiveness to audience preferences does not translate into more pro-Western or pro–United States in content. In fact, as is illustrated in chapter 4, that responsiveness and open forum provide a stage for extremist views. The second is the economic dilemma. Dependence on government financing for television channels in the Middle East has severely restricted the kinds of programming that could be broadcast. Dependence on private enterprise imposes less obvious restrictions, which are vividly demonstrated by the precarious financial situation of Al Jazeera. After the initial loan from the government of Qatar, the channel had hoped to be profitable and financially independent within five years. This objective has not yet been achieved. Al Jazeera obtains some revenue by selling footage to other channels. It has agreements with Fox News, CBS, CNN, and several European channels. But its controversial content has discouraged many Middle Eastern and U.S. companies from advertising, a significant constraint on its profits and even viability, in spite of its success in attracting an audience of millions, an estimated forty million in the Arab world.[66] Al Jazeera launched a new English-language news channel in November 2006 with eight hundred employees from fifty-five countries and a potential audience of eighty-five million households.[67] In the United States both versions are available on the Internet, but as of 2007 Al Jazeera has been unable to obtain a deal with a major cable television company to broadcast nationwide.

The popularity of Al Jazeera boosted satellite access in Middle Eastern homes, which, in turn, has provided incentives for more Pan-Arab satellite networks, both government and private, to be launched. More than 150

Arab satellite television channels were on the air in 2005.[68] These include not only other news networks, notably Al Arabiya, Abu Dhabi TV, and the Lebanese-based Al Hayat/LBC, but also an array of channels that include both Arabic and Western entertainment and cultural programming. All these channels broaden the scale of cross-border Arab interaction, and many act as transnational networks to reach diasporic audiences in Europe and North America.[69] These networks have created a worldwide market based on linguistic and cultural similarities, what some scholars have called a "geolinguistic region."[70]

Latin America: Regional Demographics and Global Markets

Latin America is the base of another but very different example of a geolinguistic media market. It is the home of two regional media conglomerates, Televisa and Globo, which have created niches for themselves, based on language and culture, in the global media market.

Televisa, based in Mexico, has effectively exploited the commercial potential of a large region of contiguous states, in which, with the exception of Brazil, the majority of inhabitants speak a common language.[71] Since the 1960s, with the invention of videotape, Televisa has maintained a lively trade in program exports to other countries in Latin America, to Spain, and to the United States. Not surprisingly its foreign expansion has centered on the Spanish-speaking population in the United States, now at least thirty-five million people. Televisa began to open up stations in the United States in 1960, in partnership with U.S. citizens, and later formed a network to distribute programs, which became Univision. Televisa eventually had to divest these stations, as the Mexican company was found to be in breach of the foreign ownership provisions of the U.S. Communication Act. In the meanwhile, a nationwide audience had been built up for Televisa programming.

In the 1990s Televisa expanded its international involvement through direct investments in media companies in Latin America, Spain, and the United States, including a new partial ownership arrangement with the Univision network. With other media companies it established arrangements for supplying programming. Televisa has become the leading producer and exporter of Spanish-language programs.[72] It has also established an international satellite service, Galavision, which is fed directly to the United States, Europe, and forty-five other countries.[73]

Brazil's Rede Globo ranks among the larger multimedia conglomerates in the world. It owns Brazil's leading newspaper, Globosat, the Globo radio system, a publishing firm, a music company, and a telecommunications network, as well as Globo Television network.[74] TV Globo exports to a wider range of countries than Televisa because Portuguese is spoken in fewer countries. The export of a single programming genre, the telenovela, has contributed substantially to TV Globo's international visibility.

The company's venture into the international market began in 1975 with exports of telenovelas, or soap operas, to Portugal, where they became extremely popular. The export of telenovelas in dubbed versions expanded dramatically and found favorable receptions in some unexpected places. The broad appeal of this genre is illustrated in the spectacular success of one particular telenovela, a historical romance called *Escrava Isaura* (Slave Girl Isaura), in France, Italy, Poland, the former Soviet Union, and especially China, where it was watched by an estimated 450 million viewers. Building on the popularity of the telenovela, TV Globo has developed a wide export market for a broad range of entertainment-oriented programming, which has been viewed in 130 countries.[75]

The international expansion of Televisa and Globo has made Mexico and Brazil, two developing countries, major international media production centers. Export profits constitute only a very small percentage of the total revenue for both companies, however. The financial success of these two companies is based largely on the revenues from their respective domestic advertising markets, which they dominate. Advertising in both countries, as in much of Latin America, is minimally regulated. In contrast to Europe and much of the developing world, commercial stations historically have predominated over public channels in Latin America. Most countries in the region have followed a U.S. market model. The dependence of Televisa and Globo on revenues from domestic advertising markets leaves the companies vulnerable to the vicissitudes of the domestic economies and their programming highly influenced by advertisers' bottom lines.

Televisa and Globo illustrate how the multiplicity of channels makes transnational niche broadcasting feasible. Satellite broadcasting has provided opportunities to expand beyond exports to the direct international transmission of programming. But the proliferation of channels has also brought more competition. For example, PanAmSat, which carries most of Televisa's new channels, also opens up Latin American markets to U.S. cable channels producing programs in Spanish or Portuguese.

Transformation of the Mass Media: The Big Picture

The combination of new technologies and government policy shifts toward deregulation and privatization has multiplied the number of channels for communicating and for transmitting media products. The result is an environment with more diverse sources of information that are accessible to a larger segment of the human population. It is a complex and dynamic environment with contradictory tendencies. There is both concentration and diffusion in the production and transmission of media products. The technologies and policies that give multinational corporations transcontinental reach, expanding their economic power, also provide a host of opportunities for new regional, national, and subnational actors. Deregulation paved the way for a wave of mergers and alliances that produced enormous conglomerates controlling production and distribution not only within a single medium but also across different media in different countries. Satellite technology increased enormously the potential reach of these megacorporations.

But the end of government monopolies in much of the world and the availability of satellites also encouraged the proliferation of national and regional channels for transmitting media products. New entrepreneurs, producers, and distributors have emerged in the South as well as the developed countries at the transnational as well as national levels. Regional and transnational niche networks based on linguistic and cultural similarities have emerged. Al Jazeera has completely transformed the media environment in the Middle East and has expanded to serve Arabic speakers beyond the region. CNN broadcasts during the Gulf War and the success of Al Jazeera (in terms of audience size, not profits) encouraged other Arab countries and entrepreneurs to acquire their own satellite systems. Other broadcasters in the South, both governmental and private, have established services to diasporic communities. In some cases these expand beyond the linguistic communities to gain a larger audience. Al Jazeera now produces news in English.

The widespread shift to a more liberal model for broadcasting in the 1980s opened the way for a massive flow of foreign content from international, primarily U.S., media companies. This flow was the product of a push-pull effect. For the international media companies it was the search for profits and market share that pushed them to expand their horizons abroad. For the newly created channels and networks there was the lure of ready-made media products from the United States, much cheaper to import than to produce from scratch. This attraction still exists. Over time, however, production capabilities improved for the novices (and sometimes the price of imports increased). The result was that indigenous channels sometimes became more successful than the big international companies because their content and context was local. According to David Hulbert, president of Walt Disney Television International, "The worldwide television market is growing, but America's place in it is declining."[76] There is considerable evidence that viewers of television tend to prefer homegrown programs that reflect local tastes and culture. A

2001 survey by Nielsen Media Research found that 72 percent of the top ten programs in sixty countries were locally produced. One explanation comes from Bibiane Godfroid, an executive at the French channel Canal Plus, which operates in eleven European countries. He suggests that "the more the world becomes global, the more people want their own culture."[77]

This constraint has prompted the international media companies in many cases to pursue a localization strategy, the adaptation of Western programs to the local context. Typically, this means producing in the local language rather than dubbing a Western product. It may also involve collaboration with regional or national producers and performers. A notable and ubiquitous example is MTV, which has a network of seventy-two international channels operating in eighty-three countries. The president of MTV International, Bill Roedy, provided a sample of the company's localization strategy and consequent cultural diversity in a *Fortune* magazine interview. "MTV India is very colorful, self-effacing, full of humor, a lot of street culture. China is about family values, nurturing, a lot of love songs. In Indonesia, with our largest Islamic population, there's a call to prayer five times a day on the channel. Brazil is very sexy. Italy is stylish, elegant, with food shows because of the love of food there."[78] Although MTV began as a Western pop music channel, it shifted its approach in many countries to appeal to local preferences when it looked more profitable.

The above discussion indicates that one of the most salient features of the new global television environment is the growth and spread of the U.S. commercial model in which entertainment becomes the dominant form of programming in order to attract large audiences—potential consumers—for advertisers. By the 1990s television almost everywhere was becoming increasingly dependent on advertising revenue, while the mass distribution of consumer products increasingly depended on television advertising. Television had become, in the words of a historian of the medium, "an unexpected prop for the whole economic system."[79]

Internet Diffusion: Patterns and Obstacles

In many respects, the Internet represents a culmination of historical developments in information and communication technologies. It performs the functions of the earlier technologies—with enhancements. Like the telegraph, it provides instant, long-distance communication but is not limited to truncated text and is far more convenient and accessible (to those who are "wired"). Like the telephone, it can exchange messages with a particular individual but also with many others at the same time through e-mail and chat rooms. The Internet is also a mass medium that performs similar functions to the press and broadcast media in the sense that one person or group can send a message, document, image, or song to a mass audience, but one that has no physical boundaries. In fact, newspapers and periodicals, as well as radio stations, are launching websites to broaden their audience. Even journals and books appear on the Internet. A significant advantage of the electronic version is that the audience is not limited to a particular locality. Expatriates everywhere can stay connected to the home country and keep up with developments there. Anyone anywhere connected to the Internet can discover different perspectives on world events by accessing newspapers and radio stations in almost every country.

What began as an experiment connecting four host computers has become a global network of networks. As recently as 1988 only eight countries, mainly English speaking, were connected to the Internet. It spread rapidly over the next decade, and by 2004 almost every country in the world—209 according to the International Telecommunications Union—had a direct connection to the Internet. The number of Internet users increased from 4.4 million in 1991 to over 1.1 billion in 2007, but this figure represents only about 17 percent of the world's population.[80] As impressive as the growth and spread of the Internet is, great disparities in access to the Internet both among and within countries are a prominent feature of the world today. This "digital divide" is discussed in chapter 5 along with changes in the distribution of Internet usage.

Most advanced industrial countries have followed a pattern of government support to build and maintain a "national backbone." The initial network system, often linking academic and research institutions, usually expands over time to cover a larger public.[81] Most developing countries face two major obstacles to building a national backbone. The first is the enormous financial outlay required to establish even a modest system of networked computers. The problem is not only the lack of funds for this purpose but also the competition from more urgent needs. Another hurdle that all too often must be overcome is a substandard national telephone system.

There are other obstacles to Internet diffusion in developing countries. The power supply is often insufficient and unreliable, a serious impediment to running networked computers. To establish and run a system requires a much larger pool of engineers, information technology specialists, and technical support personnel than is likely to be available. The demand for these technical skills outstrips the supply even in the most advanced countries. In addition there is the problem of language, which restricts the benefits of Internet access to those who are fluent in English, the language that dominates the discourse that traverses through the networks. Finally, government policies may prevent or limit Internet connectivity for cultural or political reasons. A notable example is in the Middle East, which, as indicated in table 5.1, is highly underrepresented among Internet users of the world.

The diffusion of the Internet among developing countries has proceeded along a variety of different paths. The most common pattern is a very modest version of the national backbone model, beginning with government support for a very small project, then improving capacity incrementally with increased demand and experience. In most cases the network began as a university research project.[82] An example of a small-scale beginning is the network established under the initiative of the University of Zambia, linking the ministry of health with all the provincial hospitals. The network was gradually extended to other users.[83]

International organizations have provided assistance for many of these initial undertakings. The Organization of American States has sponsored various programs that encourage the development of networking in Latin America.[84] The United Nations Development Programme (UNDP) helped to establish the first Internet networks in several nations, including India as far back as 1989.[85] National aid agencies, such as USAID, have also implemented programs promoting Internet connectivity. One way in which both international and national aid agencies help to diffuse the Internet is by establishing their own networks in the countries in which they operate. Two examples are the UNDP, which has connectivity in more than one hundred countries, and the World Health Organization (WHO), which supports networks dedicated to information and communication regarding health services.[86] Initiatives such as these on the part of national and international agencies not only provide financial and technical assistance to promote Internet connectivity, but they also play a very important catalytic role in the diffusion process. Once connections began to be made in a country, there is a demonstration effect that stimulates demands for broader access.

Nongovernmental organizations (NGOs) have also served as catalysts for developing connectivity by supporting and establishing networks and providing other forms of aid. Some NGOs have dedicated themselves to "grassroots connectivity," among key actors in the development process. The independent information organization Panos London claims that a considerable amount of Internet use in the South in the earlier years (1993–1995) was attributable to low-cost NGO networks and that "the earliest disseminators of Internet use and technology were organizations belonging to the Association for Progressive Communications (APC), such as Green Net (London) and the Institute for Global Communications (San Francisco)."[87]

Business and commercial enterprises are the most obvious catalyst to the diffusion of the Internet. Sometimes the spread of the Internet in a country may be more the consequence of "piggybacking" off the networking infrastructure of businesses than the result of government policies.[88] Having made an investment a corporation may extend opportunities for access to the Internet to academics, as well as to other commercial organizations.

Another commercially driven impetus to the expansion of access to the Internet is the proliferation around the globe of cybercafes or Internet cafes, which offer good, relatively cheap public access to the Internet. As of July 2007, there are 4,208 Internet cafes in 141 countries, according to a website that contains a database.[89] Often a large portion of the clientele consists of tourists and other foreigners. Even when tourists are the main targets of opportunity, cybercafes help to create constituencies of local users, which expand over time. The key here, of course, is the cost of access, and that in turn depends at least to some degree on government policies. For example, high costs for leased lines and high taxes on equipment will be passed on to users.

Commercial Internet service providers (ISPs) play an important role in improving and extending access to the Internet. The various "free" services such as hotmail and gmail, where they are offered, significantly broaden access to e-mail. For commercial ISPs to operate they must be permitted under government regulations and an infrastructure must be in place. Legislation passed in November 1998 in India, for example, ended the government's monopoly as an international telecommunications service provider and threw open Internet access to vigorous competition among private ISPs. One year later there were 175 ISPs, and the user population burgeoned. Even when commercial ISPs are permitted, Internet use can be limited by laws that prohibit certain kinds of material. As indicated in the case study of China in chapter 6, a combination of appropriate software, personal monitoring, and political intimidation can restrict the flow of information when applied to ISPs and any public Internet access.

In summary, the impetus for a developing country to connect to the Internet may spring from any number of sources. As indicated in the above discussion, countries have followed very different diffusion patterns, and some have led to broader access than others. One essential condition for establishing Internet connectivity is a strong domestic constituency, preferably with political influence, which provides a push for movement in that direction. Universities and research centers often provide the initiative to mobilize government policy and resources for the first steps. Even when the initiative lies with the government, success depends on the existence of technical skills to implement the policies. Academics who have studied abroad and who have had experience with global networking are likely candidates for this catalytic role. Recent moves among the Persian Gulf countries to increase connectivity to the Internet provide an example of this kind of influence. Two observers of Internet development, Grey E. Burkhart and Seymour E. Goodman, believe that younger members of key families, who have used the Internet at foreign educational institutions, are one of the constituencies that have pushed the cautious conservative governments in the Persian Gulf toward acceptance of the Internet.[90] Other constituencies that are likely to push for the establishment and improvement of the Internet are domestic businesses, which recognize the need to operate internationally, and resident foreign companies. Business enterprises may even invest in networking infrastructure, which can become a base for expansion of connectivity.

Most governments are motivated to connect to the Internet in order to make their countries, industries, and companies more competitive in the global economy. In some cases, notably that of China, there is an ongoing struggle to advance economic objectives while containing political consequences deemed negative to the regime. The Internet can contribute to economic growth both indirectly by reducing the knowledge gap and directly by enhancing the productivity and competitiveness of local businesses and connecting them with more opportunities. If realizing the commercial potential of the Internet overwhelms all other purposes, however, broader development and informational objectives will be compromised.

Conclusion: The Revolution Continues

Innovations in information and communication technologies are proliferating, and frantic efforts are underway to invent the "next big thing." Some ideas that seemed a sure thing, such as the videophone, which would enable people to see each other while they conversed on the telephone, never became widespread. On the other hand, who would have predicted that instant messaging, laboriously typing in messages with the thumb on a small gadget with a miniature keyboard, would spread like wildfire among the younger generation in many countries? Although the future is uncertain, the information revolution appears to be moving in three different directions.

The first is a trend toward convergence. The fact that all forms of information—sound, images, and data—can be processed and transmitted digitally makes it possible to move from one conduit to another. As the three major branches of communication move to digital processing, the lines between them become less distinct, and the telecommunications, computer, and audiovisual industries converge. Telephone lines and cables connect computers, and computers are conduits for all forms of information and communication. Telecommunications industries are becoming more reliant on software and complex computer systems for delivery of services.[91] A technology known as Voice over Internet Protocol (VoIP) makes Internet-based telephony possible. Software from a small firm called Skype, for example, allows people to make free telephone calls to any other Skype user anywhere and also cheap calls to traditional telephones. Satellite and cable technologies deliver both television and radio to individual sets, creating a global marketplace. Hundreds of newspapers from all over the world appear on the World Wide Web, often with frequent updates. Many radio stations and even some television programs can be accessed online.

Not only are technologies, industries, and services converging but also the devices that access them. New services are constantly being offered for the mobile cellular telephone, as new generations of the technology are developed. When connected to the Internet they can provide for e-mail exchange, browsing, downloading of music and video files, and navigation assistance from the Global Positioning Navigation System (GPS). They double as cameras and have created a popular form of communication among the younger generation in text messaging. Television companies are anticipating more demand for their programs on mobile media and are moving in that direction. Podcasting distributes many radio and television programs to mobile media through the Internet. The introduction of the iPhone represents a new stage in digital convergence by combining personal computing and mobile technologies in a way that no device has done before. Cell phones are beginning to look more like personal computers.[92]

The cell phone has been limited as a medium of international communication by the lack of technological standardization. The Europeans established a single standard, Global System for Mobile Communications (GSM), which is now one of the leading digital cellular systems, widely used in Asia and Africa as well as Europe. Users may connect with service providers in different countries by switching removable Subscriber Identification Module (SIM) cards. However, U.S. cell phones are not compatible with the European system. Special phones or arrangements are necessary for use in most countries. Purchase or rental of a compatible phone in the destination country is another solution. Service for calling internationally from the United States varies with the providers, but rates are difficult to decipher and expensive.

Although the cell phone currently is not an affordable, readily available means of international communication for most users, the invention may nevertheless have an impact on world politics in a variety of ways. Because it is quicker and cheaper to install cellular networks than landlines, more people in the world are gaining access to the economic and other benefits of telephones. Cell phones also facilitate political mobilization and coordination for demonstrations, revolutions, terrorist acts, and other efforts to bring about political change, as discussed in chapter 6.

The spectacular growth of mobile telephones and the convergence of various functions on them illustrate a second trend—toward wireless communication.[93] A new generation of wireless technologies provides improved cell phone access to the Internet. Laptop computers are now equipped with a variety of wireless options to connect the user with the Web. Wi-Fi provides "hot spots" for access in many hotels, airports, and other locations, and some cities are planning municipal wireless networks. One new option is a mobile broadband card that provides laptop access to the Web where the user has cellular service. A number of wireless technologies are being developed to expand the range of signals and to provide high-speed, always-on Internet access. Looking toward the future, the *Economist* predicted that "we are heading towards a networked society of ubiquitous, mobile communications capable of constant monitoring."[94]

A third trend is toward more participatory and interactive media. There is even a very controversial piece of cyber jargon that is circulating to describe this trend toward more user-generated content and interactive participation on the Internet. "Web 2.0" does not refer to a new version of the Web or a new technology but rather to new applications, services, and ways of using the Web that are based on "the architecture of participation."[95] The popularity of online video sharing, social network services, wikis (websites that allow anyone to add or edit content), and especially weblogs exemplify this trend.

Weblogs (or blogging) come in a variety of forms, but all are based on the idea that users create material on a website for the purpose of sharing information, opinions, and experiences and receiving feedback from other users. Generally defined as "a personal online journal," they sometimes take the form of an online diary but may also be oriented more toward news and commentary on particular topics.[96] They contain hyperlinks and, typically, a list of links along the side of the blog page to other blogs and websites that relate to the topic. This feature of blogs explains how a story, picture, or piece of information can spread rapidly and often be picked up by the mainstream media. In fact, many newspapers, television networks, and radio stations, which have established a presence on the Web, have also become part of the "blogosphere," as they add blogs for audience feedback and commentary.

Technorati, a search engine for blogs, estimated in 2006 that a new blog was created every second of every day and that the number had doubled every five months since 2003.[97] Initially, only those who knew how to create web-sites produced blogs. But the idea was appealing, and soon blog hosting services and software tools emerged to make it easier for more people to become bloggers. The idea quickly gained popularity in other countries. In fact, only 28 percent of the blogs tracked by Technorati in 2006 were in English; 41 percent were in Japanese and 28 percent in Chinese.[98]

As with most new technologies, there are optimistic and pessimistic views about the potential impact of blogs and other Web 2.0 applications. Optimists point out that expressing individual opinions and sharing them with others is inherently democratic. Blogs give voice to those who would not otherwise be heard. The "Global Citizen's Media Project," for example, seeks to realize this potential by collecting blogs and other self-published content from around the world—"shining light on places and people other media often ignore."[99] It is a cooperative effort of contributors from every continent and dozens of countries, which also seeks to "amplify the global conversation online."

Optimists also stress the informational value of self-organizing and information-sharing tools such as blogs, social networks, and wikis. These tools "leverage the wisdom of the crowds . . . harnessing collective intelligence, turning the web into a kind of global brain."[100] The value of these tools in some appropriate adaptation has even been considered by some top-level officials in the U.S. intelligence community. A paper entitled "The Wiki and the Blog: Toward a Complex Adaptive Intelligence Community" won the intelligence community's Galileo Award for 2004 for the best idea on information sharing.[101] The author, a CIA technology officer, explored the reasons that these tools are so useful in providing information and then boldly asserted that "once the Intelligence Community has a robust and mature Wiki and Blog knowledge sharing web space, the nature of Intelligence will change forever."[102]

Another testimonial from a surprising source came from the head of BBC Global News, who told a meeting of the World Editor's Forum that social networks can provide a faster source of news than his own organization. He explained that "any subject you want to write or broadcast about someone in your audience will know a lot more than you do," so it is useful to be able to tap into that expertise. He acknowledged that he finds out much more about what is happening from networks of colleagues and experts on social media sites like Facebook than from the traditional media.[103]

Skepticism about the value of Web 2.0 applications abounds and is usually part of a larger set of arguments about the Internet itself. Many of these have been pungently summarized in the book *The Cult of the Amateur: How Today's*

Internet Is Killing Our Culture.[104] This interactive version of the Web has no standards and no vetting for accuracy, he argues; amateur, unreliable, and predominantly frivolous content threatens to overwhelm vital information. Worse yet, all this "user-generated nonsense" undermines the authority of the professional, carefully edited mainstream media, leaving only "opinion chaos, a cacophony of amateurs."[105] Wikipedia, the online encyclopedia created and edited by Internet users, is a favorite example of the critics.

These divergent assessments reflect the extraordinary range of purposes for which the Internet can be used. The Internet combines the text of the printing press, the audio of the radio, and the video of television. More significantly, participation is inherent in its architecture. In this sense it is fundamentally different from the traditional mass media (radio, television, and film), in which identical messages are sent from a central point to a large audience in a one-way process. The mass media audience listens to or watches what is provided from that central point, while the Internet user interacts with a computer and with other users, often creating his or her own content to distribute to another user or to a multitude.

But this distinction is eroding, as the mass media are also becoming more participatory and interactive. Radio and television call-in shows are among the most popular programs in vastly different cultural settings. Some radio and television programs have contests in which members of the audience vote their preferences by calling in or voting online. Many television programs suggest to viewers that they can find out more on that subject by clicking on the website. Vigilant organizations regularly track viewer preferences for programs, which are often modified in response. At a minimum level mass media audiences today have become more active participants by being able to choose among a larger selection of programs than existed in the past. Videocassette recorders (VCRs) and digital video recorders (DVRs) allow users to select the time they wish to watch.

The discussion in this book focuses sometimes on one medium and at other times on another—with emphasis on satellite television and the Internet—in order to demonstrate the variety of ways in which the new technologies are affecting world politics. The terms "new media" and information and communication technologies (ICTs) are comprehensive and inclusive terms used to portray the "big picture," that is, the cumulative effect of the array of technologies that have radically changed the environment of world politics. The trend toward convergence of these technologies and their applications warrants this approach.

This chapter first traced the development of technologies that have created global networks for communication and information access. Fiber-optic cables, geosynchronous satellites, and the Internet are "technologies without boundaries" with the technical capacity to connect any two places on earth for instant communication. The trajectory of these globalizing technologies has demonstrated how their expansive properties have pushed governments to reduce restrictions on information flows, leading to widespread changes in policies that triggered worldwide entrepreneurial activity. But technologies, governments, and markets are not the whole story. Individuals have also shaped the current media environment, as they will continue to shape the impact of future technological innovations. The ARPA scientists who believed that computers could be used for communication as well as calculation; the collection of journalists who decided to establish the independent BBC-type Arab satellite news channel that became Al Jazeera; and the hundreds of "cable wallahs" in India who strung cables across trees to provide television service from the newly established AsiaSat are all examples of the way in which the social uses of a technology also affect its trajectory and impact.

The combination of these expansive new technologies, market pressures, and government policies has spurred the growth of a privatized global communication structure and has created a new, complex, and dynamic media environment. Cable, satellites, and the Internet have created vast new entrepreneurial opportunities just as governments were eliminating restrictions on private enterprise in telecommunications and broadcasting. One consequence is the concentration of economic power in the form of enormous communication conglomerates—the driving force behind the globalization of communication. Paradoxically, another consequence is the proliferation of new and diverse media actors in developing as well as developed countries at the regional, national, and even local levels.

New technologies continue to develop global networks for communication and information access. Other technological developments are aimed at the personal level, increasing channels of communication and sources of information and entertainment.

More transcontinental channels of contact are available to more people in the world at far less cost than ever before in history. Computers, digital technologies, and the Internet have vastly increased the human capacity to store, retrieve, and disseminate information.

The revolution continues.

Notes

1. Marshall McLuhan, *Understanding Media* (London: Routledge and Kegan Paul, 1964), 11.

2. Al Gore, Speech to the International Telecommunications Union, Argentina, March 21, 1994.

3. Walter B. Wriston, *The Twilight of Sovereignty: How the Information Revolution Is Transforming Our World* (New York: Charles Scribner's Sons, 1992), 43.

4. Calvin Sims, "New Atlantic Cable Makes More Calls Possible," *New York Times*, December 14, 1988, A1.

5. Simon Romero, "Shining Future of Fiber Optics Loses Glimmer," *New York Times*, June 18, 2001, A17.

6. Ken Belson, "New Undersea Cable Projects Face Some Old Problems," *New York Times*, May 10, 2004, C4.

7. Heather E. Hudson, *Communication Satellites: Their Development and Impact* (New York: Free Press, 1990), 16, 23.

8. Hudson, *Communication Satellites*, 23.

9. Jonathan F. Galloway, *The Politics and Technology of Satellite Communications* (Lexington, Mass.: Lexington Books, 1972), 69.

10. Intelsat, "2000 and Beyond: The Future Is Now," at www.intelsat.com/about-us/history/intelsat-2000s.asp (accessed September 21, 2007).

11. Karen J. Bannan, "Continental Drift," *Internet World* 7, no. 5 (March 1, 2001): 64–66.

12. The story of this first computer is told in Scott McCartney, *ENIAC: The Triumph and Tragedies of the World's First Computer* (Berkeley, Calif.: Berkeley Publishing Group, 2001). See also transcript of interview with the author on National Public Radio, Morning Edition, August 19, 1999.

13. Ronald J. Deibert, *Parchment, Printing, and Hypermedia: Communication in World Order Transformation* (New York: Columbia University Press, 1997), 121.

14. *Encyclopaedia Britannica Online*, "The Personal Computer Revolution," at http://www.britannica.com/eb/article-216069/computer (accessed July 13, 2001).

15. Howard Rheingold, *The Virtual Community: Homesteading on the Electronic Frontier*, revised ed. (Cambridge, Mass.: MIT Press, 2000), 58–59. See also Katie Hafner and Matthew Lyon, *Where Wizards Stay Up Late: The Origins of the Internet* (New York: Simon and Schuster, 1996). Especially important is an account by nine individuals who helped to make the history of the Internet. See Barry M. Leiner et al., *A Brief History of the Internet*, Internet Society, 2000, at www.isoc.org/internet/history/brief.shtml (accessed October 15, 2006).

16. Leiner et al., *A Brief History of the Internet*, 2.

17. Rheingold, *The Virtual Community*, 59.

18. Janet Abbate, *Inventing the Internet* (Cambridge, Mass.: MIT Press, 1999), 10–21.

19. Abbate, *Inventing the Internet*, 21–35.

20. Hafner and Lyon, *Where Wizards Stay Up Late*, 241–43.

21. Abbate, *Inventing the Internet*, 201.

22. John S. Quarterman, *The Matrix: Computer Networks and Conferencing Systems Worldwide*, cited in Abbate, *Inventing the Internet*, 202.

23. Abbate, *Inventing the Internet*, 245.

24. Abbate, *Inventing the Internet*, 210. These figures are taken from reports of the Michigan Educational Research Information Triad (MERIT), which managed the NSFNET for some time.

25. Bruce R. Schatz and Joseph B. Hardin, "NCSA Mosaic and the World Wide Web: Global Hypermedia Protocols for the Internet," *Science* 265:895–901. Cited in Abbate, *Inventing the Internet*, 217.

26. Abbate, *Inventing the Internet*, 6.

27. Wilson P. Dizard Jr., *Meganet: How the Global Communications Network Will Connect Everyone on Earth* (Boulder, Colo.: Westview Press, 1997), dust jacket.

28. United Nations Development Programme (UNDP), *Human Development Report 1999* (New York: Oxford University Press, 1999), 30.

29. Dizard, *Meganet*, 66.

30. Daya Kishan Thussu, *International Communication: Continuity and Change* (London: Arnold, 2000), 83.

31. Global Information Infrastructure Commission, *Building the Global Information Economy* (Washington, D.C.: Center for Strategic and Information Studies, 1998), 8; Edmund Andrews, "68 Nations Agree to Widen Markets in Communications," *New York Times*, February 16, 1997, A1.

32. International Telecommunication Union (ITU), *Trends in Telecommunication Reform, 1999* (Geneva: Author, 1999).

33. *Telegeography 2002: Global Traffic Statistics and Summary*, executive summary online, at www.telegeography.com/ (accessed October 14, 2004).

34. ITU, "Key Global Telecom Indicators for the World Telecommunication Service Sector," at www.itu.int/ITU-D/ict/statistics/at_glance/KeyTelecom99.html (accessed October 15, 2006).

35. *Telegeography 2002*, 9.

36. ITU, "Key Global Telecom Indicators."

37. ITU, *World Telecommunication Development Report, 1998* (Geneva: Author, 1998), 15.

38. ITU, "ICT Statistics Database," at www.itu.int/ITU-D/icteye/Indicators/Indicators.aspx# (accessed June 12, 2007).

39. ITU, *World Telecommunication Development Report, 1998*, 15.

40. *New York Times*, World Briefing, May 23, 2007, A8.

41. ITU, "ICT Statistics Database."

42. ITU, "ICT Statistics Database."

43. Denis McQuail and Karen Siune, *Media Policy: Convergence, Concentration, and Commerce* (London: Sage, 1998), tab. 3.1. Quoted in Pippa Norris, *A Virtuous Circle: Political Communications in Postindustrial Societies* (New York: Cambridge University Press, 2000), 91, 94.

44. William Hoynes, "Why Media Mergers Matter," *Media Channel*, at www.mediachannel.org/ownership (accessed August 15, 2002).

45. Frank Gibney, "Score One for AOLTW," *Time*, December 25, 2000, 138.

46. Thussu, *International Communication*, 121.

47. See the network's website, www.startv.com/ (accessed August 15, 2002).

48. See Bertelsmann's website, www.bertelsmann.com/ (accessed August 20, 2002).

49. *Economist*, "Survey of Television," April 13, 2002, 11, 12.

50. See, for example, John Sinclair, Elizabeth Jacka, and Stuart Cunningham, eds., *New Patterns in Global Television: Peripheral Vision* (New York: Oxford University Press, 1995), 8.

51. United Nations Educational, Scientific and Cultural Organization (UNESCO), *World Communication Report: The Media and the Challenge of the New Technologies* (Paris: Author, 1997), 187.

52. UNESCO, *World Communication Report*, 186.

53. Anita Pratap, "Challenge or Threat?" *Time*, October 21, 1991, 51.

54. "India's Television History," at www.indiantelevision.com/indianbrodcast/history/historyoftele.htm (accessed July 18, 2003).

55. David Page and William Crawley, *Satellites over South Asia: Broadcasting, Culture, and the Public Interest* (New Delhi: Sage, 2001), 89.

56. Page and Crawley, *Satellites over South Asia*, 217, and the entire chapter 6 on regional broadcasting in South Asia.

57. Subash Joshi, "25 Years of Satellite Broadcasting in India," at www.orbicom.uqam.ca/ (accessed July 7, 2003); "Satellites Covering India," at www.indiantelevision.com/satreckon/satelliteindia/satellitesoverindia.htm (accessed July 27, 2003).

58. Thussu, *International Communication*, 197–99, provides an excellent discussion of Zee TV as an example of "cultural hybridity."

59. Page and Crawley, *Satellites over South Asia*, 149.

60. Mark Landler, "A Glut of Cable TV in India," *New York Times*, March 23, 2001, C1; Barry Bearak, "Many, Many in India Want to Be a Millionaire," *New York Times*, August 30, 2000, A1.

61. *Economist*, "Murdoch's Twinkler," July 26, 2003, 59.

62. Thussu, *International Communication*, 210.

63. S. Abdallah Schleifer, "An Interview with Ali Al-Hedeithy," *Transnational Broadcasting Studies*, no. 9 (Fall/Winter 2002) , at www.tbsjournal.com/ (accessed August 5, 2003).

64. Jane Perlez, "U.S. Courts Network It Once Described as 'All Osama,'" *New York Times*, March 20, 2003, A24; Naomi Sakr, *Satellite Realms: Transnational Television, Globalization, and the Middle East* (New York: I. B. Tauris, 2001), 16.

65. The first quote is from the PBS *Wide Angle* documentary, "Exclusive to Al-Jazeera," July 10, 2003, and the second, by Al Jazeera's managing director, Mohammed Jasim al-Ali, is from Mohammed El-Nawawy and A. Iskandar, *Al Jazeera: How the Free Arab News Network Scooped the World and Changed the Middle East* (Boulder, Colo.: Westview Press, 2002), 176.

66. Allied Media Corp., "Al Jazeera TV Viewer Demographic," at www.allied-media.com/aljazeera/JAZdemog.html (accessed September 21, 2007).

67. Delinda C. Hanley, "Al Jazeera English: The Brave New Channel They Don't Want You to See," *Washington Report on Middle East Affairs 87554917* 26, no. 7 (September/October 2007): 24.

68. Philip Seib, "Hegemonic No More: Western Media, the Rise of Al-Jazeera, and the Influence of Diverse Voices," *International Studies Review* 7, no. 4 (December 2005): 605.

69. Mohammed El-Nawawy and Leo A. Gher, "Al Jazeera: Bridging the East-West Gap through Public Discourse and Media Diplomacy," *TBS Journal*, no. 10 (Spring/Summer 2003), at www.tbsjournal.com/ (accessed December 15, 2005).

70. Sinclair, Jacka, and Cunningham, *New Patterns in Global Television*, 8.

71. Except as otherwise noted, information on Televisa is from John Sinclair, "Mexico, Brazil, and the Latin World," in *New Patterns in Global Television: Peripheral Vision*, ed. John Sinclair, Elizabeth Jacka, and Stuart Cunningham, 33–66 (New York: Oxford University Press, 1995).

72. UNESCO, *World Communication Report*, 195.

73. Sinclair, Jacka, and Cunningham, *New Patterns in Global Television*, 57.

74. Information on Rede Globo is from Thussu, *International Communication*, 211–17.

75. Thussu, *International Communication*, 216–17.

76. Quote and figures from Suzanne Kapner, "U.S. TV Shows Losing Potency around the World," *New York Times*, January 2, 2003, 1.

77. *Economist*, "Survey: Television," April 11, 2002.

78. Marc Gunther, "MTV's Passage to India," *Fortune*, August 9, 2004.

79. Anthony Smith, ed., *Television: An International History* (New York: Oxford University Press, 1995), 7.

80. Internet World Stats, "Internet Usage Statistics: The Big Picture," at www.internetworldstats.com/stats.htm (accessed June 30, 2007); ITU, "Market Information and Statistics," at www.itu.int/ITU-D/ict/statistics (accessed October 16, 2006).

81. S. E. Goodman, L. I. Press, S. R. Ruth, and A. M. Rutkowski, "The Global Diffusion of the Internet: Patterns and Problems," *Communications of the ACM* 37, no. 8 (August 1994): 27.

82. Goodman et al., "The Global Diffusion of the Internet," 27.

83. Goodman et al., "The Global Diffusion of the Internet," 27.

84. Goodman et al., "The Global Diffusion of the Internet," 28.

85. Grey E. Burkhart, Seymour E. Goodman, Arun Mehta, and Larry Press, "The Internet in India: Better Times Ahead?" *Communications of the ACM* 41, no. 11 (November 1998): 22.

86. Goodman et al., "The Global Diffusion of the Internet," 28.

87. Panos, "Can the Internet Improve Life in Developing Countries?" *Monthly Public Opinion Surveys* 44, no. 2 (November 1998): 20.

88. Goodman et al., "The Global Diffusion of the Internet," 28.

89. Cybercafes, "Database," at www.cybercafe.com/ (accessed July 4, 2007).

90. Grey E. Burkhart and Seymour E. Goodman, "The Internet Gains Acceptance in the Persian Gulf," *Communications of the ACM* 41, no. 3 (March 1998): 24.

91. See *Economist*, "Survey of Telecoms Convergence," October 14, 2006.

92. Martin Fackler, "Chasing the iPhone," *New York Times*, July 2, 2007, C1.

93. See *Economist*, "A World of Connections: A Special Report on Telecoms," April 28, 2007.

94. *Economist*, "Survey of the Internet Society," January 25, 2003, 3.

95. This phrase and the term "Web 2.0" originated in the speeches and writings of Tim O'Reilly, founder of O'Reilly Media Company, and a supporter of free software and open source movements. See his chapter "The Open Source Paradigm Shift," in *Perspectives on Free and Open Source Software,* ed. Joseph Feller, Brian Firzgerald, Scott A. Hissam, and Karim R. Lakhani (Cambridge, Mass.: MIT Press, 2007), 461–81; and Tim O'Reilly, "What Is Web 2.0: Design Patterns and Business Models for the Next Generation of Software," September 30, 2005, at www.oreillynet.com/pub/a/oreilly/tim/news/2005/09/30/what-is-web-20.html (accessed June 18, 2007).

96. A sample of blogs listed by category can be found in Rich Meislin, "Blogs 101," at http://nytimes.com/ref/technology/blogs_101.html (accessed June 21, 2007).

97. *Economist,* "Survey: New Media," April 20, 2006, at www.economist.com/surveys/displaystory.cfm?story_id=6794172 (accessed June 19, 2007).

98. *Economist,* "Survey: New Media."

99. Global Voices, "About," at www.globalvoicesonline.org/about (accessed August 3, 2007).

100. O'Reilly, "What Is Web 2.0."

101. D. Calvin Andrus, "The Wiki and the Blog: Toward a Complex Adaptive Intelligence Community," September 10, 2005, at http://papers.ssrn.com/sol3/papers.cfm?abstract_id=755904#PaperDownload (accessed June 22, 2007).

102. Andrus, "The Wiki and the Blog," 24. This paper reflects the views of the author only, but it was part of the discussion in the intelligence community. See Clive Thompson, "Open-Source Spying," *New York Times Magazine,* December 3, 2006, 54.

103. Oliver Luft, "BBC Global News Chief Gets Web 2.0 News via Facebook, not Beeb," *Online Journalism News,* June 5, 2007, at www.journalism.co.uk/news/story3342.shtml (accessed June 22, 2007).

104. Andrew Keen, *The Cult of the Amateur: How Today's Internet Is Killing Our Culture* (New York: Doubleday, 2007).

105. Interview on National Public Radio with John Ydste, Saturday Weekend Edition, June 16, 2007.

CHAPTER FOUR

↶

War and Peace in the Information Age

How can a man in a cave outcommunicate the world's leading communication society?

—Richard Holbrooke[1]

Words seem ethereal and ideas ephemeral next to bullets and bombs, but the two modes of interaction seem increasingly linked.

—Monroe E. Price[2]

Two trends are changing the world in which foreign policy makers, diplomats, and the military must operate. One is a new information environment, which has enlivened an old controversy and raised new questions about the influence of the media on foreign policymaking. The second is the proliferation of nonstate actors empowered by these technologies to participate actively in world politics, creating a new political environment. If the cliché "information is power" is correct, then it is a significant development in world politics that more people today have access to more information from more diverse sources than ever before, as well as the ability to spread information and to mobilize support for or opposition to particular positions and policies. Public diplomacy, which is "the promotion of the national interest by informing, engaging, and influencing people around the world," has become a more important instrument of foreign policy because the conduct of international relations has become more public, and the public has become more involved.[3]

Foreign Policymaking in the New Information Environment

New technologies expand the reach and availability of the old ones. Batteries make cheap radios work even where there is no electricity. Fiber-optic cables and satellites now connect countries and continents with telephones and a plethora of television channels. Mobile phones now exceed landlines, and the fastest growth is in Africa. Other technologies are completely new. Internet-connected computers combine the capacity to store and process information with the ability to transmit messages and images almost instantly around the world. Satellite remote sensing imagery makes information, once classified, readily available.

A combination of technological innovations has revolutionized the news media, notably, laptop computers, video phones, and mobile satellite hookups—ever smaller and more portable. These devices replace the tons of equipment that were previously necessary to transmit reports from remote locations. The camcorder replaced the tape recorder, and video formats allowed images to be transmitted electronically rather than being physically transported. The first live transmissions involved mobile satellite uplink units that were large, cumbersome, expensive to deploy, and subject to local broadcasting regulations. Smaller, more mobile transmission equipment was developed in the latter part of the 1990s. These breakthroughs included the video phone, which involved merely a camera, digital compression unit, and satellite telephone that could fit onto an airplane luggage rack.[4] The convenience of these improvements makes it possible to report events from places hitherto inaccessible to a television audience that watches the events in real time, that is, as they occur. All of the mass media—newspapers, radio, and especially television—have changed their operations to take advantage of satellite technology in order to provide more timely news. In the 1970s fewer than half of all television news stories were shown on the day they happened, whereas today most news is broadcast the day it is taped, if not live.[5]

Although the three major television networks had covered events live from time to time before 1980, it was the launching of Cable News Network (CNN) in that year that gave impetus to this shift. As an upstart network and one with the radical idea of twenty-four-hour news coverage, CNN experimented with new ideas regarding institutional organization and programming content in order to succeed. CNN's founder, Ted Turner, was committed to making the fullest use of the technological developments that would allow the network to broadcast as much "breaking news" as possible. He was also committed to the idea of an international news network, establishing affiliates abroad for news exchange and transmitting the news regularly via satellite to as many countries as possible. CNN's live reporting from Iraq during the Gulf War in 1991 inspired the creation of other international and regional news channels, and spurred the demand for live global television reporting, for seeing history as it unfolds. New television stations and networks multiplied, as more cable and satellite services became available.

There is general agreement that the instantaneous transmission of news accelerates the decision-making process and creates pressures for an immediate response. When government officials discuss the impact of satellite television, they almost invariably highlight this change. Gordon Smith, deputy minister of the Canadian Ministry of Foreign Affairs, told a conference on "Virtual Diplomacy" that "the most important long-term trend is the change in the pace of the game . . . responses must now be almost instantaneous."[6] David Gergen, recalling before the same conference his own experience as adviser to four presidents, explained, "With instantaneous media coverage, the media wants a government opinion before government officials have had any time to formulate an official position, let alone a response."[7]

Policy makers often receive pictures of events and television reports before they can receive information and analysis about the event from their own diplomats or intelligence officials. Initial impressions are formed, and emotion-laden images can sway officials as well as the public. Leaders and their constituents may have access to the same initial reports about an event and receive them at about the same time. Pressure builds for an immediate response before more complete information about the event and its context can be acquired from an array of experts and advisers. Those who are consulted will also be monitoring the news media accounts, their graphic images, and interpretive spins. The pressure of time is built into the decision-making process and is part of the very definition of crisis. The technologies that transmit information instantaneously to a large number of people intensify those pressures.

The spread of satellite television and the decline of state-owned monopolies have also created a more transparent environment, "a condition in which information about governments' preferences, intentions, behavior, and capabilities is widely available to the global public."[8] It is harder for governments to keep secrets, and they are under greater scrutiny from more sources. Increased transparency and visibility also reduces flexibility for policy makers. When a statement is made on television, it becomes recorded history that can be, and often is, replayed later to remind the audience of any changes of position, inconsistencies, or inaccurate predictions. As the insurgency gained strength in Iraq, reports of the number of deaths were occasionally accompanied by the image of George Bush making a speech aboard the battleship USS *Abraham Lincoln* under the banner "Mission Accomplished."

The Internet, which is multipurpose, interactive, and transnational, provides even more opportunities for scrutiny, as the sources of information and political orientations are more diverse than in the mainstream media anywhere. Information can also spread rapidly on the Internet. Foreign newspapers and broadcasts are easily accessible, as are websites from a multitude of sources, reliable and unreliable.

Besides accelerating the decision-making process and increasing the transparency of government actions, satellite television also enhances the importance of images. Long before the advent of satellite television, Robert Jervis wrote a book that stressed the power of images in international relations. "A desired image can often be of greater use than a significant increment of military or economic power," he wrote. "An undesired image can involve costs for which almost no amount of the usual kinds of power can compensate and can be a handicap almost impossible to overcome."[9] Images have always been important in international relations, but the advent of global television has magnified the role of this element of power. It has increased the importance of "soft power," the power to attract through the force of ideas, values, institutions, and culture.[10] Because much of the television and film seen around the world and much of the music heard is from the United States, its image is widely projected to a very diverse audience. Insofar as there is admiration for this programming *and* the values embedded in it, the U.S. image and its ability to attract is enhanced. But those values are perceived in very different ways. To some, U.S. culture exemplifies a free and spontaneous lifestyle. Others, especially some in the Muslim world, are repelled by what they see as vulgarity and indecency. The ubiquity of U.S. cultural fare in the global media has both positive and negative effects on its image.

Images and messages are refracted through a national and cultural lens. A message designed to mobilize support from a domestic audience may well make its way to a foreign audience and produce unintended consequences. A single word, whether a slip of the tongue or not, can enrage a foreign audience and complicate future policy with unintended effects. In a press conference the weekend after the attacks on the World Trade Center and the Pentagon, President George W. Bush declared, "This is a new kind of evil, and we understand, and the American people are beginning to understand, this crusade, this war on terrorism, is going to take a while."[11] The use of the word "crusade" provided ammunition for those who wanted to portray the "war on terror" as a war against Islam, and Bush has struggled ever since against that interpretation.

Not only the words but also nonverbal signaling and body language take on a new importance in the television age. Televised messages can convey information through facial expressions and body language that cannot be deci-phered in the written form. Seeing a message can be more compelling than reading it. Christer Jonsson, who has studied the impact of television on diplomatic signaling, points to the need for world leaders to be skilled tele-vision performers on what is literally a world stage. Television has "expanded the scope of theatricality . . . every encounter, every gesture, every handshake is watched, interpreted, and reviewed."[12] Invitations to visit the White House, to stand side by side with the president in the Rose Garden or, in the second Bush administration, to visit the ranch in Crawford are intended to symbolize a close relationship between two countries. Handshakes and re-fusals to shake hands have always symbolized friendship and hostility respec-tively, but the visibility when transmitted live to a worldwide audience adds significance to the implicit message.

Do the Media Set the Foreign Policy Agenda?
Satellite television expands the scope of concerns of leaders and their con-stituents when graphic images of crises in distant and unfamiliar parts of the world demand attention. Earthquakes, floods, revolutions, atrocities, wars, and much more appear on screens in homes around the world as these events are occurring. The history that the world has watched unfold on television has been full of dramatic and powerful images. The first featured television event of the post–Cold War era was the spectacular Gulf War in 1991, which brought convincing pictures of smart bombs, smart generals, and the "high-way of death" into living rooms around the world. Then a host of humani-tarian crises in the disintegrating Yugoslavia and in Africa produced heartrending images of atrocities, refugees, and starving children. The col-lapsing World Trade Center towers and the array of images from the war in Iraq and its aftermath introduced the new century.

How and to what extent does the emotional impact of these images trans-late into influence over policy? Can television propel certain items onto the foreign policy agenda and, by the sheer emotional power of its images, create pressures to alter government priorities? Are the news media seizing the ini-tiative from policy makers? How has the proliferation of information chan-nels affected the ability of governments to manage the news and mobilize support for their policies?

Walter Wriston, a former CEO of Citicorp, argued in his book *The Twi-light of Sovereignty* that "the national and international agendas of nations are increasingly being set not by some grand government plan but by the media: policymakers have to spend a good share of their time and energy dealing with whatever crises or pseudocrises have been identified by the media that particular day."[13] This agenda-setting role is more controversial than the impact of the media as accelerant. The dramatic technological developments of the 1990s that facilitate reporting from the field allow reporters to roam freely, lending credence to the view that the media select the issues for policy makers to address. A catalytic event generating debate on this question was the intervention of the United States in Somalia in the fall of 1992 to ensure the distribution of food supplies, where a violent conflict among warlords exacerbated a famine and anarchy ruled. A widespread public perception developed that television images of starving children had pushed the United States to intervene in Somalia, and then, when U.S. troops became part of the conflict, images of a dead soldier being dragged through the streets of Mogadishu forced the United States to withdraw.

So compelling was this interpretation of television's influence on policy that it popularized the term "CNN curve" to describe the medium's ability to incite popular demands to "do something" quickly, while heightening the political risk of the response.

It was this double bind that, in retrospect, doomed the humanitarian effort in Somalia from the start. The emaciated children cried out to be fed, yet the source of their plight was not only a drought but also the lack of effective governing institutions and a vicious struggle between heavily armed militias. Solving the fundamental problems, that is, reducing the level of arms, negotiating a settlement, and helping to establish a functioning government, would have involved a level of commitment that no government, including the United States, wanted to make. To impose peace would put American lives and political careers at risk. To respond with a purely humanitarian effort to distribute food would minimize those risks, or so it seemed. But when this effort escalated into a full-scale conflict, the media highlighted the disastrous consequences. The term "CNN effect" has circulated with a variety of meanings, all attempting to convey various ways in which global real-time media are exerting a significant impact on policymaking.

Challenging the assumption that the media are performing a significant agenda-setting role in world politics, many skeptics insist that the media now, as in the past, continue to be heavily dependent on official government sources to identify what is news, how it is interpreted, and which issues become the focus of public debate. This skepticism is grounded in much of the scholarship on the relationship between the media and foreign policy, in addition to new empirical research inspired by the concept of the CNN effect. There are multiple variations on the theme that the inherent advantages of political power, combined with the effect of journalistic norms, ensure that news content continues to be shaped more by the preferences of political officials than by any independent news media priorities.[14] Political officials are a major source of news for the media. In dictatorships, the practice results from lack of choice. In democracies it is a product of journalistic norms based on the democratic imperative to keep the public informed about the government's words and actions.[15] Regardless of the form of government, the national media are obliged to report the statements and actions of its officials on matters of state. In addition to having routine access to media coverage, governments also have the organizational capabilities and resources to initiate or to stage events in order to gain attention, influence opinion, or make a policy point. The term "photo-op" has been coined to describe the use of this particular strategy for managing the news.

Framing the News
Because political leaders have easy access to the media, they have ample opportunity to "frame" events in a manner designed to elicit public support. The frame is the meaning or interpretation that is given to events so that they can be understood. Framing events involves, according to Robert Entman, highlighting some facets of events or issues and making connections among them so as to promote a particular interpretation, evaluation, or solution.[16] It uses familiar images and symbols to explain what is happening, what is at issue. President George H. W. Bush's framing of Saddam Hussein as a modern-day Hitler when the Iraqi dictator invaded Kuwait in 1991 is an example of a very effective use of this power. Having defined the problem as one of a cruel aggressor with an appetite for expansion, the solution could only be to oppose him.

Because of their ready access to the media, their resources, and the fact that they represent the authoritative voice of the government, political leaders have a significant advantage in determining how an event or issue is framed in the media. According to W. Lance Bennett and Jarol B. Manheim, two political scientists who analyzed the role of the U.S. news media during the Gulf War, journalists tend to take their cue from political leaders. "As a practical matter, news organizations routinely leave policy framing and issue emphasis to the political elites (generally government officials)"[17]—routinely, perhaps, but not always.

At least four variables affect the ability of political leaders to maintain control over the framing of an event or issue.[18] The first is the "cultural congruence" of the frame. A frame needs to resonate with the basic cultural assumptions of a society and invoke familiar patterns of thinking. For opposing elites to successfully challenge the leaders' frame, they need to be unified in posing a counterframe that resonates within that particular culture. In his book on framing and U.S. foreign policy, Robert Entman argues that "those frames that employ more culturally resonant terms have the greatest potential for influence."[19] The second variable is the degree of consensus among the relevant policy makers, which tends to discourage the media from providing an alternative interpretation to the official one. Significant and sustained debate among the political elite can either provide a counterframe or suggest one that the media can construct. The third variable is the amount of control over the flow of information. The nature of the event is the fourth variable that affects the ability of the leaders to maintain control over the way in which it is framed in the media. They are more likely to control the framing of events they initiate than those they do not anticipate. Some events are more ambiguous, more open to multiple interpretations, than others, and these open possibilities for dissent and counterframing by journalists and elites.[20]

The conflict in the disintegrating multiethnic state of Yugoslavia in the early 1990s is an example of an ambiguous situation. The rise of nationalist leaders to power, especially in the republics of Croatia and Serbia, strengthened the centrifugal tendencies inherent in the fragile multiethnic federation. When Croatia and, subsequently, Bosnia-Herzegovina, seceded and declared themselves to be independent states, the Serbian inhabitants of those states felt threatened and were determined not to remain under "foreign rule." First in Croatia, then Bosnia, the Serbs attempted to expand their control by armed force, with the help of the federal army, and to remove forcibly non-Serbs from the areas under their control ("ethnic cleansing"). Among European and U.S. leaders there was considerable confusion about the appropriate frame for this conflict. Was this a story of "ancient hatreds," "Serbian atrocities," "power hungry leaders," or something else? The Clinton administration, for example, on some occasions described the conflict as Serbian aggression and at other times a three-sided civil war.[21] Because there was uncertainty and disagreement over the definition of the problem, there was also lack of clarity about the policy response. In such situations divisions within and among governments are inevitable, and the task of formulating a policy is more formidable. The resulting policy vacuum leaves the task of framing the conflict to the reporters, and this is what happened in the Balkan conflict.

The Media-Policy Nexus

The advent of live television news coverage stimulated renewed interest in the role of the media in policymaking. Obviously this role is country specific in many respects, and much of the research has focused on the United States,

where the degree of independence from government has remained a matter
of controversy. Journalists tend to see themselves as public watchdogs,
whereas many scholars have challenged the idea of an adversary press, as indicated above.[22] The new information environment adds another layer of
controversy to this traditional debate and extends its geographical relevance.
The basic question is whether this new environment enhances the capacity
of the media to influence the foreign policies of governments. Two issues in
particular arise from this basic question. Does live global television news increase the media's influence over the formulation and implementation of foreign policy? Does the abundance of information sources make it more difficult for governments to maintain control over their interpretation of events
and their ability to mobilize support for their responses?

Much of the research on individual cases to test for the "CNN effect" has
found the influence of the mass media on key policy shifts to be much less
than is popularly assumed, and certainly more complex. Two studies of media influence on the decision to airlift food to the people of Somalia, for example, reached the same conclusion—that the media did not suddenly propel Somalia onto the foreign policy agenda. In fact, the bulk of the news
coverage *followed* the initial key decision and came in response to an array of
pressures from Congress, executive agencies concerned with Africa, and
other official sources. The media became a means for political officials dis-
satisfied with existing policy to pressure higher officials to change it.[23] Other
studies concluded that it was not the images of Somalis celebrating over the
dead corpses of American soldiers, a dead soldier being dragged through the
streets of Mogadishu, and the captured pilot being interrogated that led to
withdrawal of U.S. forces. In fact, the Clinton administration had already
planned a policy shift aimed at withdrawal before these images were repeatedly shown on television.[24] This more complex picture of media influence on
decision making in the case of Somalia is significant because it was so widely
perceived as a prime example of media-driven foreign policy.

Warren Strobel also puts the "CNN effect" to an easy test by focusing on
five "peace operations," the type of foreign policy activity he considers most
likely to be subject to media influence. Peace operations, such as the inter-
ventions in Bosnia and Somalia, are limited military missions where less than
"vital" interests are involved. They provide more opportunities for the media
to influence policy than do conventional wars, he explains, because the goals
and the adversary are likely to be less clear-cut and the policy will be more
difficult to explain. Support is more difficult to mobilize in the absence of
clear national security threat, and casualties harder to justify. There is likely
to be more scrutiny from the international media because a multiplicity of

actors is involved, such as peacekeeping units from other countries and non-governmental organizations. Restrictions on the media are harder to justify than in a conventional war. There is more ambiguity inherent in these situations, and it is more difficult to mobilize and maintain support for this kind of policy.[25] In spite of the special vulnerabilities of peace operations to media influence, Strobel found "not a single instance where the news media, with their dramatic images and words, their pervasive reporting, their persistent questions, were the sole cause of a reversal in policy."[26] This conclusion was based on interviews with more than seventy relevant policy makers, journalists, and administrators in international agencies.

Strobel's findings provide a good summary of various skeptical arguments against enhanced media influence in the information age. His main point is that leadership is critical as a determinant of media influence, that the media are unlikely to exert a significant impact when the political leaders are strongly committed to a clearly articulated policy, which they have effectively explained and justified.[27] Second, he maintains that when the media appear to be driving foreign policy, it is usually diplomatic, political, and strategic considerations that motivate the decisions. The media pressures merely reinforce other motivations. What appears to be the initiative of the media in identifying an issue for the policy makers' agenda is often the product of other actors' efforts to put that issue on the media's agenda. Third, Strobel and other skeptics claim that when the media do have an impact on policy, it is likely to be modest, provoking only a shift in tactics, a "rhetorical adjustment" or, at most, a "minimalist response."[28] For example, to defuse pressures to do something about a humanitarian crisis in which officials do not wish to become involved, they may combine appropriate rhetoric of concern with some assistance rather than making a real policy change that would address the fundamental causes of the crisis. Nik Gowing, a major presenter for BBC World TV, quotes in his study of the CNN effect a low-level official who asserted, "Now ministers and officials have learned to adapt by making instant responses which make the most limited commitments possible."[29]

Even if these skeptical arguments are accepted, the impact of the new media environment on foreign policymaking is substantial. Taking the last argument first, minimalist responses to humanitarian crises may become the norm because real-time television makes it impossible to ignore completely images of violence and human suffering at the same time it highlights the risks and the costs involved in ending these crises. If the pervasiveness of television does encourage that kind of "minimalist" policy response, then that is a very important impact. In some cases the minimalist response may be worse than none at all, or at least, it may have unanticipated negative consequences. President Bush's emergency food airlift to Somalia is an example. It was a low-risk way to appear to be addressing the problem of starvation. It did not solve that problem and, in fact, made it worse by giving the warring factions something else to fight over. Most of the food did not reach those who needed it because there was no control over the distribution. The lack of success led to a deeper commitment but one still far less than would be necessary to solve the underlying problem of the famine, the civil war, and lack of effective political institutions.

Even if the media exert their impact on foreign policy decisions only in conjunction with other influences, or as a catalyst to accelerate a change in direction, this does not negate their importance. It is a rare decision that would have a single cause. Also, the fact that the media are so often the tools of other actors in a struggle for influence, rather than autonomous actors driving international politics, does not make them less important. Indeed, the competition over the news media is part of the larger struggle for influence and power in world politics.[30] The new information and political environments, where the number of media channels and actors seeking to use them are proliferating, intensifies that competition and enhances the importance of the media.

Finally, even if leadership does determine the extent of media influence on policy, the new media and political environments make the task of effective leadership more difficult. The pervasiveness of media scrutiny highlights any uncertainties that governments might have about their policies. It has become more difficult to "fake it." Further, the proliferation of news media sources may affect the ability of political leaders to impose a dominant interpretation on events and to mobilize support for their policy choices. Broadcasting systems traditionally served primarily national audiences, and for reasons discussed above, even in liberal democracies the range of views was limited by the values and assumptions of the given political culture. Satellite news channels and Internet news sites reduce these geographical limitations and increase the diversity of views and information available to those with the appropriate connections—at least potentially. By 2001 there were more than three thousand U.S. newspapers online and more than 1,500 from outside the United States.

One of the few empirical studies of online foreign news found that approximately one-fourth of a sample of Internet users in the United States during the conflict with Iraq obtained news from an online foreign source.[31] Just how and to what extent individuals will use this abundance of resources is not known, but governments must be prepared to deal with information and counter arguments that originate beyond the national boundaries. Entman suggests that the increased accessibility of foreign sources on the Internet may affect public opinion and policy indirectly as well by stimulating independent counterframing by journalists. He indicates that journalists used foreign critiques to balance the debate over the intervention in Iraq and that perspective helped to build pressure for taking the issue to the United Nations.[32]

In sum, the CNN effect, interpreted as the media driving foreign policy, may be a "straw man," too easy to knock down. The media alone are not likely to propel issues onto national and international agendas or change policies. They are not likely to provide an alternative interpretation of events and issues except under certain circumstances, for example, when leadership does not convey a clearly defined policy and culturally resonant rationale, when there is significant debate among policy makers, or when the situation is highly ambiguous. But those circumstances may be more likely to occur in the new media environment.

Open Diplomacy on the Fast Track

The conduct of international relations today takes place on a world stage that is crowded with players. In the broadest sense diplomacy is the communication process through which the official representatives of states try to advance their national interests and reconcile conflicting interests by words rather than force. The narrow meaning of diplomacy refers to what diplomats do. Traditionally, diplomats, especially those stationed abroad, have performed four important functions. They provide a routine channel of communication between governments. They represent and symbolize their home country but serve as a kind of honest broker, conveying the views of the home country and the host country to each other. They are the eyes and ears of the home country, providing information and analysis regarding not only people and events but also the general mood of the host country. They also provide a routine means of negotiation between countries, a way of dealing with problems at a lower level before they become serious enough to make the television cameras or the front pages of the newspapers.

Diplomacy in both the broader and narrower sense has been transformed by the speed of new communication technologies and the more open, pluralistic international political environment. Many analysts began to see potentially negative effects of new communication technologies on traditional diplomacy even before the advent of satellites and cable. One of the most distinguished pioneers in international relations theory, Hans Morgenthau observed more than three decades ago that the increased speed of communications was eroding traditional diplomacy. He wrote, "Diplomacy owes its rise in part to the absence of speedy communications. . . . Diplomacy owes its decline in part to the development of speedy and regular communications."[33] The assumption here is that with faster, more direct communication between government officials readily available, there would be less reliance on the diplomatic channel.

Traditionally, diplomatic reports from the field, or dispatches, were sent in diplomatic "pouches" by courier or by cabled telegrams, then they would have to make their way through the bureaucratic channels before those who actually made the decisions would see them. In the 1990s, when satellite television was broadcasting more and more news of events as they happened, that is, in real time, the Internet and e-mail communication were in the early stages of development. Top officials frequently saw reports and pictures from satellite television before they had access to reports from the embassy abroad, especially in times of crisis. Marlin Fitzwater, press secretary to presidents Ronald Reagan and George H. W. Bush, recollected a critical event just prior to the beginning of the Gulf War in 1991, which illustrates how the timing issue could relegate diplomats to the background. "There was no talk of cables back to the embassies or phone calls back to heads of state. In most of these kinds of international crises now, we virtually cut out the State Department and the desk officers. Their reports are still important, but they often don't get here in time for the basic decisions to be made."[34]

Most foreign affairs bureaucracies, including the U.S. Department of State, did not begin to establish new structures and procedures for communication, taking advantage of new digital technologies, until the end of the decade. During his tenure as secretary of state, Colin Powell took a special interest in updating and standardizing the department's information technology capabilities. As they began to modernize, the speed of diplomatic reporting began to catch up with that of the journalists, and officials could no longer claim that they could not wait for reports from the field. Direct, immediate communication from the field to specific contact persons in Washington is now possible through a variety of means. Classified satellites transmit encrypted cables and messages to and from secure satellite phones. Secure Telephone Units (STUs) work like an ordinary telephone but are set up to encrypt messages at the push of a button and to communicate with anyone anywhere with a similar unit. Digital Video Conferencing (DVC) and Secure Video Conferencing (SVITS) provide a method of connecting immediately the White House and various departments and agencies.

In the new technologies and the way they have been adapted, there is the potential for much improved efficiency, speed, and coordination and less reason to ignore diplomatic reports from the field. Communication channels are faster and more reliable, and recipients can be directly targeted. But messages still must make their way through the layers of bureaucracy and compete for the attention of busy officials overwhelmed with information, which is even more voluminous from the multitude of sources available today. Routine reports from embassies abroad provide important context for foreign policymaking. They can provide early warning signals regarding crises that might be prevented if appropriate, timely action is taken. But there is more compelling urgency in the television images of the latest crisis.

New technologies have affected the role of diplomats as not only sources of information but also the primary channel of communication between home and host governments. Satellite television is sometimes used as a direct channel of communication between world leaders, thus undermining the ambassador's role in conveying an important message. The event that Fitzwater was recollecting above was a speech by Saddam Hussein, translated excerpts of which were broadcast live on the U.S. networks. He appeared to be making a peace overture, even as the U.S. preparations for the Gulf War were reaching their final stages in January 1991. President George H. W. Bush responded by dispatching his spokesman to issue a statement rejecting Hussein's proposal before the television cameras. Within two hours statements from Baghdad appeared on television to indicate that the message had been received.[35] Throughout the ensuing war both Bush and Hussein monitored the events on CNN as they occurred. Both knew that both were watching. Other leaders also stayed tuned and sometimes made their own appearances on the world television stage. With the increase in the number of twenty-four-hour international news channels, and the dispersion of attention among them, CNN might have lost some prominence as a channel of direct communication. But satellite television offers unprecedented opportunities for leaders to send signals and messages to not only each other but also to a wider audience both at home and abroad.

The Public Diplomacy Imperative
In the new information and political environments, world leaders are finding they must communicate—effectively—with this wider audience. A Department of Defense task force conveyed this imperative in its 2004 report on public diplomacy: "In an age of global media, the Internet revolution, and powerful nonstate actors—an age in which almost everything governments do and say is understood through the mediating filters of news frames, cul-

ture, memory, and language—no major strategy, policy, or diplomatic initiative can succeed without public support."[36] Satellite television enhances the capacity of world leaders to communicate directly with the citizens of other countries, to make convincing arguments for their policies, and to project a positive image to a wide audience. But there are competing images and messages.

Satellite television and other new information and communication technologies also empower those who wish to challenge those policies or lobby for others. The proliferation of diverse sources of information, particularly on the Internet, provides opportunities for ordinary citizens and nongovernmental organizations to conduct independent analyses of political issues, which may challenge official interpretations.[37] Further, e-mail and, especially, chat rooms and blogs on the Internet allow for critical discourse that is not available in the mainstream media, thus widening the parameters of debate, especially in times of crisis when the "rally around the flag" phenomenon is at its peak. Most significantly, groups do not merely debate over the Internet, but they also organize and mobilize to advocate policies.

The same technologies that give more people access to more information also provide new ways for them to participate in international politics. The Internet, through e-mail, Listservs, and websites, serves as a source of information, which can be quickly disseminated around the world, and a means of communication to join together individuals and groups with a common political objective. It can contribute to a sense of common purpose and help to coordinate political advocacy and action. It diffuses ideas and tactics. Websites publicize information, arguments, positions, and plans. Cell phones and faxes also facilitate the coordination and implementation of plans for direct action, such as demonstrations. Newsworthy direct action gains more publicity when it makes the newscasts on television. The number and diversity of international television channels increase the opportunities for coverage.

These new forms of communication have spurred the growth of transnational groups, organizations, and networks with the capacity to use basic tools of political influence in the international arena, namely, persuasion, agenda setting, and framing.[38] One widely cited example of this phenomenon is the International Committee to Ban Land Mines, an umbrella organization of over one thousand nongovernmental organizations (NGOs) from over sixty countries. Under the leadership of a single individual, Jody Williams, the committee organized and coordinated a worldwide campaign to mobilize public opinion to pressure reluctant governments to draft and ratify a treaty to prohibit the use, stockpiling, production, and transfer of antipersonnel land mines. The committee also managed to persuade some governments directly, notably the Canadian government, and to work with them to build support. The Canadian government benefited from this relationship with an NGO initiative because it projected a desirable image of a government that promotes a human security agenda, and this kind of cooperative effort has been labeled the "Ottawa process," to denote the location of the final drafting.

The treaty has been signed by 158 states, although the U.S. government was one of the few that remained unpersuaded, in spite of an extensive lobbying campaign. The committee clearly put the issue on the international political agenda. They were successful in their efforts at persuasion in part because the way they framed the issue, that is, the way they defined the problem, was so compelling. The problem of hundreds of innocents being killed and maimed, especially children, turned out to be more convincing than the arguments of military necessity of the treaty's opponents. A Canadian government official has observed that, without the efforts of this committee, the treaty would not have been signed, and without e-mail the committee could not have mobilized so rapidly or coordinated their efforts so effectively.[39]

The campaign to ban land mines illustrates the trend toward growing participation of nonstate actors in international politics. Another example would be the campaign to influence public opinion and to pressure target governments to sign the statute establishing an international criminal court. Yet another example was the campaign to lobby *against* an international agreement among the members of the Organisation for Economic Co-operation and Development, that is, the governments of the most developed countries. The Multilateral Agreement on Investment (MAI), which would have established rules favorable to investment, was on its way to conclusion before the anti-MAI coalition helped to take it off the organization's agenda. A number of studies have established the vital role of the Internet and the World Wide Web in mobilizing opposition to this agreement, which, in turn, contributed significantly to its demise in 1998.[40] The strength of the anti-MAI lobby was part of an evolving antiglobalization movement, which has been mobilizing large demonstrations and protests at international economic meetings since the World Trade Organization meeting in Seattle in 1999.

The use of new technologies by NGOs and social movements is discussed more extensively in chapter 6. Here the important point is how this use creates a new international political environment that affects the conduct of diplomacy and the relations between states. The enabling power of new information and communication technologies is allowing individuals and organizations to be significant actors in world politics. The fact that more people can and do use the tools of political influence to affect international outcomes increases the need of governments to gain popular support for their policies—or at least to defuse opposition.

Winning Hearts and Minds in the War on Terror

Public diplomacy has become more important as not only an instrument of foreign policy but also a vital part of national security strategy. In the national security strategy document that was submitted to Congress one year after the attacks on the World Trade Center and the Pentagon, President Bush pledged to "wage a war of ideas to win the battle against international terrorism." For this purpose, the document said, "We need a different and more comprehensive approach to public information efforts that can help people around the world learn about and understand America."[41]

Public diplomacy had been an important instrument of U.S. foreign policy during the Cold War, which was, in part, a war of ideas to win the battle against international communism. As early as 1953 a special agency was established, the U.S. Information Agency (USIA), with the mission to "tell America's story to the world." The emphasis was on people-to-people contacts rather than government to government. It was a soft sell approach to creating a positive image of the United States and its policies. Two hundred American cultural centers became a focus of intellectual life in 125 countries, with well-stocked libraries, information services, visiting speakers, and cultural programs. The Voice of America beamed news and other programming in many languages. When the Soviet Union collapsed, many assumed that because the United States was the only remaining superpower, the need to tell America's story was less important, that it mattered less what ordinary people in foreign countries thought.[42] The sentiment was widespread that we did not need to spend a lot of resources projecting a good U.S. image after the demise of the Soviet propaganda machine. Congress reduced the budget of USIA, which led to the closure of many American cultural centers, including centers in Pakistan, Turkey, and Jordan, and downsized others. In 1999 Congress downgraded the USIA as an independent agency and folded it into the State Department.

Suddenly, on September 11, 2001, came the shock that there were people in the world who had a very negative image of the United States and that their attitudes constituted a serious threat to national security. The task of winning the hearts and minds of ordinary people abroad, especially in the Muslim world, where Osama bin Laden already had a head start, suddenly took on a sense of urgency. An aggressive, multipronged approach was launched to mobilize support for the "war on terrorism," to market American values, and to counter negative publicity.

The most immediate challenge was the war in Afghanistan. The White House was slow to recognize the significance of the change in the international media environment with the emergence of the Arab-language satellite television channel, Al Jazeera, and the spread of its popularity. Eventually, interviews were scheduled on the channel with various U.S. spokespersons. Meanwhile Al Jazeera was providing pictures of destruction from U.S. bombs, buildings, villages, and casualties, and playing tapes of Osama bin Laden. These reports and images constituted the bulk of available information from Afghanistan, as the Pentagon limited media access to its operations and restricted information about them to Pentagon briefings.[43] The U.S. television networks were persuaded not to broadcast Osama bin Laden's tapes, on the grounds that coded messages might be embedded in them. But the relevant Islamic audience got the messages from Al Jazeera, and they subsequently appeared on scores of Arab Internet sites. Reflecting on Osama bin Laden's success in reaching Muslim audiences, Richard Holbrooke rhetorically asked the 9/11 Commission during his interview with them: "How can a man in a cave outcommunicate the world's leading communication society?"[44]

A method of communication from earlier wars, the dropping of leaflets from planes, was used to explain to the Afghan people why they were being bombed. The messages explained that the air attacks were necessary to destroy the terrorist network that had attacked the United States, insisted that the bombs were not directed at the Afghan people, and warned them to stay out of potential targets. The Pentagon briefings emphasized the care that was being taken to avoid civilian casualties. But the pictures of bombs falling on a poor country that had been a victim of two decades of war were hard to counter.

To counter enemy "propaganda" about civilian casualties and the progress of the war, with "corrections" and positive messages, a network of communication offices was set up in Islamabad, London, and Washington. Each morning American and British communication directors in the three "coalition information centers" conferred to develop and coordinate the administration's daily messages. The nerve center was the White House "war room," where representatives of various agencies worked together to devise appropriate strategies and coordinate responses. Karen Hughes, senior adviser to the president, was the director of the U.S. news management team, which also included other veterans from various presidential campaigns.[45] The news center in Islamabad, which is ten hours ahead of Washington, made possible timely rebuttals to Taliban accusations. A campaign to publicize the harsh treatment of women in Afghanistan under the Taliban brought in the two first ladies, Laura Bush and Cherie Blair.

The creation of the Office of Strategic Influence in the Pentagon represented an even more aggressive approach to promoting U.S. policies and influencing public opinion abroad, using not only the foreign media and the Internet but also covert operations. According to a special article in the *New*

York Times regarding the office, it was a response to concerns that the United States was losing support for its war on terrorism, especially in Islamic countries, after the bombing attacks in Afghanistan.[46] Leaked classified proposals indicated plans to use such techniques as planting news items in foreign media organizations and sending journalists and civic leaders e-mail messages that promoted U.S. views or attacked unfriendly governments. The Pentagon's identity as the source would be concealed. Providing false information to foreign news media was also contemplated. The mission of the office and the various proposals regarding its operations were highly controversial even within the Defense Department, where many feared the impact on the credibility of information provided by the military. As soon as information about the office became public, it was closed down by Secretary of Defense Donald Rumsfeld, less than four months after it was created.

Yet another approach to winning hearts and minds drew on the techniques of public relations to sell the administration's foreign policy and its war on terrorism. This campaign was carried out by the undersecretary of state for public diplomacy, Charlotte Beers, a former advertising executive. The focus of her efforts was the need to change perceptions regarding the United States in Muslim-majority countries because, as she testified to the Congressional Appropriations Committee, "a poor perception of the United States leads to unrest, and unrest has proven to be a threat to our national and international security."[47] In order to counter what she saw as a widespread belief that the United States was anti-Islam, she launched a number of initiatives under the rubric of "shared values." A set of four videos was produced with that title (by an advertising company), portraying happy and prosperous Muslims in the United States, an open and tolerant society. The series was eventually suspended because so few countries (four) agreed to broadcast the videos. It was also shown on the Middle East Broadcasting Channel, headquartered in London. At one live showing where opportunity for feedback was provided, several in the audience said they would prefer to have the cultural center that was closed in the 1990s, where they could read in a pleasant, friendly atmosphere.

Several of the Beers initiatives were focused on young people. A new radio network for Arabic-speaking youth in the Middle East was created. It was called Radio Sawa, which means "together" in Arabic. It continues today to broadcast Arabic-language popular music, interspersed on the hour with newscasts with an American perspective. One example of Beers's efforts to foster dialogue was a live televised satellite hookup between a selection of young people in the United States and in Indonesia. "Common values, common challenges," printed large in Indonesian as a studio backdrop in Jakarta, was the theme of the program that was designed as a dialogue about everyday life in the two countries.[48] Yet another initiative to appeal to the younger set was the publication of a new "consumer lifestyle" Arabic-language magazine, called *Hi*, and sold at newsstands in the Middle East.[49]

All of this effort to market a positive image of the United States took place as the United States moved closer to war with Iraq. Just before the invasion of Iraq in March 2003, Charlotte Beers resigned, and the office of Undersecretary for Public Affairs remained vacant throughout the war until December. The headquarters for winning hearts and minds had already shifted to the White House, where President Bush had created the Office of Global Communications (OGC) to advise him on the most effective ways "to communicate American policies and values with greater clarity" and to coordinate the work of the various agencies in order to "convey a few simple, powerful messages."[50]

The use of state-of-the-art media and technology for this purpose was encouraged in the executive order creating the office. One means of coordination was a daily "Global Messenger," a sheet of "facts and talking points" sent each day to American ambassadors, foreign diplomats, congressmen, and reporters. Besides providing consistent positive messages about U.S. policies, another important role was "countering propaganda and disinformation," which the OGC performed with alacrity. Two months before the invasion, it produced "Apparatus of Lies," a collection of Saddam Hussein's propaganda. The White House website describes some of the efforts of this office, which includes "telling the stories of torture and brutality in Saddam's Iraq and updates on the liberation of the Iraqi people."[51]

With the invasion of Iraq, promoting a positive image of the United States among Muslim countries became a Herculean task. The OGC devised the theme "Iraq: From Fear to Freedom," which cast the war as a humanitarian venture to liberate the Iraqi people. The message was promoted to Middle Eastern television outlets and newspapers, accompanied by scenes of marines passing out food and military doctors providing medical help to Iraqi people.[52] But these images had to compete with more compelling ones of civilian casualties, and there was a much wider array of media coverage than during the war in Afghanistan. Commenting on the ineffectiveness of what he called the "feed and kill policy," a Washington-based correspondent for the Middle East News Agency declared, "Throwing bombs in Baghdad and throwing food at the people—is not winning hearts and minds."[53] The news frame of a Muslim country invaded and occupied by a foreign force tended to overwhelm the liberation from tyranny frame.

Public opinion surveys confirmed the failure of U.S. public diplomacy leading up to, during, and following the fall of the Hussein regime. The Pew

Research Center for People and the Press conducted six cross-national surveys from the summer of 2002 to May 2005, which included questions about opinions of the United States, the war in Iraq, and the war against terrorism. These surveys showed opinion in Europe plummeting just before the war in Iraq began, then improving slightly in May 2003, after Bush declared "Mission Accomplished," but favorable ratings remained well below the levels of 1999 and 2000. Among most of the predominantly Muslim countries sampled at the end of major hostilities, the vast majority indicated unfavorable opinions of the United States. The Pew surveys conducted in May 2003 indicated that favorable views of the United States were held by only 27 percent of the people in Morocco and Lebanon, 15 percent in Indonesia and Turkey, 13 percent in Pakistan, and 1 percent in Jordan.[54] In a summary of general world trends in 2005, the Pew Research Center concluded that "anti-Americanism is broader now than at any time in modern history. It is most acute in the Muslim world, but it spans the globe—from Europe to Asia, from South America to Africa."[55] A State Department survey of editorials and op-eds in seventy-two countries in April 2004 found media commentary to be consistent with these views, as 82 percent were negative.[56]

Survey results such as these, in addition to the observations transmitted from embassies abroad, prompted more than fifteen studies of the inadequacy of U.S. public diplomacy between September 11, 2001, and the end of 2004. One of the most widely publicized was the bipartisan report "Changing Minds, Winning Peace: A New Strategic Direction for U.S. Public Diplomacy in the Arab and Muslim World." The study, which was prepared at the behest of a congressional subcommittee, was chaired by Edward Djerejian, a former ambassador in the Middle East. It reached similar conclusions regarding public diplomacy to those of the Pentagon advisory panel (the Defense Science Board), which looked at the larger U.S. "strategic communication."[57]

Both reports deplored the extent to which public diplomacy had been downsized and underfunded after the end of the Cold War (reducing personnel by 40 percent) and linked this neglect directly to the security threat facing the United States. The Djerejian report warned, "A process of unilateral disarmament in the weapons of advocacy over the last decade has contributed to widespread hostility toward Americans and left us vulnerable to lethal threats to our interests and our safety."[58] Both concluded that the level of commitment and amount of creativity that went into Cold War public diplomacy was essential, but so was an understanding of how the information environment and the strategic situation had changed. "Disseminating scarce information to closed societies was central during the Cold War," the Defense Board report explained. "Today there are few closed societies. Satellite

TV, the Internet, computers, and cell phones mean political struggles are about gaining attention and maintaining credibility."[59] Adversaries of the United States are benefiting from an open environment where information can flow freely through multiple channels. The critical problem for U.S. diplomacy was not crafting the right message for the right target, the report argued, but the fact that the United States had lost its credibility in the Muslim world.

Ironically, at the same time this advisory board to the Defense Department was emphasizing the importance of credibility as the key to U.S. influence and security, the idea of a secret propaganda program resurfaced in the Pentagon. According to a *New York Times* report, the purpose of the program was to "shape perceptions" abroad with such techniques as planting positive messages to counter anti-American ones and disinformation to confuse and discredit adversaries.[60] Although Secretary of Defense Rumsfeld had closed down the Office of Strategic Information when similar proposals were publicized almost three years earlier, the issue continued to be debated at various levels in the Pentagon. One year later, at the end of 2005, there was yet another disclosure—that pro-U.S. news articles written by American troops had been placed in Iraqi news media without identification of the U.S. source.[61] While many in the military worried about the credibility issue, and no representative would publicly make the arguments justifying the planting of stories, the case was clearly made by retired army lieutenant colonel Ralph Peters on Public Television's *NewsHour with Jim Lehrer*. "Our adversaries are planting and otherwise circulating negative information about our policies, which needs to be countered," he emphasized, because "in postmodern conflict, if you lose the media battle, you lose."[62]

Historically, covert, deceptive information techniques, or information operations, have been used on the battlefield in wartime to ensure the success of military operations. Public affairs communications from the Defense and State Departments are intended primarily to inform the U.S. media and public with factual information about the government's activities. The purpose of public diplomacy is engaging, informing, and influencing international audiences.[63] The conduct of information operations tends to undermine the credibility that determines the success of both public affairs and public diplomacy, especially in today's transparent environment where covert operations are likely to be revealed and information sources are abundant. The confounding of the war on terrorism and the struggle for the hearts and minds of the Arab and Muslim world encouraged an array of simplistic, hard sell tactics that focused on delivering the message without taking the first important step of listening to the targeted audiences and trying to understand their values and worldviews.[64]

This discussion of U.S. efforts to win hearts and minds in the Arab and Muslim world suggests some of the challenges that confront any government's public diplomacy in the new information and political environments. First, it is an essential component of foreign policy. Evan Potter, the special adviser for communications for the Canadian Department of Foreign Affairs and International Trade, makes this point unequivocally in his assertion that "few foreign policy objectives can now be achieved without an enabling environment sustained by innovative public diplomacy initiatives designed to understand, inform, and influence publics at home and abroad."[65]

Second, the new information environment provides new ways to seek public support among more audiences, but it also makes this task more difficult. There is more competition with growth in the numbers of nonstate actors, in their access to new information and communication technologies, and in their political assertiveness. The main challenge of public diplomacy today is so many competing messages from so many sources saying so many things. Even terrorist organizations are practicing public diplomacy. Bernard Haykel, a scholar of the jihadist movement, explained in a television interview that "these terrorists have a public, they have an audience, and they're constantly trying to engage with this audience."[66]

Third, in the information age, the ability to influence perceptions and attitudes rests largely on the ability to gain attention and to establish credibility. Because there is so much information available from so many sources, attention becomes the scarce resource and politics becomes a contest of competitive credibility, observes the Harvard political scientist Joseph S. Nye.[67] That credibility becomes more difficult to establish as a more transparent information environment subjects the statements and actions of governments to greater scrutiny.

Conflict and War in the Information Age

Fighting wars has always involved a considerable amount of uncertainty, even when there is a high degree of asymmetry between the belligerents. New information, communication, and military technologies vastly improve the organization of combat and the accuracy of weapons, but they cannot eliminate miscalculation and unpredictability. Indeed, calculations regarding the effective use of force are more complex in the new information and political environments. Weapons are more accurate, but the threats, the targets, are likely to be more diffuse, dispersed, and ambiguous. Multiple sophisticated surveillance systems can provide images and data from vast distances, and computers can sift, integrate, and convert this information into the knowledge to conduct precision strikes against the enemy. But the human element, and hence the possibility of error, cannot be eliminated.

The Revolution in Military Affairs

Many military analysts claim that the information revolution is altering the nature of combat, producing a "revolution in military affairs."[68] The new information and communication technologies are the central element of this revolution, enhancing organizational and operational capabilities in three ways. First, they have the potential to "lift the fog of battle" by providing the entire command structure from field to headquarters "an omniscient view of the battlefield in real time, by day and night, and in all weather conditions."[69] A network of sensors, including satellites, unmanned aerial vehicles, reconnaissance aircraft, and special operation forces on the ground, can generate three-dimensional images, which indicate the precise location of enemy units, as well as one's own, for nearly instantaneous strikes. Other valuable information, such as terrain, weather, and the movement of supplies can also be conveyed.

Second, computerized networks provide unprecedented speed and effectiveness in the command, control, and intelligence functions of combat. Information, briefings, and commands can be communicated almost instantly to and from distant locations. Forces in remote locations are part of this network with satellite and cellular communications. Third, new information and communication technologies are making weapons "smart," with internal guidance systems that either sense a target from a laser beam or pick up a signal from a global positioning satellite. This precision in targeting capabilities lessens collateral damage, that is, death and destruction that does not contribute to the military objectives. Targets can be identified and destroyed precisely from remote locations. An array of sensors, vehicles, and weapons can be operated by remote control. Unmanned planes, or drones, can provide more sustained surveillance than manned aircraft, and they have the potential to attack when a defined target is recognized. These technologies are in varying stages of development and deployment.

The war in Afghanistan provided a testing ground for some of these technologies and demonstrated how much progress has been made since the Gulf War, which introduced the public to this information approach to war. Ninety percent of the bombs dropped on Afghanistan were precision guided, whereas only about 10 percent in the Gulf War were. During the Gulf War the navy could not receive its orders electronically, so printouts were delivered by hand to aircraft carriers. In contrast, in Afghanistan pilotless surveillance aircraft piped streaming video of Taliban and Al-Qaeda movements to command posts in Saudi Arabia and the Pentagon. Commanders at these command posts could then transmit target coordinates to navy and air force pilots and call almost immediate, precise air strikes on those targets. Surveillance aircraft, manned and unmanned, were part of a constellation of information systems that also included imaging satellites and small groups of Special Forces on the ground in Afghanistan. Using lasers to illuminate targets for smart bombs, these troops helped to clear the way for the anti-Taliban armies, the Northern Alliance, to advance against the Taliban. It was the integration of the information-gathering systems, the dispersed forces on the ground, and the aerial bombing that destroyed the Taliban as an effective army.[70]

These spectacular technologies seem straight out of science fiction, but they are reorienting the way the United States prepares for and fights its wars. Critics worry about some of the possible consequences. Anyone who has ever used a computer is frequently reminded of "Murphy's law," which promises that "anything that can go wrong will go wrong." Computers are not infallible. They crash or succumb to other mysterious malfunctions. In any case, human beings tell them what to do and interpret the data they provide, and "to err is human." During the NATO bombing of Belgrade in the war over Kosovo, the Chinese embassy was accidentally bombed. The satellite-steered, two-thousand-pound bombs hit their target precisely, but the site turned out not to be a Yugoslav arms agency, as indicated on the faulty CIA map. The Chinese media claimed the strike must have been deliberate, given the sophistication and accuracy of U.S. weapons and targeting systems.[71] Heavy reliance on these technologies also creates vulnerabilities that can be exploited by an adversary with "cyberattacks," the corruption or destruction of information sources or computer networks with computer viruses, and hacker attacks.[72]

The "Counter-Revolution in Military Affairs"
Even more significant for the future of warfare is the combination of low-technology weaponry and traditional guerilla tactics, with new information and communication technologies, to counter the advantage of superior weapons technology.

Two scholars in media studies, John Downey and Graham Murdock, have described this phenomenon as the "counter-revolution in military affairs" or the "globalization of guerilla warfare."[73] Scholarly interest in irregular warfare, notably terrorist tactics and nonstate insurgencies, intensified after the attacks on the World Trade Center and the growth of the insurgency in Iraq that followed the military victory. Interest came from two directions in particular—

from military analysts concerned with the need to adapt U.S. defense policy and from communications scholars who focused on the potential of new information and communication technologies to transform unconventional as well as conventional warfare.

As early as 1989, a small group of military analysts, mostly officers, began to discuss in military journals a phenomenon they called "fourth-generation warfare" (4GW), irregular warfare dominated by terrorists and nonstate insurgencies, as the major threat to international security.[74] The 4GW proponents are primarily military officers who are skeptical of what they see as undue emphasis in the U.S. military budget, training, strategy, and doctrine on conventional warfare fought with high-technology weapons against large, identifiable enemies with professional standing armies. They claim that the overwhelming military superiority that provides conventional deterrence also pushes America's enemies into greater reliance on irregular warfare, ways of fighting that do not test U.S. strengths.[75] Certain characteristics of 4GW are typically emphasized. It is asymmetric warfare, that is, a vast discrepancy exists between the resources, the capabilities, and the philosophies of the combatants. Asymmetric warfare tends to increase the level of uncertainty and the potential for tactical, operational, and strategic surprise.[76] Avoidance of confrontation, dispersion of forces, and surprise attack are the traditional hallmarks of guerilla warfare, which are designed to mitigate the effectiveness of a superior military. Guerilla forces typically do not wear uniforms and are difficult to distinguish from civilians. They present few targets that are vulnerable to conventional attack.

What is new, and what makes irregular forces more formidable than in the past, is their empowerment by new information and communication technologies, which enhance their organizational and operational capabilities and strengthen their ideological cohesion. Numerous dispersed small groups, using such technologies as cell phones and the Internet, can act conjointly across great distances to form networks.[77] These networks facilitate the planning and coordination of actions, making it easier for small, nonstate entities to tie down and possibly wear out much better equipped armies. The Internet and the multiplicity of media channels also provide unprecedented opportunities for terrorists and insurgents to mobilize support and influence perceptions of the conflict.

The Internet's unique configuration of attributes has made it a valuable tool and resource for these irregular warriors. It is easy to access, unregulated, anonymous, a source of vast information, and a means of fast communication. It can address multiple audiences. An extensive survey by Gabriel Weimann, professor of communication at Haifa University, Israel, found hundreds of websites serving multiple purposes for terrorist groups.[78] These sites are first and foremost the sinews of networks, each linking an array of loosely connected groups spread over different countries. Besides keeping these groups in contact with each other, the Internet is a means of obtaining and sharing information about everything from potential targets to instructions for making a bomb and carrying out attacks. Information about transportation facilities, power plants, ports, and other vital centers is readily available, as is access to satellite maps. According to the author of two books on terrorism, Daniel Benjamin, "Master bomb-makers are instructing their protégés, probably from a distance of thousands of miles, on the finer points of bomb-building."[79] In a search for the key words "terrorist" and "handbook" on the Google search engine, Weimann found nearly four thousand matches that included references to guidebooks and manuals. As grandly stated by a British journalist, "Whether Bin Laden, al-Qaida's Egyptian theorist Ayman al-Zawahiri and their colleagues are on a mountain in the Hindu Kush or living with their beards shaved off in a suburb of Karachi no longer matters to the organization. They can inspire and guide a worldwide movement without physically meeting their followers—without even knowing who they are."[80]

Besides training, instruction, and communication, the Internet is used to plan and coordinate specific attacks. The most dramatic example was the use of Internet communications by Al-Qaeda to coordinate precision attacks on the World Trade Center and the Pentagon with very small, dispersed units—a total of nineteen attackers. These communications were coded to hide their identities and their messages. Subsequently, with the arrest of Abu Zubaydah, the alleged mastermind of the attacks, federal officials found thousands of encrypted messages on his computer.[81] There are a variety of ways in which identities are hidden, including various types of encryption software and changes in network accounts. Public computers, such as those in cyber-cafes and libraries, can be used to hide further the source of messages.[82]

The Internet is also used for fundraising, recruiting, mobilizing supporters, and getting appropriate messages out to different audiences. Bulletin boards, chat rooms, and e-mail lists identify potential recruits, create solidarity, and publicize the cause. Websites and videos can be widely distributed and are designed to broaden and deepen support. Two rhetorical approaches are commonly used to justify the use of violence.[83] One line of argument is that there is no other choice when the oppressor is a militarily powerful state. This approach enhances the political power of the weak because it turns the struggle into a David and Goliath contest—and who roots for Goliath?[84] Violence is sometimes justified with Islamic legal and theological arguments. The second approach is to delegitimize the adversary by emphasizing its brutality, insensitivity to civilian casualties, and the malevolent motivations for its actions.

The use of the Internet by Iraqi insurgents has been closely analyzed by the International Crisis Group, a nongovernmental research organization that produces field-based reports. Its report "In Their Own Words: Reading the Iraqi Insurgency" emphasizes the importance to the insurgency of its legitimacy, which relies on opposition to the occupation and anger at some of its specific practices.[85] It found an evolution in the discourse of Iraqi insurgent groups, demonstrating an ability to learn from mistakes and increasing concern for their public image. Beheadings and other grisly images were more rarely distributed on the Internet after a significant negative response to this practice. The research of Bernard Haykel, a New York University scholar of the jihadist movement, confirms this sensitivity to public opinion. The leaders of Al-Qaeda, he claims, are constantly "trying to gauge what the tolerance level of their public is for the kind of violent activities that they're engaged in."[86]

The Internet is only one of the many media channels used by insurgents and terrorists to advance their cause. Most Iraqi insurgent groups have their own multimedia enterprise with journalists equipped to provide photographs and videos of events they wish to publicize. These can be loaded onto the Internet and distributed even more widely on videos. Osama bin Laden and other Al-Qaeda spokesmen tape messages from time to time that are sent to one or more television stations for broadcasting. These are picked up by other stations around the world and also circulated on the Internet. The rapid circulation of information and images through the transnational media can also aid efforts to delegitimize adversaries, as was illustrated by the pictures of the abuses at the Abu Ghraib prison.

It is often assumed that publicity in the mass media encourages terrorism because it enables the perpetrators to intimidate as large an audience as possible. Dramatic images on television certainly focus attention on any group that claims responsibility. But the direction of influence will depend to a great extent upon the way the action is framed in the media and the predispositions of the audience, as is illustrated in the cliché "one man's terrorist is another man's freedom fighter."

U.S. officials have frequently acknowledged the fact that managing the way their war on terrorism is represented and perceived among multiple publics is a vital part of the conflict itself. In a speech to the Council on Foreign Relations in February 2006, Secretary of Defense Donald Rumsfeld quoted approvingly the following statement of Osama bin Laden's chief lieutenant, Ayman al-Zawahiri: "More than half of this battle is taking place in the battlefield of the media. We are in a media battle in a race for the hearts and minds of Muslims." Rumsfeld then commented, "They know . . . that a single news story, handled skillfully, can be as damaging to our cause and helpful to theirs, as any other method of military attack."[87]

The War in Iraq: The Triumph and Failure of Spin
The Bush administration was spectacularly successful in persuading the American people of the need for an invasion to change the regime in Iraq in March 2003. It met with limited success elsewhere and failed in the Arab world. The struggle to win the hearts and minds in the Arab world was discussed above as part of the larger public diplomacy effort that followed the attacks on the World Trade Center and the Pentagon.

Here some of the reasons are explored for the success on the domestic front in shaping public perceptions and in maintaining the dominant interpretation of the event in the media during the course of major combat operations. The "framing of the war" was the key to this success.[88]

Framing the War

The effective communication strategy began with the framing of the response to the September 11 attacks as the "war on terror," and the representation of the overthrow of the regimes in Afghanistan and Iraq as part of that war. Implicit in the war on terrorism frame was an open-ended and global conflict that could be directed against any adversary.[89] This frame also met three conditions that enable political leaders to maintain control over the framing of an event. First, the conflict was represented as a threat to basic cultural values. In his remarks to the nation following the attacks, President Bush explained, "America was targeted for attack because we're the brightest beacon for freedom and opportunity in the world. And no one will keep that light from shining."[90] Entman, emphasizing the importance of a frame's "cultural congruence," postulates that when leaders manage to frame an event so that it strongly resonates with the basic cultural assumptions of a society, especially when it is framed in terms of a threat to dominant values, that frame is likely to dominate media coverage.[91] The second condition was the absence of a sustained and significant debate among the political elite that could have provided the basis for more "dissenting" coverage in the media. The third condition lay in the nature of the situation itself. There were potential ambiguities in the attacks of September 11, but the situation clearly called for a response. It was the communication strategies used by the administration, together with journalistic norms and career motivations, that managed to transpose the threat to the regime in Iraq.

According to a *Washington Post* survey in August 2003, 69 percent of Americans believed that Saddam Hussein was involved in the September 11 attacks.[92] Although President Bush himself never explicitly made this connection, mentioning "Saddam Hussein" and "September 11" frequently enough in the same paragraph or sentence helped to make the link. The link was made indirectly on a number of occasions, as illustrated in his speech to the nation just before the invasion of Iraq. "There is no doubt that the Iraq regime continues to possess and conceal some of the most lethal weapons ever devised," the president said. The regime had already used weapons of mass destruction against its neighbors and its own people, he continued, and it has a record of aiding terrorists. The danger is clear, he warned, "using chemical, biological or, one day, nuclear weapons, obtained with the help of Iraq, the terrorists could fulfill their stated ambitions and kill thousands or hundreds of thousands of innocent people in our country, or any other."[93] Having framed the issue of Saddam Hussein as a key element of the terrorist threat, there could be no other course than to eliminate him.

More than a year after the war was launched and after the absence of weapons of mass destruction in Iraq had been clearly established, two major newspapers, the *New York Times* and the *Washington Post*, published articles that attempted to explain to their readers why they had not been more aggressive in questioning the information they had provided regarding the issue of Iraq's weapons and possible connection with terrorists.

Their explanations provide considerable insight into the relationship between the media and the government, especially at the onset of war. They both acknowledged that the administration's assertions generally went on the front pages, even when they were repetitive, whereas any skeptical views or qualifications usually ended up in the back pages. The *Washington Post* pointed out that from August 2002 through March 19, 2003, when the war was launched, the newspaper ran 140 front-page stories that focused heavily on administration rhetoric against Iraq with headlines such as "War Cabinet Argues for Iraq Attack" and "Bush Cites Iraqi Threat." But, the editor who covered the prewar diplomacy for the newspaper admitted, "The caution and the questioning was buried underneath the drumbeat. . . . The hugeness of the war preparation story tended to drown out a lot of that stuff." She explained further, "We are inevitably the mouthpiece for whatever administration is in power. If the President stands up and says something, we report what the President said." The executive editor of the newspaper made a similar confession: "We were so focused on trying to figure out what the administration was doing that we were not giving the same play to people who said it wouldn't be a good idea to go to war and were questioning the administration's rationale. Not enough of those stories were put on the front page. That was a mistake on my part."[94]

So one part of the explanation is the journalistic norm to publish official statements, and there were plenty of them to fill the front pages. Another journalistic norm, the need for a newsworthy story, provides another part of the explanation. The *New York Times'* article admitted that it had relied too heavily on the claims of Iraqi defectors and exiles who were bent on regime change. Articles based on their dire claims about Iraq tended to get prominent display, whereas follow-up articles that called these claims into question were buried—or there was no follow up at all.[95] For example, one front-page article was published under the headline "Illicit Arms Kept till Eve of War, an Iraqi Scientist Is Said to Assert." The newspaper acknowledged that it never checked on the veracity of that story or followed it up.

Implicit in these two articles is the reality that war rhetoric is exciting news material, whereas skepticism and qualification are not. In any case, skepticism does not provide an alternative frame and certainly not a culturally resonant one. The official interpretation of Iraq as an imminent and dangerous threat to American values and security was compelling. Challenging this interpretation posed potential risks for the careers of journalists and politicians alike. There was not a significant, sustained, unified opposition among the political elite, either in the executive branch or in Congress, to suggest an alternative frame to focus the attention of the media. The *Washington Post's* self-analysis article concluded with the executive editor's defensive assertion that critics of the newspaper's coverage "have the mistaken impression that somehow if the media's coverage had been different, there wouldn't have been a war." That would seem to be an open question.

During the combat phase of the war itself, both the rhetorical and the institutional aspects of an effective communications strategy were managed with great skill. Words and phrases were carefully selected to support the administration's policy and used so repeatedly that they became the accepted language of the war.[96] For example, the progress of the combat operations was generally attributed to "coalition forces," even though there were only two major armies actually in combat, the United States and the British. "Liberation" was the preferred term over "occupation." The war rhetoric was effective but fairly traditional. The institutional side was more creative, making good use of new information and media technologies. The Office of Global Communication, which was set up two months before the war, centralized the communication strategy in the White House and managed to flood the twenty-four/seven media with a steady stream of messages and to keep them consistent. There were regular news briefings every two hours in the morning by an administration official, beginning with the 7:00 A.M. report from Brigadier General Vincent K. Brooks from the U.S. Central Command's Forward Headquarters in Doha,

Qatar. This live report was timed to appear on the morning news shows. The White House spokesman, Ari Fleischer, would hold another two or three sessions with reporters during the rest of the day. The Pentagon and the State Department also held frequent briefings.

But the big news was from the battlefield itself, thanks to the Pentagon's decision to embed more than five hundred reporters and photographers in the invasion force. As one *New York Times* reporter wrote, "Planners must have contemplated advances in media technology and decided that if they can't control the press, they may as well use it."[97] With their ever more portable satellite phones (twenty pounds instead of seventy pounds during the 1991 Gulf War), journalists provided firsthand accounts of the war as it unfolded, conveying the excitement of battle and stories about life with the troops. Television viewers became involved in the war as spectators. The news media were flooded with dramatic footage that guaranteed a large audience. "Embedded journalism" combined with the advances in media recording and transmission technologies provided a more intimate and multifaceted view of the war than was possible in earlier wars.[98] But in some ways the coverage was quite restrictive. Because it was technically possible to file reports live continually, there was pressure to do so. Yet, the information and perspective each reporter could provide was limited to his or her immediate military unit. Therefore, much of the saturation coverage of the war conveyed unconnected bits with little context. Nevertheless, the overall effect was to generate sympathy for the troops and support for the war.

The War on Terror versus the Clash of Civilizations

Managing the way the war in Iraq was represented and perceived proved to be far more difficult in the rest of the world than it was in the United States. It was also much more difficult than it was in the first Gulf war. Between the first and second U.S. wars in Iraq the media environment changed dramatically, especially in the Middle East. The international news monopoly of the U.S. and other Western media came to an end in this part of the world as Pan-Arab satellite television channels and other news outlets proliferated.[99] First and most significant was Al Jazeera. Launched in 1996, the channel had already acquired a large audience before the war in Iraq and had gained considerable popularity and credibility among Arabs in the Middle East and elsewhere with its intensive reporting on the Israeli-Palestinian conflict. Al Jazeera achieved international prominence with its coverage of the war in Afghanistan from its bureau in Kabul. Because it was able to remain in areas under Taliban control when most Western journalists were ordered to leave, Al Jazeera's footage began to appear on Western television channels with an increasingly familiar logo.[100] The channel attracted even more attention when it became the exclusive recipient of tapes from Osama bin Laden, which it aired, much to the distress of the U.S. government. What the United States called a war on terror, Osama bin Laden called a U.S. war on Islam.

By the beginning of the war in Iraq in March 2003, the number of Arab satellite news channels was growing rapidly. Al Arabiya, Al Hayat/Lebanon Broadcasting Corporation, Abu Dhabi, and Nile News were among the most widely viewed. According to observers in the region, news on these channels was watched not merely by elites but also by all levels of society.[101] Restaurants and neighborhood coffee shops with transnational stations were turned into crowded news cafes with special sections for watching live transmissions from Baghdad. And the war they saw unfold was very different from the one the Americans were watching. Whereas U.S. cable and network channels focused on military movements and strategies, rarely showing the consequences, the Arab transnational media focused on the dead and wounded Iraqis and the destruction of population centers. Indeed, the proliferation of Pan-Arab channels encouraged competition to air the goriest images. The U.S. government criticized the Arab media for inflaming their viewers with these images. The Arab media criticized the American media for sanitizing the war, for ignoring the human cost, and for presenting it as a video game.[102]

Although there was considerable variation in the press and television coverage, the senior editor of the *Transnational Broadcasting Studies Journal*, Hussein Amin, claims that all Arab transnational television looked at American troops as invaders, not as liberators. The news from the field was generally framed not as a war on terror or as the liberation of the Iraqi people from tyranny but rather as a brutal and humiliating assault on defenseless Arabs. Amin describes how the image of an American flag draped over Saddam Hussein's statue was transmitted to tens of millions of Arab viewers, contributing to "a sense of humiliation of their Arab brothers and their fears of American imperialism." This is an excellent example of the power of transnational satellite broadcasting, he notes, that "one soldier makes an individual gesture and an entire region watches in astonishment."[103]

Saddam Hussein had tried to frame the Gulf War twelve years earlier in similar terms, as an example of Iraqi victims of Western, especially U.S., imperialism. This interpretation was not very convincing, when it was Hussein who had invaded and occupied a neighboring Arab country, Kuwait. The U.S. "law and order frame" made more sense in that case.[104] Further, Operation Desert Storm was carried out under the aegis of a UN resolution, and the coalition that the United States mobilized to push Hussein out of Kuwait included a half dozen Arab states in addition to the major Western powers. According to the political communication scholar Gadi Wolfsfeld, the legitimacy of this U.S. campaign was rarely questioned by most international news media.[105] There were examples of alternative frames in the media, such as the *Times of India*, which saw the war as an example of the dangers of the new unipolar world. But these individual examples did not have the capacity to influence perceptions beyond their domestic base.

The contrast in the U.S. efforts to prevail in the framing of the two wars in Iraq illustrates how four variables affect the ability of political leaders to dominate the framing of an event, namely, the cultural resonance of the frame, the amount of political consensus, the degree of control over the flow of information, and the level of ambiguity inherent in the event, that is, how open it is to multiple interpretations. Even under the most favorable circumstances, it is more difficult to promote a frame in the international context than the domestic because of differences in political culture. But in the case of the first war in Iraq, where the territorial integrity of a sovereign nation had been violated, the law and order frame had the advantage of resonating with basic cultural values that were widespread. The need to expel an invader from his neighbor's territory was also a simple story with little ambiguity regarding the aggressor in this situation.

The situation that led to the second war in Iraq was much more complex and ambiguous. The United States insisted that Saddam Hussein had not complied with a series of UN resolutions, especially one requiring him to demonstrate that he was not producing weapons of mass destruction. He was a tyrannical leader who had abused his people. A military intervention would liberate the people of Iraq and remove the threat of these weapons to the region and the world. The complexity of the situation and the uncertainties about the nature and imminence of this threat hampered the U.S. efforts to impose its interpretation of the rationale for the war. The ambiguity of the situation left it open for a framing contest, in which American imperialism, Arab humiliation, and variations on these themes had more cultural resonance in the Arab countries than themes of liberation and international security. The crusades and the Mongol sack of Baghdad were sometimes used as synonyms for the American-led invasions of Iraq.[106] Arab media journalists both reflected and reinforced the existing climate of opinion.

The fact that the Arab media became the major source of information in the Middle East, and that their journalists tended toward the more culturally resonant frames, ensured that the United States would face a Herculean task influencing the perceptions about the war in this region. Besides the growth in the number of Pan-Arab satellite television channels, other new media technologies contributed to the difficulties that the United States experienced in imposing its representation of the Iraq War. The Internet was also spreading in the Middle East, providing yet another source of information and rumor, completely out of U.S. control. Further, the prevalence of digital cameras and the ease with which anybody's images could be posted on the Web and widely circulated was yet another obstacle to controlling the flow of information and thus dominating the interpretation of the war.

Another major obstacle was the existence of significant and sustained dissent among a number of relevant policy makers at the international level, which also encouraged alternative frames for the media. France and Germany, for example, disagreed with the U.S. claims that previous UN resolutions authorized military action against Iraq, which they viewed as a rush to war. Only four West European countries were members of the "coalition of the willing," half the number in the earlier war. Whereas the Gulf War coalition contained eight Arab countries, not a single Arab country joined the coalition in the second war with Iraq. The existence of significant dissent among relevant governments, the ambiguity of the situation, and a less Western-dominated international media environment produced genuine competition over the meaning of the conflict, in which the most culturally resonant frames prevailed—the U.S. frame in the United States and the Arab frame in the Middle East.

Conclusion

The development and diffusion of new information and communication technologies has transformed the environment in which international relations are conducted and wars are fought. Political leaders communicate more quickly and easily through a variety of channels, and more information is readily obtainable than ever before. The downside is that the accelerated information flow means that decisions and responses must be made more quickly—in a more transparent environment where actions and their consequences are visible to a much larger, more diverse public. Risks are greater because failures and shortcomings are more obvious, if not greatly magnified. Local events can suddenly become global issues, as in the case of the cartoons with Muhammad's image, published in an obscure Danish newspaper but circulated around the world, generating controversy and exacerbating tensions.

New technologies offer greater opportunities for political leaders to influence the perceptions of foreign as well as domestic publics, bypassing other states' controls. But gaining public support for their policies has become more challenging for governments in many ways, even as it has become more important.

The Western mainstream monopoly of the news has come to an end, and the effort of any government now to influence perceptions is complicated by the general availability of abundant and diverse news sources. Information is no longer restricted to the policy elites. Access to new information and communication technologies enables nonstate actors to form transnational networks and use the tools of political influence (and sometimes violence) to affect international outcomes. In this new political environment effective public diplomacy is essential for governments to accomplish their foreign policy objectives and to prevail in conflict and war.

In this era of live global television, managing the way a conflict is represented and perceived among multiple publics has become even more important than in the past. "The way the mass media represent the conflict is part of the conflict," the political communication scholar Robin Brown explains. "Shaping the perceptions of opponents, supporters, and neutral groups influences whether they become involved and how they participate."[107] The combination of new information, communication, and weapons technologies potentially revolutionizes warfare with computers, lasers, sensors, unmanned combat aerial vehicles, and networks of communication that would allow machines to conduct much of the battlefield activity. But some of the new information and communication technologies can also be combined with low-technology weaponry and traditional guerilla tactics to enhance the organizational and operational effectiveness of irregular combatants, such as insurgents and terrorists. The Internet, for example, is used not only for training, planning, and coordinating actions but also as a means of mobilizing support and influencing perceptions of the conflict.

Because leading government officials in every country have privileged access to the media, their interpretation of events tends to prevail in the domestic context, especially when the meaning they give to the event has a strong resonance within the culture and there is no unified opposition among political elites posing a culturally resonant counterframe. These traditional advantages probably persist in the new information environment, and media attention—even with its graphic, emotion-laden images—is unlikely to be the sole impetus for an issue to appear or disappear from a government's foreign policy agenda. But the task of influencing perceptions of events and mobilizing support for the policy response has become far more complex and problematic in this new environment.

In the world of global media, global audiences, and porous borders, messages skillfully designed to persuade the domestic audience can have serious negative repercussions when they reach other audiences with different perspectives and assumptions. A successful foreign policy, in peace and war, must have some understanding of the attitudes and cultures of those who will be affected by it, and the framing of the policy must reflect that understanding. Even domestically, there will be more competition to influence perceptions because the volume and diversity of information sources makes it easier for alternative views to gain attention. Politics in the international arena is a contest for attention and, most important, credibility. No video or blitz of press conferences can establish credibility. It is a long-term process.

Notes

1. Richard Holbrooke, National Commission on Terrorist Attacks upon the United States, *The 9/11 Commission Report* (New York: W. W. Norton, 2004), 377.

2. Monroe E. Price, *Media and Sovereignty: The Global Information Revolution and Its Challenge to State Power* (Cambridge, Mass.: MIT Press, 2002), 250.

3. Edward P. Djerejian, "Changing Minds, Winning Peace: A New Strategic Direction for U.S. Diplomacy in the Arab and Muslim World," Report of the Advisory Group on Public Diplomacy for the Arab and Muslim World, submitted to the Committee on Appropriations, U.S. House of Representatives, October 1, 2003, 13.

4. Technical information is taken from Steven Livingston and W. Lance Bennett, "Gatekeeping, Indexing, and Live-Event News: Is Technology Altering the Construction of News?" *Political Communication* 20, no. 4 (October–December 2003): 371.

5. Walter B. Wriston, *The Twilight of Sovereignty: How the Information Revolution Is Transforming Our World* (New York: Charles Scribner's Sons, 1992), 48; Oswald H. Ganley and Gladys D. Ganley, *To Inform or to Control? The New Communications Networks*, 2nd ed. (Norwood, N.J.: Ablex, 1989), 59.

6. Gordon Smith, "The Challenge of Virtual Diplomacy," speech at the U.S. Institute of Peace Conference on "Virtual Diplomacy," April 2, 1997, at www.usip.org/virtualdiplomacy/publications/vdpresents.html (accessed December 5, 2005).

7. Hilary McLellan, summary of U.S. Institute of Peace Conference on "Virtual Diplomacy," April 2, 1997, at www.tech-head.com/diplomacy (accessed December 5, 2005).

8. Bernard I. Finel and Kristen Lord, *Peace and Conflict in the Age of Transparency* (New York: Palgrave, 2000); Kristen Lord, "War and Peace in the Age of Transparency," *Georgetown Journal of International Affairs* 4, no. 2 (Summer/Fall 2003): 130–34.

9. Robert Jervis, *The Logic of Images in International Relations* (New York: Columbia University Press, 1989), 6.

10. The term was first publicized by Joseph S. Nye Jr. in "Soft Power," *Foreign Policy*, no. 80 (Autumn 1990): 155–74.

11. Todd S. Purdum, "After the Attacks: The White House," *New York Times*, September 17, 2001, A2.

12. Christer Jonsson, "Diplomatic Signaling in the Television Age," *Harvard International Journal of Press/Politics* 1, no. 3 (Summer 1996): 26–27.

13. James Schlesinger, "Quest for a Post-Cold War Foreign Policy," *Foreign Affairs* 72, no. 1 (Winter 1993): 17; Wriston, *The Twilight of Sovereignty*, 144.

14. See, for example, Leon Sigal, *Reporters and Officials: The Organization and Politics of Newsgathering* (Lexington, Mass.: D. C. Heath, 1973); W. Lance Bennett, "Toward a Theory of Press-State Relations in the United States," *Journal of Communication* 40, no. 2 (Spring 1990): 103–25. For a more economic explanation for government dominance of the media, see Edward S. Herman and Noam Chomsky, *Manufacturing Consent: The Political Economy of the Mass Media* (New York: Pantheon, 2002).

15. W. Lance Bennett, "The News about Foreign Policy," in *Taken by Storm: The Media, Public Opinion, and U.S. Foreign Policy in the Gulf War*, ed. W. Lance Bennett and David L. Paletz (Chicago: University of Chicago Press, 1994), 27.

16. Robert Entman, *Projections of Power: Framing News, Public Opinion, and U.S. Foreign Policy* (Chicago: University of Chicago Press, 2004), 5.

17. W. Lance Bennett and Jarol B. Manheim, "Taking the Public by Storm: Information, Cuing, and the Democratic Process in the Gulf Conflict," *Political Communication* 10, no. 4 (October–December 1993): 332.

18. These variables combine points made by two authors: Entman, *Projections of Power*; and Gadi Wolfsfeld, *Media and Political Conflict: News from the Middle East* (Cambridge, UK: Cambridge University Press, 1997).

19. Entman, *Projections of Power*, 6.

20. Entman, *Projections of Power*, 18.

21. Warren P. Strobel, *Late-Breaking Foreign Policy: The News Media's Influence on Peace Operations* (Washington, D.C.: U.S. Institute of Peace Press, 1997), 99.

22. Wolfsfeld, *Media and Political Conflict*, 37, 38.

23. Steven Livingston and Todd Eachus, "Humanitarian Crises and U.S. Foreign Policy: Somalia and the CNN Effect Reconsidered," *Political Communication* 12, no. 4 (October–December 1995): 413–29; Jonathan Mermin, "Television News and American Intervention in Somalia: The Myth of a Media-Driven Policy," *Political Science Quarterly* 112, no. 3 (Fall 1997): 386–403. Both compare the sequence of events with analysis of news coverage.

24. Strobel, *Late-Breaking Foreign Policy*.

25. Strobel, *Late-Breaking Foreign Policy*, esp. chap. 3.

26. Strobel, *Late-Breaking Foreign Policy*, 9. These points summarize one theme of his book.

27. Also a major conclusion of Jonathan Mermin, *Debating War and Peace: Media Coverage of U.S. Intervention in the Post-Vietnam Era* (Princeton, N.J.: Princeton University Press, 1999), 142.

28. Strobel, *Late-Breaking Foreign Policy*, 163.

29. Nik Gowing, "Real-Time Television Coverage of Armed Conflicts and Diplomatic Crises: Does It Pressure or Distort Foreign Policy Decisions?" Working Paper 94-1 (Cambridge, Mass.: Joan Shorenstein Center on the Press, Politics, and Public Policy, 1994), 9.

30. See Wolfsfeld, *Media and Political Conflict*, for his "political context" model for understanding the role of the media in political conflict.

31. Samuel J. Best, Brian Chmielewski, and Brian S. Krueger, "Selective Exposure to Online Foreign News during the Conflict with Iraq," *Harvard International Journal of Press/Politics* 10, no. 4 (2005): 53, 65.

32. Entman, *Projections of Power*, 153.

33. Hans J. Morgenthau, *Politics among Nations*, 3rd ed. (New York: Alfred A. Knopf, 1966), 546.

34. Quoted in Timothy J. McNulty, "Television's Impact on Executive Decision-making and Diplomacy," *Fletcher Forum of World Affairs* 17, no. 1 (Winter 1993): 67.

35. This account is from McNulty, "Television's Impact," 70–71.

36. Defense Science Board Task Force, *Strategic Communication* (Washington, D.C.: Office of Under Secretary of Defense, 2004), 12, at www.acq.osd.mil/dsb/reports/2004-09-Strategic_Communication.pdf (accessed December 5, 2005).

37. Steven Livingston, "Diplomacy in the New Information Environment," *Georgetown Journal of International Affairs* (Summer/Fall 2001): 111–12.

38. Robin Brown, "Information Technology and the Transformation of Diplomacy," *Knowledge, Technology, and Policy* 18, no. 2 (Summer 2004): 25–26.

39. Quoted from an interview in Rhiannon Vickers, "The New Public Diplomacy: Britain and Canada Compared," *British Journal of Politics and International Relations* 6, no. 2 (2004): 185.

40. Peter J. Smith and Elizabeth Smythe, "Globalisation, Citizenship, and Information Technology: The Multilateral Agreement on Investment (MAI) Meets the Internet," in *Culture and Politics in the Information Age: A New Politics?* ed. Frank Webster, 183–206 (London: Routledge, 2001).

41. *The National Security Strategy of the United States*, September 2002, at www.whitehouse.gov/nsc/nss.pdf (accessed November 25, 2005), 6, 31.

42. Stephen Kinzer, "The World: The Untold Story: Why They Don't Know Us," *New York Times*, November 11, 2001, 5(4).

43. Elizabeth Becker, "Hearts and Minds: In the War on Terrorism, a Battle to Shape Opinion," *New York Times*, November 11, 2001, A1.

44. Holbrooke, *The 9/11 Commission Report*, 377.

45. Becker, "Hearts and Minds," 1.

46. James Dao and Eric Schmitt, "Hearts and Minds: Pentagon Readies Efforts to Sway Sentiment Abroad," *New York Times*, February 19, 2002, A1.

47. Victoria de Grazia, "The Nation; The Selling of America, Bush Style," *New York Times*, August 25, 2002, 4(4).

48. Jane Perlez, "Satellite TV Tries to Bridge a Culture Gap," *New York Times*, February 9, 2003, 13.

49. Amy Cortese, "Media Talk: U.S. Reaches Out to Younger Readers, in Arabic," *New York Times*, February 17, 2003, C7.

50. White House Office of Global Communications website, at www.whitehouse.gov/ogc/aboutogc.html (accessed December 1, 2005). All quotations about this office are taken from this White House website.

51. White House Office of Global Communications website.

52. Elizabeth Becker, "The American Portrayal of a War of Liberation Is Faltering across the Arab World," *New York Times*, April 5, 2003, B10.

53. Khaled Abdelkariem, quoted in Becker, "The American Portrayal," 10.

54. Pew Research Center for the People and the Press, "Views of a Changing World, 2003," June 2003, at http://pewglobal.org/reports/pdf/185.pdf (accessed December 4, 2005).

55. Pew Research Center for the People and the Press, "Global Opinion: The Spread of Anti-Americanism, Trends 2005," January 20, 2005, at http://pewresearch .org/trends (accessed December 4, 2005), 106.

56. Quoted in Defense Science Board Task Force, *Strategic Communication*, 15.

57. The two reports are Djerejian, "Changing Minds, Winning Peace," and Defense Science Board Task Force, *Strategic Communication*.

58. Djerejian, "Changing Minds, Winning Peace," 13.

59. Defense Science Board Task Force, *Strategic Communication*, 83.

60. Thom Shanker and Eric Schmitt, "Hearts and Minds: Pentagon Weighs Use of Deception in a Broad Area," *New York Times*, December 13, 2004, A1.

61. Eric Schmitt, "Military Admits Planting News in Iraq," *New York Times*, December 3, 2005, 11.

62. Jeffrey Brown, "Opposing Views on Planting Stories," *The NewsHour with Jim Lehrer*, December 12, 2005, at www.pbs.org/newshour/bb/middle_east/july-dec05/ media_12-02.html (accessed December 5, 2005).

63. See Defense Science Board Task Force, *Strategic Communication*, 12, for this distinction.

64. Defense Science Board Task Force, *Strategic Communication*, 38, 41.

65. Evan Potter, "The Role of Advocacy: Mass Media and the New Diplomacy" (paper presented at the International Studies Association Annual Meeting, Portland, Ore., February 26, 2003), 5.

66. Steve Inskeep, "Changes Seen in al-Qaeda Structure," Morning Edition, National Public Radio, November 23, 2005.

67. Joseph S. Nye Jr., *The Paradox of American Power: Why the World's Only Superpower Can't Go It Alone* (New York: Oxford University Press, 2002), 67–68.

68. See, for example, John Arquilla and David Ronfeldt, *Networks and Netwars: The Future of Terror, Crime, and Militancy* (Santa Monica, Calif.: Rand Corporation, 2001); Bruce Berkowitz, *The New Face of War: How War Will Be Fought in the 21st Century* (New York: Free Press, 2003); Bill Owens, *Lifting the Fog of War* (New York: Farrar, Straus and Giroux, 2000).

69. Owens, *Lifting the Fog of War*, 14–16. Owens identifies these three advantages in the military terms "battle awareness, C4I (Command, Control, Computers, Intelligence), and "precision force use."

70. Information in this paragraph was taken from Thomas E. Ricks, "A New Way of War," *Washington Post National Weekly Edition* (December 10–16, 2001), 6; and James Dao and Andrew C. Revkin, "A Revolution in Warfare," *New York Times*, April 16, 2002, D1.

71. Eric Schmitt, "Smart Bombs, Dumb Map," *New York Times*, May 16, 1999, 6; Elizabeth Rosenthal, "China's Mood: Real Public Rage Stoked by Propaganda Machine," *New York Times*, May 14, 1999, A13.

72. John Downey and Graham Murdock, "The Counter-Revolution in Military Affairs: The Globalization of Guerilla Warfare," in *War and the Media*, ed. Daya Kishan Thussu and Des Freedman (Thousand Oaks, Calif.: Sage, 2003), 79.

73. Downey and Murdock, "The Counter-Revolution in Military Affairs," 70–71.

74. William S. Lind and a group of other military officers initiated this line of thinking with the article "The Changing Face of War: Into the Fourth Generation," *Marine Corps Gazette* (October 1989): 22–26. A symposium on the subject appears in *Contemporary Security Policy* 26, no. 2 (August 2005), see esp. introduction, 185–88. A website for "Defense and the National Interest" contains many articles and debates on this subject, at www.d-n-i.net/ (accessed March 7, 2006).

75. Jeffrey Record, "Why the Strong Lose," *Parameters* 35, no. 4 (Winter 2005/2006): 17–18.

76. Clinton J. Ancker III and Michael D. Burke, "Asymmetric Warfare," *Military Review* (July–August 2003): 18, 22.

77. Arquilla and Ronfeldt, *Networks and Netwars*, 2.

78. Gabriel Weimann, "www.terror.net: How Modern Terrorism Uses the Internet" (Washington, D.C.: U.S. Institute of Peace Press, 2004), at www.usip.org/pubs/specialreports/sr116.pdf (accessed March 7, 2006), 1. See also Gabriel Weimann, *Terror on the Internet* (Washington, D.C.: U.S. Institute of Peace Press, 2006).

79. Daniel Benjamin, "Changes seen in Al-Qaeda Structure," interview on Morning Edition, National Public Radio news transcript, November 23, 2005.

80. Paul Eedle, "Terrorism.com," *Guardian*, July 17, 2002, 4(G2).

81. Weimann, "www.terror.net," 10.

82. Timothy Thomas, "Al Qaeda and the Internet: The Danger of 'Cyberplanning,'" in *Through Alternative Lens: Current Debates in International Relations*, ed. Daniel J. Kaufman, Jay M. Parker, Patrick V. Howell, and Kimberly Field (Boston: McGraw-Hill, 2004), 155.

83. Weimann, "www.terror.net," 6.

84. John Sayen, "4GW—Myth, or the Future of Warfare?" Defense and the National Interest, at http://d-n-i.net/fcs/sayen_4gw_reply.htm (accessed February 2, 2006).

85. International Crisis Group, "In Their Own Words: Reading the Iraqi Insurgency," Middle East Report No. 50, February 15, 2006, at www.crisisgroup.org/ (accessed February 2, 2006).

86. Bernard Haykel, "Changes Seen in Al-Qaeda Structure," interview on Morning Edition, National Public Radio news transcript, November 23, 2005.

87. Donald H. Rumsfeld, speech to Council on Foreign Relations, New York, February 17, 2006, at www.defenselink.mil/speeches/speech.aspx?speechid=27 (accessed March 9, 2006).

88. Robin Brown, "Spinning the War: Political Communications, Information Operations, and Public Diplomacy in the War on Terrorism," in *War and the Media*, ed. Daya Kishan Thussu and Des Freedman (Thousand Oaks, Calif.: Sage, 2003), 94.

89. Daya Kishan Thussu and Des Freedman, "Introduction," in *War and the Media*, ed. Daya Kishan Thussu and Des Freedman (Thousand Oaks, Calif.: Sage, 2003), 1.

90. George W. Bush, transcript, *New York Times*, September 12, 2001, A4.

91. Entman, *Projections of Power*, 17.

92. Paul Waldman, "Why the Media Don't Call It as They See It," *Washington Post*, September 28, 2003, B4.

93. George W. Bush, "President Says Saddam Hussein Must Leave Iraq within 48 Hours," Office of the Press Secretary, March 17, 2003, at www.whitehouse.gov/news/releases/2003/03/20030317-7.html (accessed January 5, 2006).

94. Howard Kurtz, "The Post on WMDs: An Inside Story," *Washington Post*, August 12, 2004, A1.

95. *New York Times*, "The Times and Iraq," May 26, 2004, A10.

96. Elisabeth Bumiller, "Even Critics of War Say the White House Spun It with Skill," *New York Times*, April 20, 2003, B14.

97. Lucian K. Truscott, "In This War, News Is a Weapon," *New York Times*, March 25, 2003, A17.

98. Amy Harmon, "Technology: Improved Tools Turn Journalists into a Quick Strike Force," *New York Times*, March 24, 2003, C1.

99. Philip Seib, "Hegemonic No More: Western Media, the Rise of Al-Jazeera, and the Influence of Diverse Voices," *International Studies Review* 7, no. 4 (December 2005): 601.

100. Seib, "Hegemonic No More," 602.

101. Hussein Amin, "'Watching the War' in the Arab World," *Transnational Broadcasting Studies Journal* (Spring/Summer 2003), at www.tbsjournal.com/Archives/Spring03/amin.html (accessed January 14, 2006).

102. Amin, "'Watching the War.'"

103. Amin, "'Watching the War.'"

104. The term "law and order frame" is from Wolfsfeld, *Media and Political Conflict*, chap. 8.

105. Wolfsfeld, *Media and Political Conflict*, 185.

106. Susan Saches, "Arab Media Portray War as Killing Field," *New York Times*, April 4, 2003, B1.

107. Brown, "Spinning the War," 87.

ー

The Information Revolution, the Global Economy, and the Distribution of Wealth

Quantitative changes in the patterns of transcontinental communication and information exchange—more, faster, cheaper connections—have produced qualitative changes in the way governments and societies relate to each other. The information revolution has been a propelling force behind the process of globalization, defined here as the "widening, deepening, and speeding up of worldwide interconnectedness in all aspects of social life."[1] Economic, political, social, and cultural relations across borders and regions have increased in volume, scope, intensity, and density, creating networks of connections and interdependence. Advances in information and communication technologies (ICTs) have encouraged these trends by increasing the technical capacity to act and interact across great distances on a sustained, regularized basis. Nowhere has their impact been more profound than in the economic sphere. This chapter examines their role in the process of economic globalization and puts the debate over their impact into the larger context of the debate over globalization.

ICTs and the Global Economy

"Economic globalization" is a concept that is commonly used, yet hotly contested, both in academic texts and in popular discourse. The controversy involves such questions as, what is new about it; how, why, and to what extent is it actually occurring; how inevitable is the trend; and most important, what are the distributional consequences? Even the meaning of the concept itself is a source of dispute. The role that ICTs play in the process of economic globalization is also the subject of controversy, which centers on contending views regarding technology and historical change. Before addressing these issues, it is important to provide evidence of a globalizing economy and to indicate how new ICTs have facilitated some of the major changes that are occurring. These include an increase in the volume and scope of cross-border economic activities and changes in the nature and organization of production and finance. Cumulatively, these changes suggest that a transformation or qualitative shift in the organization of the world economy is occurring.[2]

Trade

The dramatic expansion of trade in the post–World War II period began with the idea among the victors that international trade was the key to economic growth and prosperity. The General Agreement on Tariffs and Trade (GATT) was established in 1947 as a forum for negotiating reductions in barriers to trade, and it involved commitment on the part of its members to work toward that end. Over the next fifty years a series of rounds of negotiations reduced the average tariff on manufactured goods to less than 5 percent. The World Trade Organization (WTO), which was established as a successor to GATT, expanded the membership and embarked upon efforts to reduce barriers to trade in services and nontariff barriers to trade.

In an increasingly open trading environment, trade in goods and services rose from 574 billion in 1973 to 10.1 trillion dollars in 2003.[3] For most of the period since the end of World War II, world trade has actually grown faster than world output. Merchandise exports (that is, tangibles such as raw materials and manufactured goods) equaled 5 percent of the world gross domestic product (GDP) in 1950, 10 percent in 1973, and more than 17 percent in 1998.[4] This means that more and more of what the world produces is produced in one country and exported to another and that most countries are becoming more dependent upon trade as a source of economic growth. This ratio of export growth to GDP growth has been considered a measure of the increasing integration of economies and of globalization.[5] Downturns in one economy mean it will import less from others.

International trade has become more complex with the involvement of more actors than ever before, changes in the composition of trade, new patterns of specialization, intensified competition, and an emerging new global division of labor. The world trading system today, according to David Held et al., "is defined both by an intensive network of trading relations embracing virtually all economies and by evolving global markets for many goods and some services." This shift toward global markets has been facilitated by improved worldwide communications and transportation networks, the widespread adoption of liberal trade policies, and the internationalization of production.[6]

There are now many more states actively involved in world trade. Two developments contributed to this expansion. One was the rapid growth of a few Asian countries and a shift among many developing countries from inward-oriented development strategies with high tariff barriers to more export-oriented strategies. The other was the collapse of the Soviet Union into fourteen independent states, the disintegration of the Soviet economic trading bloc, and the end of Communist Party monopoly of power in Russia and Eastern Europe—all these events occurring in the early 1990s. New governments in the former Eastern bloc, eager to expand their trade beyond that region, moved toward more liberal foreign economic policies. One indication of the expansion of the international trading system is the comparison of the original membership of GATT, which was twenty-three states, with the current membership of 148 in the WTO. All are committed by their membership to reducing trade barriers and expanding trade, but they are also aggressively competing for shares in the world markets.

Significant shifts have occurred in the composition of international trade—what is being traded. Prior to World War II the majority of international trade was in primary goods—agricultural products and raw materials such as copper and oil. Since the end of that war the share of manufactured goods in world trade has steadily increased to become a majority of trade flows by the mid-1960s and three-quarters today.[7] Trade in services has also increased—on average 6 percent a year in the 1990s, accounting for 20 percent of total world trade in 2003.[8] International trade in services is extremely diverse, including such activities as transportation, telecommunications, financial services (banking, insurance, and accounting), distribution, and computer-enabled business services. Production and trade in goods and services are increasingly interlinked, as many of these services are what have been called "circulation activities within the production chain."[9] Goods that are produced for international trade have to be marketed, transported, distributed, financed, and tracked, and may involve a host of other services. Two key sectors that have been particularly affected by ICT developments—financial and information technology (IT) services—will be considered after the discussion on changes in production.

A new division of international labor is evolving—a far more complex trading system. Although the economically advanced countries continue to dominate world trade (about 70 percent of the total), this concentration masks both the intensity of the competition and changing patterns of trade.

The developing countries' share of world trade has increased from 23 percent in 1985 to 31 percent in 2004. More significantly, their share of world exports in manufactured goods has increased from 10 percent in 1980 to 27 percent in 2004.[10] No longer are former colonies and other developing countries confined to their historic role as exporters of raw materials and importers of manufactured goods from the industrialized countries. Half of their exports today are manufactured goods, in contrast to only 10 percent in 1960. This shift is attributable in large part to the rapid growth of a few East Asian countries in the 1980s, fueled by their manufactured exports, followed by a second tier in Southeast Asia in the next decade.

Then during the 1990s China developed one of the fastest growing economies and has managed to become a major player in the global economy. The internationalization of production, a trend toward the dispersal of various aspects of the production process across different regions, has brought many other developing countries into production and integrated them into the global economy.

Production
Changes in production are closely related to changes in patterns of trade, and they are propelled by the same forces—liberalization, ICT advances, and competition for advantage in a worldwide, competitive marketplace. Reductions in national restrictions on foreign investment have removed barriers to expanding production beyond territorial boundaries. Electronic communication and better, cheaper telephone service provide the physical conditions necessary for producing where it is most efficient (and profitable) to produce, and intensified competition provides a powerful incentive to do so. These forces in combination have transformed the way in which the world's goods are produced and distributed.

Historically, production was a national affair that took place in a national context to serve, primarily, a national market.[11] Today, multinational corporations (MNCs) are internationalizing the production and distribution of the world's goods and services, and the information revolution is facilitating that process.[12] Advances in communication technologies have improved the capacity of firms to organize and manage production at a distance and have increased their flexibility to disperse various aspects of the production across different national locations. Producing abroad can provide a firm with certain advantages, such as lower labor costs, lower taxes, fewer regulations, and better access to a foreign market.

Because different locations have different advantages, corporations seeking greater efficiency and competitive advantage can choose to locate various components of the production process in different countries. For example, in the automobile industry, the design and the production of more complex parts, such as engines and transmissions, may be allocated to an industrially advanced country, while the more labor-intensive stages of assembly may be allocated to a less industrially developed country with lower labor costs. So parts of the automobile may be made in different countries, assembled in yet a different country, and distributed to many others. The cumulative effect of these decisions of individual firms is a general trend toward corporate restructuring and a diffusion of the production process across national boundaries.

In the early stages of MNC growth in the 1960s, many U.S. firms relocated labor-intensive parts of the manufacturing process "offshore" to lower-cost locations, such as Taiwan and Korea. The production facilities were generally part of the firm itself, affiliates, or subsidiaries. The recent trend is toward offshore outsourcing, that is, contracting out certain business functions or aspects of the production process to external firms abroad. These functions might be advertising, accounting, or various parts of the production process itself. Nike, the athletic shoe company, illustrates a new organizational form in which all the production and almost all other functions are subcontracted except for central coordination and marketing the main company's brand. The company does not own any production facilities, and no Nike employee makes shoes in a factory. The four to five hundred thousand workers who do make Nike shoes are employees of one of the subcontracted supplier firms. The main job of Nike as the core company, which employs only about twenty-three thousand, is to manage the production and distribution networks, to sell the products, and to design new ones.[13]

A global communication infrastructure facilitates subcontracting and other forms of transnational collaboration, or "strategic alliances," because the tasks of supervision and coordination among the dispersed elements of the production and distribution processes are much more easily conducted than in the past. Other forms of transnational collaboration include joint ventures, in which two or more firms share ownership; coproduction arrangements; licensing; and franchising agreements. Strategic alliances have proliferated because they serve a variety of purposes. They allow firms to benefit from complementary capabilities, advantages, skills, and technologies. They expand the size of the market and thus allow firms to benefit from economies of scale. They help a firm to share the costs and risks of research and development. They also allow a firm to operate in an economy otherwise restricted by, for example, regulations on foreign ownership. MNCs have far greater flexibility in the way they structure their organizations, functionally and geographically.

There is tremendous variety and complexity in the organizational structures of MNCs today, and they are increasingly connected into international production networks.

Corporate organizational restructuring is related to the widespread shift in the mode of production toward a more "lean" and "flexible" model. Production is lean and flexible because many activities that were previously done within the corporation are done by other firms. A key feature of the lean and flexible model is the use of computer-based systems known as Electronic Point of Sale (EPOS) to provide timely information that will allow "just-in-time" deliveries in order to keep inventories at a minimum. Technologies using the bar code enable retailers to track every sale in detail—model, size, color, source, and so forth. Sale information can be conveyed immediately to relevant suppliers so that production at every stage of the process can be adjusted according to the preferences revealed in this information. Not only is there a tremendous cost saving in the avoidance of overstocks and warehouse costs, but these technologies also allow firms to respond to changing needs and market demands, as well as to accommodate local conditions. Another aid to supply chain management is Radio Frequency Identification Technology (RFID). More data can be transmitted by a product containing an RFID tag and RFID reader than with bar codes, and no contact is necessary to read the data.

One company that has achieved spectacular success with an innovative use of the bar code is the giant U.S. discount retailer Wal-Mart.[14] Timely information embedded in the bar code about what was being sold and at what price enabled Wal-Mart to develop an efficient global supply chain but, even more significant, to make specific demands on the suppliers regarding product, price, and timing of delivery. According to Jon Lehman, a former manager of six Wal-Mart stores, the bar code essentially gave the company access to all of its suppliers' books and completely changed the communication process between them. As the volume of Wal-Mart sales increased its buying power—number 1 in the United States, for clothing, sporting goods, groceries, and toys—it was able to dictate prices to manufacturers to accommodate or else lose Wal-Mart's lucrative business. In order to meet its promises to customers of "always low prices," Wal-Mart not only began to look abroad for low-cost suppliers of goods but also, by insisting on rock bottom prices from U.S. manufacturers, forced most of them to move their production facilities abroad—or go out of business. By the mid-1990s Wal-Mart was the leading company in terms of global sourcing, according to Gary Gereffi, professor of sociology at Duke University, much of it from China. Wal-Mart gives its Chinese suppliers specifications for Wal-Mart products, including timing, delivery, and acceptable price. In a sense, he says, "Chinese suppliers learn how to export to the U.S. market through large retailers like Wal-Mart."[15]

These changes in the organization and management of production have created a "global manufacturing system in which production capacity is dispersed to an unprecedented number of developing as well as developed countries."[16] The trend toward outsourcing and dispersal of different components of the process opens up new opportunities for small- and medium-sized enterprises (SMEs), as well as developing countries, to become part of global production networks. SMEs involved in contractual arrangements as suppliers might even expand their production units through franchising or other kinds of cooperative arrangements. Some are becoming small-scale MNCs by establishing operating facilities in two or more countries and maintaining managerial control over them (foreign direct investment or FDI). FDI outflows from developing countries have grown rapidly since the 1990s, faster than those from developed countries. By 2003 they represented one-tenth of the world's total stock. In the late 1980s there were only 3,800 indigenous MNCs in developing countries, but this number had more than doubled a decade later. Three companies from developing countries made the list of top nonfinancial MNCs in 2002.[17]

Finance

The image of millions of dollars being transferred instantly thousands of miles away with the click of a mouse illustrates the profound effect that the information revolution has had on the financial relations among states. International financial relations include all types of cross-border capital flows, including international lending, portfolio investments (stocks, bonds, and investment funds), currency trading, and FDI as discussed above. Since the 1980s all types of cross-border financial transactions have increased dramatically. International issues of shares increased from eight billion in the 1980s to three hundred billion in 2000. The number of multinational banks, which have been vehicles for large international financial flows, has proliferated since the 1980s. Transborder bank lending increased from two trillion in 1983 to over eleven trillion in 2001.[18] The average *daily* turnover in foreign exchange markets, that is, the buying and selling of currencies, was 1.9 trillion in 2004, more than double the 818 billion in 1992.[19]

New information and communication technologies that became widespread in the 1990s were a powerful force propelling forward a trend of increasing international financial activity that began to take off in the 1970s. Two events in that decade were crucial. The first was the shift after 1973 from a fixed to a flexible or floating exchange rate system. Thereafter, exchange rates would be determined by day-to-day trading, by the buying and selling of currencies, rather than a rate fixed in relation to the dollar or gold, as it was under the Bretton Woods system. This shift made exchange rates more volatile and encouraged the growth of foreign exchange markets by encouraging speculators to buy and sell currencies at a profit.

The second major event was the quadrupling of oil prices in 1973–1974. As oil transactions were conducted in dollars, oil-producing states soon found themselves with huge surpluses of "petrodollars," which they deposited in Western banks. The banks, flush with these petrodollar deposits, eagerly sought new clients and found many of them in developing countries that were eager to borrow. This flood of petrodollars and the availability of loans for the rest of the decade created new channels of financial activity—and enormous debts for the developing world.

Developments in the 1980s further expanded and extended international financial markets. The United States experienced throughout the decade record highs in its trade and balance of payments deficit, which means that it was paying out more for goods and services than it was receiving for the goods and services it was selling in international markets. Deficits increase the demand for credit, which usually has the effect of raising interest rates to attract funds. The rising deficits of the United States coincided with the rise of Japan as the world's second largest economy, and one with a significant balance of payments surplus. Japan and other European countries provided the funds to finance these deficits with investments in the stock market, treasury bonds, and foreign direct investments. This flow of capital from abroad into the United States contributed much to the globalization of capital.[20]

One of the most important developments in the international financial system during the 1980s and continuing into the next decade was the widespread deregulation of financial services. The initial steps were taken by the United States, then the UK, inspired by the laissez-faire perspectives of their respective leaders, Ronald Reagan and Margaret Thatcher. Thatcher opened up the London stock market to foreign dealers in 1986. In order to prevent the loss of capital to these centers, most other developed countries soon thereafter began to remove controls on the flow of capital across borders, to open up their stock markets, and to allow international banks. In the latter part of the decade and beginning of the next, many East Asian states opened up their economies to foreign investment, and in the 1990s the move toward financial liberalization spread to other parts of the developing world. Many countries without stock markets developed them, and many that had been closed were opened. Deregulation of financial markets in developing countries, especially those in East and Southeast Asia that were experiencing phenomenal growth rates, led to a rush of short-term capital inflows. The collapse of the Soviet economic system and the Soviet economic bloc created still more channels for international financial activity in the 1990s. As these states tried to make a transition from command to market economies and to enter the global economy, they required considerable external capital.

Financial services are fundamental to the conduct of all economic activities, but they are also commodities in their own right in the sense that they are produced and traded like manufactured goods.[21] The widespread diffusion of ICTs has facilitated the phenomenal growth of international financial transactions by making them easier, quicker, and less costly—because money, unlike goods such as clothing, can be used, transferred, and delivered electronically.[22] One of the many advantages of electronic transactions is the tremendous savings in interest payments when funds are transferred instantly. Technically, finance should be the sector least bound by geography, as the global communication infrastructure makes possible twenty-four-hour electronic trading in all financial services. However, true twenty-four-hour global trading is still evolving and currently most well developed in certain kinds of transactions, most notably in foreign exchange and in U.S. government bonds.[23]

Trading in currencies has contributed more than any other form of cross-border financial transactions to the emergence of a global capital market. Historically, currencies were bought and sold primarily to facilitate international trade in goods and services. Increasingly, the foreign exchange market has taken on a life of its own where large banks and corporations, and even individuals, trade currencies for the purpose of profiting from changes in value. Trade in currencies now far exceeds the value of international trade in goods and services, and the gap is increasing. In 1986 foreign exchange trading was twenty-five times the level of world trade; by 2001 it was fifty-seven times.[24] As the volume of this trade expands, it becomes more difficult for governments to intervene by buying or selling their own currencies in order to maintain their value. This trade is highly speculative and based on rapid responses to fluctuations (or anticipated changes) in currency values.

Major changes have occurred not only in the scale of international financial activity but also in the organization and conduct of financial services. The Internet has prompted the development of new platforms, most notably online financial services, that expand the reach of these services and broaden access to them. According to the *Economist*, almost every financial firm "from the swankiest Wall street investment bank to the provider of microcredit for

the poor" has developed an Internet presence. For example, FOREX.com offers access to the foreign exchange market with "superior trading tools,
twenty-four-hour customer support, and a secure online trading experience."
The cautious but curious might even open a mini–virtual account for as little
as $250.[25]

Cross-border trading in stocks is also easier, cheaper, and more accessible
with online services. The *Economist* claims that online stockbroking is "one
of the Internet's big success stories," with spectacular growth in the United
States and Europe and great potential in Asia. The stock market with the
highest proportion of online trading is, in fact, in Seoul, South Korea. Multinational discount stockbrokers, such as E*trade and Charles Schwab, have
used the Internet to challenge the big traditional firms, and their success has
both pushed the established firms toward online services and has inspired the
creation of rivals offering even cheaper online services.

International banking is somewhat more limited by lack of organizational
infrastructure and national regulations than foreign exchange trade. There
has been tremendous growth in multinational banking, however. The number of foreign affiliates of banks increased from 202 in 1960 to 1,928 in 1985,
the period of most rapid growth.[26] The motto on the website of the world's
sixth largest bank (in 2000), HSBC, is "the world's local bank." A notewor-
thy development, which has been encouraged by ICTs, is the growth of offshore financial centers, which seek to attract business with their low tax levels and minimal regulation. The Cayman Islands is a notorious example. Of
the more than five hundred banks "located" on the island of thirty thousand
inhabitants, only seventy actually have a physical presence there, and some
are little more than a name plate in the lobby of another bank.[27] With so few
regulations and "no questions asked," some offshore financial centers have
become not only tax havens but also places where money obtained by illegal
means can be "laundered." Their use by criminal cartels and terrorists has
been of particular concern.

Finally, a major change in international financial relations is in the information environment in which they are conducted. Large institutional investors such as banks, investment firms, and mutual funds can scan the globe
for investment opportunities and carry out practically instant, costless transactions.[28] An array of resources on the World Wide Web and other media
provide up-to-date information to monitor international trading activities—
especially the performance of stocks and currency fluctuations—as well as
more general financial conditions. Instant access to much of this information
is now available not only on the home or office PC but also on mobile
phones (including satellite-enabled phones), and personal digital assistants

(PDAs). Not only is information abundant, quick, and easy to access, but these technologies make instant responses to changing conditions possible from almost anywhere.

Globalization of Finance

In sum, ICTs have contributed to the growth of cross-border financial relations by making them easier, quicker, and cheaper and by providing the technical possibilities for new ways of conducting transactions. Cross-border transactions have increased in volume and speed, and global capital markets are emerging. The phrase "globalization of finance" encompasses all these changes, but it also implies a shift to a more market-oriented, less state-based financial system, a shift in the balance of power from governments and international agencies to private financial actors, such as bankers, money managers, and currency speculators.[29] When money can flow across national borders, unhindered by capital controls, these actors will move it where it can yield the highest returns.

This mobility of capital, and the speed with which it can be moved, constrains governments and affects their ability to manage their economies through fiscal and monetary policies. For example, if a government tries to boost its economy by lowering interest rates so that it is easier and cheaper for its citizens to obtain credit for purchases, foreign investors in the stock and bond markets may transfer their money to a place where the yield is higher. Even more difficult for a government to control is the value of its currency. The volume of currency that is exchanged each day in the global foreign exchange markets far exceeds the foreign exchange reserves of most countries and can overwhelm a government's efforts to stabilize the value of its currency by buying or selling it.

The international financial structure is increasingly becoming a global system linking national financial systems and the fate of their economies. Capital mobility and market volatility in a wired world of interconnected economies increases the risk of the "contagion effect," the tendency of one country's financial crisis to spread to others and reverberate throughout the system. The risks are particularly high when large sums of short-term investments flow into a country, as happened in East Asia in 1997. Deregulation of financial markets in a number of rapidly developing countries had attracted a flood of short-term capital flows, much of it speculative, in the middle of the 1990s. When the economy began to slow in Thailand, the big international investors began to worry that the currency, the Thai baht, would be devalued. As an excellent example of a self-fulfilling prophecy, there was a stampede to sell the baht and withdraw investment capital, actions that led to a precipitous drop in the value of the currency and in the stock market. Thailand's central bank attempted to stabilize the currency but failed to do so, even after using most of its foreign exchange reserves in the effort. The "panic" spread to Indonesia, Malaysia, South Korea, and throughout much of East and Southeast Asia. A herd mentality prevailed as investors collectively perceived increased risk in holding any Asian currency or even any other that looked like an emerging market. What started as a run on Thai currency rippled throughout the region, then Russia, Brazil, Argentina, and other countries in Latin America. The operation of financial markets has been producing "manias, panics, and crashes" for centuries, as Charles Kindleberger explains in his history of financial crises.[30] Electronic trading in an environment where financial information is diffused instantaneously among the world's financial centers increases volatility and unpredictability and makes risk a structural feature of the system.

Information Technology Services
Information technology services, and IT-enabled services, represent a new and rapidly growing category of cross-national economic activity. As a new area, and one that covers a wide variety of services requiring a broad range of skills, there has been considerable confusion in terminology and lack of general agreement on a single term that encompasses all of the diverse activities. The term information technology (IT) services is sometimes used to cover the whole category but more often is used to refer more specifically to computer and information services, the high-skill end of the sector, involving such services as programming, software design, and project development. The terms "business process outsourcing," "back office," and "IT-enabled services" typically refer to such core business services as customer call centers, accounting, payroll processing, and recordkeeping. In common parlance "outsourcing" is often used as a shorthand term to cover this whole category of services, but it is misleading for two reasons. First, "outsourcing" simply refers to the contracting out of certain functions to a supplier outside a given firm, not necessarily one overseas. Offshore outsourcing is the more accurate term, but it can cover any stage of the production process as well as various business functions. Business-process offshore outsourcing has become a focus of heated controversy in the United States and Europe.

Two forces driving growth in the offshoring of these services are the intensification of competition and, of course, advances in information and communication technologies. Competition spurs firms to seek lower labor costs and governments to seek niches or specializations that will give them a comparative advantage. This strategy is particularly important for developing countries that start out in a less competitive position. But it is the advances in ICTs that have made IT outsourcing such a practical alternative and have made possible and profitable an array of new services. Internet connectivity via fiber-optic cable makes it feasible to shift a broad range of basic office functions and computer-related activities to distant locations where the labor costs are much lower, providing the requisite skills are available.

One country that has been able to capitalize on these advantages to become what the *Economist* magazine called the "Back Office to the World" is India.[31] More than half the world's top five hundred companies outsourced information technology (IT) work to India in 2003.[32] Differences in time zones mean that customer service is available round the clock for firms in North America. Projects such as software program development can continue on a twenty-four-hour basis with the Indian programmers picking up where the Americans left off at the end of the day. Or night shifts can be arranged to coincide with the working day in various zones of the United States. Salaries are a fraction of what they would be in the United States so that, by shifting business and IT services to India, costs are typically reduced by 20 to 40 percent, according to one estimate.[33] Then there is India's unique advantage of an enormous pool of English-speaking graduates of IT and computer science programs. Approximately 250,000 students at over one thousand colleges enter computer science programs each year in India. Many of these institutions are high quality and very selective. The seven campuses of the Indian Institute of Technology admit only 2 percent of their applicants each year, the Indian Institute of Science only 0.3 percent.[34]

Although Ireland and India have been the largest exporters of business services at the beginning of the twenty-first century, it is India that has been the focus of media attention and political controversy. The issues in this controversy are at the heart of the debate over economic globalization. On the negative side the major concern is the impact on employment, the jobs lost in one country when business functions are shifted to another. The issue has become such a heated and emotional one in the United States that the Democratic candidate for president in 2004 accused CEOs who send jobs abroad of being "Benedict Arnolds," that is, traitors. On the positive side, thousands of young college graduates in India now have promising futures when they might otherwise have remained unemployed or underemployed. IT and business service exports have increased from seven billion dollars in 2000 to eleven billion dollars, fueling record economic growth for the country and assuring India a niche in the global economy.[35]

Economic Globalization: The Debate

Thus far the emphasis has been on the dramatic changes that have been occurring in the world economy and on some of the ways in which ICTs have facilitated this transformation. It is important now, in summarizing these changes, to consider some of the issues typically raised in discussions of economic globalization, including a more explicit assessment of the role that ICTs have played. Is economic globalization an inevitable consequence of the globalizing technologies? Has the extent of economic globalization been exaggerated, as Robert Gilpin claims in his textbook on the global political economy?[36] What is the impact of economic globalization on the distribution of the world's wealth?

ICTs and Economic Globalization

Information technology is based on two distinct technologies: communication technologies that are concerned with the transmission of information and computer technologies that are concerned with the processing of information. It is this convergence, along with the transition to digital systems, that has made such a profound impact on the way that business is conducted today.[37] But as the discussion of changes in trade, production, and finance clearly indicates, the information revolution is a necessary but not a sufficient condition for economic globalization.

ICT advances, along with those in transportation, have reduced the constraints that time and space historically imposed on the conduct of international commerce. By increasing the ease and speed of transactions and decreasing the cost, these technologies have led to an explosion of trade, investment, and finance. A global communication infrastructure has increased the flexibility of firms to produce where and how they deem it is most efficient. ICTs make it much easier and more feasible to produce offshore and to disperse aspects of the production process to suppliers in different locations, either MNC affiliates or independent firms under subcontract, when these strategies provide a competitive advantage. Transnational collaborations of all kinds among firms have proliferated, creating networks of multiple relationships. The internationalization of production is changing patterns of trade, shifting more manufacturing to the developing countries.

Computer technologies also facilitate the internationalization of production. Computer-controlled technologies standardize the manufacture of components. By increasing accuracy and consistency across different suppliers and lowering the skill levels required, there is more flexibility in the choice of location for the supplier. Another kind of flexibility provided by electronically controlled technology is the capacity to tailor production to local requirements. So a basic model can be readily manipulated to supply an international market. These technologies also speed up the production process. In the garment industry, for example, computer-controlled cutting reduces the time to cut a suit from one hour to four minutes.[38]

ICTs have also helped to transform the last link in the production chain—retailing—the step that gets the product to the consumer. There are two ways in which a retailer becomes transnational.[39] One is by selling directly to customers in several countries by expanding its physical facilities abroad or selling to them over the Internet. The other is by sourcing products from different parts of the world. The case of Wal-Mart illustrates what many scholars see as a shift in the bargaining power from the manufacturers to the retailers, from a supplier-driven to a buyer-driven economy. In the past, it was the manufacturers who decided what to produce and then tried to get retailers to buy and sell the product. In the last ten or fifteen years the big retailers, the buyers, have used their control over information about what is being sold, plus their enormous buying power, to gain control over the supply chain, to tell the manufacturers what to produce. Gary Gereffi even asserts that "global retailers have become the most powerful companies in the global economy "because they have the ability to shape global supply chains, global sourcing networks, and make decisions about where products are made around the world, at what price and how fast things have moved."[40] Paradoxically, although new information technologies have helped to produce retail giants like Wal-Mart, the Internet also provides a new platform for small and specialized companies to sell directly to customers across the globe.

ICTs have played a vital role in the internationalization of the service sector in general, which includes transportation, telecommunications, advertising, insurance, travel, and tourism, as well as financial, business, and technical services. As these and other services are essential to the growth of international trade and production, flows of cross-border activity in this exceedingly diverse sector have accelerated at about the same rates as trade. ICTs not only increase the ease and speed of conducting and managing these activities, but they also have created new platforms for conducting them and new growth areas in this sector. Information technology services is one booming new growth area that would not exist at all without the global network of fiber-optic cables, communication satellites, and Internet-connected computers. Financial services have been transformed by technologies that transfer money and diffuse financial information electronically, almost instantaneously, across borders. Electronic global trading networks are forming global capital markets, especially in the trading of currencies. Electronic trading systems give investors direct access to a wide selection of markets.

One more notable contribution of ICTs to economic globalization is in providing new channels for global advertising and marketing. The previous chapter discussed the proliferation of cable and satellite television channels with their transnational reach. Because the vast majority of channels are now financed at least in some degree with paid advertising, the opportunities for transnational producers to market their branded products are endless. The existence of "niche" media for particular interest or ethnic groups even facilitates targeting a more susceptible audience. The Internet also has become an important medium for advertising.

In sum, new information technologies and expanding communication infrastructures are a driving force behind globalization in the economic as well as other spheres of human activity. They have facilitated the internationalization of production, massive increases in trade and financial transactions, and major changes in the world economy. But they are not the only force, and these changes were not inevitable. The globalizing technologies possessed properties that increased the physical capacity for transnational economic activities of all kinds and even provided the basis for new ways of interacting in the economic realm and new ways of conducting commerce. But both the extent of globalization and the form it has taken are the product of a conjuncture of technological, political, economic, and social forces interacting with and reinforcing each other.[41]

Firms, recognizing opportunities in the new technologies, pressured governments to liberalize and deregulate their economies, reducing barriers to trade, investment, and the flow of money across their borders. Meanwhile, an ideological shift was taking place in the 1980s in two major economies, the United States and the UK, led by President Ronald Reagan and Prime Minister Margaret Thatcher, respectively, who were convinced of the benefits of these changes. Other governments in Western Europe, and subsequently in other regions, were either persuaded of the logic of liberalization or pressured to move in that direction by their own domestic firms or by external economic and political pressures.

The governments of many developing countries shifted from inward-oriented, state-dominated development strategies to more outward, market-oriented strategies, opening up their economies to foreign trade and investment. They were persuaded to make this major change either by the lack of better results from the former strategies or by the conditions imposed on them by international financial institutions to liberalize their economies—or, most often, by a combination of the two. The spectacular growth rates that four East Asian economies, Hong Kong, Singapore, Taiwan, and South Korea, achieved from export-oriented strategies also convinced some governments that greater participation in the world economy could bring benefits.

The revolution in telecommunications and information technologies made it possible to move money across borders quickly and easily. Pressures from banks and other financial institutions that wanted to operate in a less restrictive environment encouraged governments to move toward removing controls on these flows. Following the precedent set by the United States and the UK in the 1980s, governments began to deregulate their domestic financial institutions and open them up to foreign participation. Once national controls were loosened, the flows accelerated and global markets emerged. It was the combination of globalizing technologies, market pressures, and government policies that spurred the dramatic increase in transborder financial flows and networks.

Political change at the international level also contributed to economic globalization. The disintegration of the Soviet Union and the Soviet economic bloc, followed by the transition of the successor states and former bloc members in Eastern Europe to capitalist economies, brought another group of new actors into the world economy just when the trend toward liberalization was becoming widespread. These political changes widened the scope of the international trading system. Freer trade and more actors in the trading system also increased competition at both the international and the domestic levels. The search for competitive advantage led to much corporate restructuring, including a tendency to parcel out different parts of the production process to different suppliers, based on the gains in efficiency that they could provide. This trend toward disaggregation of the production process created complex networks of transnational production that link economies more closely together.

Even individuals have influenced current trends in the global economy. In democratic systems, voters brought into office leaders who espoused less government regulation and helped to form the political climate that moved governments in the direction of liberalization. And individual consumers, voting with their feet in their search of the lowest possible prices, have helped to propel the trend toward global outsourcing.

Is It Really a Global Economy?

How and to what extent is economic globalization actually occurring? David Held et al. have provided a framework for assessing globalization in a historical context that focuses on four dimensions: the extensiveness of networks of relations (extensity), the intensity of flows (levels of activity within those networks), the velocity of interchanges, and the degree of impact.[42] There is little debate regarding the third dimension, the velocity interchanges. Satellites, fiber-optic cables, and Internet-connected computers transmit data, messages, images, songs, and anything that can be digitized at speeds that are unique in human history. The other three dimensions require further consideration.

This chapter thus far has indicated a high level of "extensity" with the involvement of an unprecedented number of states and firms in global trade and production networks. Although the nature and extent of participation in international economic activities varies significantly, there are few countries today that are not involved in and affected by global economic networks. The international trading system encompasses almost every state in the world today. Of the 191 members of the United Nations, 148 are members of the World Trade Organization, committed to expanding trade.

The number of states that are recipients of substantial (ten billion dollars or more) foreign direct investment (FDI) increased from seventeen in 1985 to fifty-one in 2000. Although the bulk of FDI comes from the advanced industrial economies, FDI from developing countries is growing and becoming more important, according to the United Nations Conference on Trade and Development (UNCTAD). By 2000, more than one-third of FDI in developing countries originated in other developing countries. The numbers of MNCs, which are the primary vehicles for FDI, continue to increase and expand their reach to almost all countries in some degree. In 2005 over sixty thousand parent MNCs were spread across the globe in over nine hundred thousand foreign affiliates. Ten years earlier there were forty thousand parent companies and 250,000 foreign affiliates.[43] The shift among MNCs toward more complex organizational and management models has decentralized and "transnationalized" the production process, dispersing various aspects of the process across countries. The result is the emergence of complex global production and distribution networks involving a diversity of firms and countries—small and medium enterprises, as well as MNCs, and developing as well as developed countries.

The "intensity" of flows through these networks is indicated by the exponential growth in the volume of activity. Trade grew twice as fast as the global economy in the 1990s, with an average annual 6 percent increase in both merchandise exports and trade in commercial services, compared to 2.5 percent increase in the world GDP. The rate of growth in trade slowed at the turn of the century but in 2004 increased 9 percent over the previous year, compared to a 4 percent increase in world production.[44] The internationalization and decentralization of production, with different components of the process in different locations, intensifies trading relations among the firms and countries providing inputs. Other than the spectacular increase in the numbers of MNCs and affiliates, noted above, the activity of MNCs is difficult to measure. Sales of foreign affiliates as a percentage of world GDP provide some indication of increased levels of intensity in international production. These sales have risen from 10 to 15 percent of world GDP in the 1970s to about 25 percent in the latter part of the 1990s.[45]

With the growth of trade, MNCs, and production and distribution networks, private financial flows also increased in volume and scope, both extensity and intensity, to support these activities. The widespread deregulation of financial markets in the 1980s, combined with the electronic revolution in the 1990s, gave an enormous boost to all kinds of cross-border financial activities, which began to take on a life of their own, particularly foreign exchange transactions. Private international financial flows and foreign currency transactions have been outpacing the value of trade by increasing amounts, and they have now reached unprecedented levels.[46]

The contemporary world of finance also involves a large part of the world today in one way or another. The expansion of foreign direct investment to more states has been noted above. New channels of financial activity opened up in the early 1970s as petrodollar surpluses from the Organization of the Petroleum Exporting Countries' (OPEC) quadrupling of oil prices were deposited in Western banks, which searched the developing world for new borrowers. Rapidly developing economies and the transition economies of Eastern Europe were incorporated into the international financial system in the 1990s when short-term investments (stocks, bonds, and investment funds) flooded in following the deregulation of their financial markets. Further expanding the extensity of the system, over one hundred countries are parties to an interim General Agreement on Trade in Services, which involves a commitment to work toward further liberalization of trade in services, including financial services. Financial activities are strongly concentrated in a few key metropolitan centers, but networks flow from these centers to connect other major cities and much of the rest of the world.

The analysis of contemporary economic change in this chapter suggests that the impact is far reaching and multidimensional. From a systemic perspective, the growing intensity, extensity, and velocity of worldwide economic interactions and networks, combined with changes in the organization of those activities, have produced a level of worldwide economic interconnectedness that is unique to the current era.[47] Global markets and global production networks are emerging. The volume and scope of cross-border financial flows are such that national financial systems are becoming increasingly "enmeshed."[48]

Evidence presented thus far of changes in trade, production, and finance suggests that economic globalization is occurring as a *process*, as "an evolving transformation or qualitative shift in the organization of the world economy."[49]

Viewed in this manner it is more accurate to think in terms of a *globalizing* world economy rather than imply that a single, integrated *globalized* economy currently exists. Further, from the discussion of the role of ICTs in this process, it is clear that the nature and extent of globalization thus far must be attributed to the conjunction of political, economic, and social, as well as technological, forces. The trajectory of this process will also be shaped by these forces inter-acting with each other; it will not necessarily be in the direction of more glob-alization.

Why such cautious terminology? Although cross-border exchanges have reached historic proportions, and the globalizing technologies that facilitate them know no boundaries, it is not a borderless world. The impact of these technologies on the state-based international systems is discussed in chapter 6. But because economic globalization is often considered to be eroding na-tional sovereignty and undermining the power of the state, the issue is briefly considered here.

Increased interconnectedness of economies arguably weakens the ability of states, even the most powerful ones, to manage their economies. Interna-tional commitments to free trade preclude policies to protect industries threatened by foreign competition. Financial enmeshment limits the flexi-bility that governments can use to steer their economies to avoid recession or inflation. The rapid mobility of capital increases vulnerability, unpre-dictability, and risk for both national economies and the global financial sys-tem. The enormous wealth and transnational flexibility of MNCs pursuing global strategies are in many respects beyond the control of national govern-ments.

But it was the leaders of governments who reduced tariffs, removed capi-tal controls, and encouraged foreign investment. There remains a broad area for national legislation to shape the impact of the globalizing economy. Gov-ernments have established international institutions with rules and proce-dures that also affect the conduct of international economic activities. Eco-nomic globalization is not necessarily diminishing state power, according to David Held et al.,[50] but it is "transforming the conditions under which state power is exercised" in the sense that it is changing the cost-benefit calculus of many policy choices that they must make.

ICTs, Globalization, and the Distribution of Wealth

The most contentious element of the globalization debate concerns the dis-tributional effects, that is, the impact of economic globalization processes on the distribution of the world's wealth. ICTs have both indirect and direct dis-

tributional effects. Indirectly, they provide the infrastructure that has facilitated the economic changes discussed in this chapter. Directly, access to
them, or the lack thereof, affects the interaction capacity, employment, and
income of states and individuals. Differential access to ICTs both among and
within countries has been the focus of much attention among scholars and
policy makers under the rubric of "digital divide." The issue under debate in
both instances is whether the changes have expanded economic opportunity
or increased inequality and marginalization.

Assessing the distributional effects of economic globalization is problematic because they are highly asymmetrical and uneven. There is great variation in the degree of participation among states, and the benefits, costs, and
vulnerabilities are distributed unevenly among states, firms, and individuals.
On the one hand, globalization processes have created a new "geo-economy,"
in which the North-South divide, the center-periphery categories, and the
historical patterns of specialization are no longer meaningful descriptions of
the world economy. A new international division of labor is evolving in
which a significant shift is occurring in the location of manufacturing from
the developed to the developing countries.[51]

A number of newly industrialized countries are emerging as major players
in the global economy, especially as exporters of manufactures. The four
"tigers," which experienced explosive growth in the 1970s and 1980s, South
Korea, Taiwan, Singapore, and Hong Kong, now have incomes equivalent to
those of many advanced industrialized countries. Their share of the global
GDP almost doubled between 1976 and 1995.[52] As they move up the ladder
of greater technological sophistication and higher wages, some production is
relocated to countries with lower wages. In the 1990s a second tier of newly
industrializing countries in Asia is becoming important as manufacturing
centers. China, once a poor, closed, isolated country, has become the world's
sixth largest economy and in 2004 was the third largest exporter and im-
porter in world merchandise trade.[53] India, another poor country with a
highly protected economy, is experiencing high growth rates following a shift
to a more open economy and is becoming a major player in IT and service
exports.

Although production is now dispersed to an unprecedented number of developing as well as developed countries, trade and foreign investment remain
highly concentrated. Developing countries as a whole increased their share
of the world's global exports in manufactured products from 10 percent in
1980 to 27 percent in 2004.[54] But that means that nearly three-fourths of this
trade was still concentrated in the advanced developed countries representing only 15 percent of world population. Less than one-third of the total

world foreign direct investment goes to developing countries. Although foreign direct investment from developing countries has increased and the
number of indigenous MNCs has doubled, 90 percent of the top one hundred
MNCs are headquartered in the European Union, Japan, or the United
States.[55]

Not only is the growth of transnational economic activity concentrated in
developed countries, but also the gains that have been made in the developing world have been concentrated in a very few states. Seven states account
for more than 70 percent of low-technology exports and 80 percent of high-
technology exports from developing countries. And 70 percent of all foreign
direct investment in developing countries is concentrated in only ten.[56]
These are the states that have experienced accelerated economic growth as
they became integrated in the world economy.

Meanwhile many other countries have experienced economic stagnation
or even decline during the globalization era. Annual GDP per capita growth
rates between 1990 and 2003 were negative for forty-one countries, and 1
percent or less for another twenty-eight countries. The United Nations Development Programme (UNDP) estimates that, on average, growth rates of
1 to 2 percent a year are necessary to halve the poverty rate over a twenty-
five-year period. At the global level the percentage of people living on less
that one dollar a day has declined from 40 percent in 1981 to 20 percent in
2001, a dramatic decline. This reduction in poverty is largely attributable to
the decline in East Asia from 57 percent to 14 percent. The rate has actually
increased for sub-Saharan Africa, from 41 to 46 percent with average incomes lower than in 1990, and ten countries in Latin America have experienced a sustained period of economic stagnation.[57]

Lack of state capacity to respond to opportunities is obviously one reason
for the asymmetrical effects of globalization processes. Inadequate transportation and communication infrastructure, for example, adds costs to producers and reduces their potential profit from export. Such deficiencies also
make producers unlikely candidates as suppliers in a global production chain.
More generally, the lack of industrial capabilities limits a state to exports involving simple assembly or cheap, unskilled labor.

External constraints also limit the ability of a state to secure gains from
globalization processes. These include structural features of the global economy, practices of individual states, and rules of international organizations
such as the WTO. The most prominent feature of globalization is the concentration of significant portions of the world's wealth and technology in giant MNCs. A list of the top one hundred economic entities in the world,
which compares the gross national product (GNP) of states with the annual

revenues of MNCs, indicates that more than half are MNCs. Only twenty countries are wealthier than the top five MNCs.[58] Combining wealth and technology with a high degree of flexibility and mobility, these transnational entities possess bargaining power that is a formidable match for governments and producers, especially small-scale producers in developing countries.

The internationalization of production, with the development of global sourcing and supply systems, provides new opportunities for small- and medium-sized firms to become suppliers in global production chains. But this participation comes on the terms of the MNCs, which typically specify low costs, quality standards, and quick deliveries. The increasing market power of MNCs poses particular problems for agricultural producers, especially small-holder farmers in poor countries. A few giant supermarkets have become essentially gatekeepers to developed country markets for agricultural produce. The top thirty chains account for about one-third of global grocery sales. One-third of grocery sales in the United States come from Wal-Mart; in the UK five supermarkets account for 70 percent of grocery sales. In Latin America the share of food sales in supermarkets has tripled since the late 1980s from 20 percent to 60 percent.[59] The fact that supermarkets draw from global supply networks makes it relatively easy for them to switch suppliers, an advantage that further augments their bargaining power. This concentration of buying power gives the large supermarket chains enormous capacity to influence prices, product standard requirements, and delivery times, putting a tight squeeze on producers and their gains. Because smallholder farmers generally lack the capabilities to meet these requirements, they are becoming increasingly marginalized or excluded altogether in favor of larger farms, especially those owned or leased by major export companies.

Another example of a structural change in the global economy that affects most significantly some of the poorest countries in the world is the long-term decline in the prices of commodities, especially agricultural products. More than fifty developing countries are dependent upon agriculture for at least one-quarter of their export revenues. Between 1997 and 2001 the combined price index for all commodities fell by 53 percent in real terms. In simple terms this decline means that African exporters had to double the volume of their exports in order to maintain their export revenue.[60] Many agricultural exporters face additional obstacles in the subsidies that the European Union, the United States, and other countries provide their producers in order to make them more competitive in the world market with lower prices.

Tariff policies can also reduce gains from trade. Imports from low-income to high-income countries tend to be on average higher than those applied among high-income countries. Developing countries account for only one-third of developed country imports but two-thirds of their revenues from tariffs.[61] The interests of wealthier states have tended to dominate the agenda of the WTO and other international financial institutions with the result that the needs of developing countries have not been adequately addressed, and some rules that have been established put them at a disadvantage. For example, WTO rules now prohibit certain government policies that were fundamental to the industrial development of East Asia, such as local content and technology transfer requirements for foreign investments.

It is not surprising that the distributive effects of economic globalization have been the focus of vigorous debate, as they are mixed, uneven, and dynamic. The evolving global structure provides both opportunities and constraints. It "reflects existing patterns of inequality and hierarchy while also generating new patterns of inclusion and exclusion, new winners and losers."[62] Clearly, although some developing countries are moving out of the periphery and are becoming significant actors in the global economy, there are many more that remain marginalized, unable to compete in a more competitive world economy. The competition has broadened, but many are still out of the competition altogether. Greater enmeshment of economies provides new opportunities for involvement but also heightened vulnerability from increased levels of trade dependence and the volatility of global financial markets.

New models of production provide opportunities for small and medium enterprises (SMEs)—including those locally based in developing countries—to participate in the global economy as links in a supply chain. The downside is that they must operate on the terms of the giant MNCs. In the larger picture, the highly fragmented nature of the production process has a negative impact on accountability. Who is responsible for sweatshop conditions—the subcontractor employer, the local government, or the MNC?

The Internet provides opportunities for SMEs with modest means and infrastructure to enter the global marketplace directly by marketing and selling their products on the World Wide Web. Although payment across national boundaries still poses obstacles because most of the world's population do not possess a credit card, and arranging for international payments is a complication for SMEs, the number and variety of small businesses with a presence on the Web is remarkable and growing rapidly. Nevertheless, the giant MNCs dominate global economic activity. And because of their wealth, size, and transnationality, they are in a particularly advantageous position to use all the mass media to help create and dominate global markets.

In sum, the new information and communication technologies affect the distribution of the world's wealth indirectly by providing the infrastructure that makes economic globalization possible and by shaping economic change in some very specific but contradictory ways. But more directly, access to ICTs, and the lack thereof, has important distributive effects, which have been the subject of great controversy. The Internet in particular has been the object of hyperbolic predictions. Optimists enthusiastically claim that the Internet has the capacity to bring knowledge and prosperity to isolated and marginalized individuals and nations. They see the digital revolution as a historic opportunity for developing countries to "take a quantum leap forward," to develop their productive capacities and become integrated into the global economy.[63] Pessimists fear that the individuals, groups, and nations that are already the most privileged will be the ones who will benefit from the Internet, leaving the others to fall even farther behind. The concept of the digital divide emerged to refer to the gap between those who have access to computers and the Internet and those who do not. The concept gradually broadened to cover differential access to ICTs generally, both within and among countries. Concern about this gap and the need to "bridge" it grew as ICTs expanded their reach and the Internet became a global phenomenon.

The Digital Divide
The 1990s were a time of innovation and dynamism in information and communication technologies. Following the invention of the World Wide Web and the launching of the first graphical Web browser, the number of users of the Internet doubled approximately every year. Software applications proliferated, and new uses of the Internet were discovered. Initially, the locus of this activity was concentrated in the United States. The Internet spread rapidly, and by the end of the decade over two hundred countries were directly connected in at least some minimal way.[64]

But the diffusion of the Internet, and ICTs more generally, has been highly uneven. Connectivity and access are minimal for the majority of countries, and the global reach of the Internet continues to be out of reach for the vast majority of the world's population. Table 5.1 demonstrates tremendous disparities in the use of the Internet among the various regions and, even more significant, the penetration levels of the Internet within each region. Only 3.6 percent of the population in Africa uses the Internet and 10 percent in the Middle East, in contrast to more than two-thirds of the North American population (69 percent). Usage of the Internet has become more widely distributed across three regions. As table 5.1 indicates, users in North America

Table 5.1.   Worldwide Internet Use, 2007

Region	Internet Usage	Percentage of Total Worldwide Users	Penetration as a Percentage of Population
Africa	33,421,800	2.9	3.6
Asia	409,421,115	36.0	11.0
Europe	319,092,225	28.2	39.4
Middle East	19,424,700	1.7	10.0
North America	230,138,282	20.4	69.0
Latin America	102,304,809	9.0	18.4
Oceania	18,756,363	1.7	54.4
World total	1,133,408,294	100.0	17.2

Source: Adapted from Internet World Stats, "Internet Usage Statistics: The Big Picture," at www.internet-worldstats.com/stats.htm (accessed June 30, 2007).

in 2007 represent less than 21 percent of the world's total; even when combined with those in Europe, they represent only half, while 36 percent are in Asia. According to a NUA survey in 1998, 79 percent of the world's users were in North America and Europe, and only 17 percent were located in Asia.[65] Although this change in distribution indicates significant growth in the numbers of Internet users in Asia, they constitute just 11 percent of the population in the region. And, according to table 5.1, only 17 percent of the total world's population is using the Internet, which leaves the vast majority of 83 percent completely out of global communication networks.

The Internet is both a means of instant, cheap, long-distance communication with a potential global reach and a revolutionary breakthrough in the human capacity to store, retrieve, and disseminate information. Access is, therefore, a key to wealth and knowledge. As the uses of the Internet multiplied, and digital technologies became more pervasive, the digital divide gained prominence on the political and public agenda. Countless governmental, intergovernmental, nongovernmental, and private sector projects were aimed at bridging this divide. One effort to create a database of worldwide efforts, by the World Resources Institute, had documented over seven hundred projects by 2003.[66]

Underlying this attention and these efforts was the assumption that access to ICTs opens the doors to wider economic and social development opportunities and has the potential to address problems of poverty and inequality. As expressed in the statement of principles of the World Summit on the Information Society, "the challenge is to harness the potential of information and communication technology" to promote such goals as "the eradication of extreme poverty and hunger; achievement of universal primary education; promotion of gender equality and empowerment of women; reduction of child mortality; improvement of maternal health and combat HIV/AIDS, malaria and other diseases."[67] On the other hand, lack of access consigns vast swaths of the world's population to be marginalized at the periphery of communication networks and the information society. While it is generally recognized that the digital divide is a reflection of other basic social inequalities—in wealth, status, and education—the assumption behind the clarion calls for urgent action is that lack of access to ICTs creates inequalities that exacerbate other inequalities.

These calls have met with some skepticism for a number of reasons. Many have questioned whether digital technologies are the best approach to promote development and to reduce poverty and inequality. Installing and maintaining the physical infrastructure for modern ICTs is extremely expensive. An enormous financial outlay is required to establish even a modest system of networked computers or a system of landlines for telephones. In any case, how can computers operate when electrical power is unavailable or erratic? And how can people who do not speak English, the dominant language on the Web, and might not even be able to read, benefit from the Internet? There is not only the problem of available funds for these investments but also a question of priorities. How justifiable is it to use scarce resources to invest in ICTs where millions of people lack adequate clean water, nutrition, health care, and basic education? Even Bill Gates—one of the world's chief evangelists for computer technology—once asked, "What good is a computer for someone who survives on one dollar per day, whose main concern is the next meal?"[68]

The Great Indian Digital Divide

In no country is the debate between the optimists and the pessimists more relevant than in India, where new centers of information technology are creating wealth and integrating some sectors into the global economy, while millions remain marginalized and deprived of the most basic human needs. No developing country has benefited more from the digital revolution than India, and in no country is the digital divide wider or deeper domestically. Information technology has created a new and dynamic economic sector, generating significant employment and wealth. India's IT software and services export revenues amounted to eighteen billion dollars in the fiscal year 2005–2006, and they are growing rapidly.[69] Indian companies have become world leaders of software development and services. A new cadre of high-technology entrepreneurs has emerged. The owner of one Indian IT company, Wipro Limited, was on *Forbes* magazine's year 2000 list of the fifty richest people in the world. According to two scholars of India's communication revolution, the software industries have produced more millionaires in India in the last five years than all other industries put together over the last fifty years. The services of India's highly skilled, English-speaking software professionals are sought after by major global corporations, and many have become founders or managers of IT companies in the United States.

On the other side of the digital divide are the 39 percent of the population who cannot read or write, the 80 percent who survive on less than two dollars per day, and those who live in the thousands of villages that do not have telephone connections. Will India's progress toward bridging the global digital divide widen the gap between the rich and the poor within the country? The pessimistic view is compelling. The new wealth is unlikely to trickle down to the poor in the villages and slums. As IT industries become more market oriented, there will be little to attract investment in telecommunications infrastructure and other investments to bring connectivity to these areas. To make India's IT competitive in the global economy the government must give a high priority to this sector. Government support for IT education and industry drains resources that are desperately needed for health and primary education for the poor.

Despite the force of these skeptical arguments, optimists have insisted that the new information and communication technologies, especially the Internet, have the potential not only to spur growth in India's economy as a whole but also to bring new opportunities to those who are mired in poverty and despair. The head of the Indian IT giant Wipro conveyed some of this spirit in an interview with the BBC: "Information technology has transformed our international image from being a land of elephants and snake charmers to a land of competent engineers. In five years, it could transform the country."[70] In the euphoria of the technology boom in the latter 1990s, the idea of wiring urban slums and remote villages, of "linking isolated rural pockets to the borderless world of knowledge," captured the imagination of journalists, scholars, nongovernmental organizations, digital pioneers, and the corporate sector.[71] As one of the world's poorest countries and simultaneously an emerging global IT power, India became a testing ground for many projects using ICTs for development, especially so-called grassroots or rural development projects. By 2002, there were at least fifty such projects, many implemented as pilot programs trying out a variety of different approaches. Although little comparative research has been conducted on all these scattered projects, the few field studies and observations that are available provide useful insights into the problems and possibilities of ICTs for development.

The Gyandoot project, a path-breaking experiment to use ICT to improve the delivery of government services and provide other useful information to a rural community, is illuminating. Its entrepreneurial business approach and low-cost wireless technology garnered praise as a model of economic sustainability. The project even won the Stockholm Challenge Award for the year 2000, out of over six hundred competing projects aimed at improving living conditions and increasing economic growth. This telecenter network of twenty-one villages in rural Madhya Pradesh was launched in 2000 by the Indian Administrative Service in consultation with the local governments (panchayats). The villages paid for the equipment and space for the kiosks, which were operated by local, educated, unemployed youth who were trained for that purpose. Small fees were charged for information on agricultural product prices, health, education, employment, and even matrimonial possibilities. But the emphasis was on connecting villagers with local government as a way of cutting out layers of bureaucracy, increasing transparency, and reducing corruption. Certain government forms, certificates, and records were available from the kiosk for electronic transaction. Arrangements were made for direct communication with the district officer, especially for lodging complaints.

Two years after Gyandoot was launched, the Indian Institute of Management in Ahmedabad conducted an extensive field evaluation along with recommendations. Its overall conclusion was that, "in achieving its intended objects, [however], Gyandoot cannot be considered a success."[72] The main conclusion was that the usage, which was "far below acceptable levels," did not justify the cost. The report identified the main reasons for lack of usage as lack of knowledge about the services provided, perceived lack of need for those services, or dissatisfaction with them. The main reason for dissatisfaction with the electronically delivered government services was that they did not significantly improve the overall quality of service. Although there was enthusiasm for the idea of sending complaints to the district administration, for example, and the electronic communication sped up responses, the solutions to the problems were no more forthcoming. Similarly, certain requirements in the use of government forms ensured that layers of bureaucracy and opportunities for corruption remained.

The two groups that appeared to derive the most benefits from Gyandoot were the young operators of the kiosks, who obtained computer training and a job, and large-scale, educated farmers, who benefited from the price and general agricultural information. The recommendations of the study focused on the need for strengthening the "backend processing" of the various government departments, meaning that the office personnel needed to be more capable and more committed to providing the services. Further, the service delivery should be centered at the kiosk, thus avoiding necessary trips and signatures. Finally, much more attention should be given to spreading the word, especially to the poorest segments, regarding the range of services.

Another project that provides useful insights was launched in 1998 by one of India's best known scientists, M. S. Swaminathan, who played a key role in the introduction of high-yielding wheat varieties in India in the 1960s.[73] This was one of the earliest and most well-publicized efforts to provide information and services to rural areas, and this one continues to expand. The project established eight and eventually twelve "village knowledge centers," linking them to each other and to wider information networks through a combination of wired and wireless technologies with solar panels for electricity. Surveys were conducted prior to the organization of the centers in order to assess the kinds of information and services that would be useful in the different villages. The focus was on creating databases on topics such as government services, agriculture, health, and education that is adapted to the needs of the specific locality. Current information such as crop prices, job listings, and ocean wave reports (for fishermen) is downloaded from the Internet by the computer operators who have been trained at the center. In addition, the intranet provides practical local information, and it has become the basis for a newsletter circulating in the villages in the project. Women volunteers are trained to manage the centers. The project is financed by the M. S. Swaminathan Research Foundation, the local government, and the International Development Research Center of Canada.

The *Economist* magazine, noting the paucity of data and even good methodologies for collecting and evaluating the results, visited some of the villages in this project and asked the residents what they thought about their knowledge center—to get a "view from the ground."[74] Although this was not a scientific opinion survey, the impressions of these skeptical observers contribute to an understanding of the potential and limits of ICT for development projects. The views of the villagers were quite mixed. Many of the older, illiterate, and lower caste villagers, important target groups of the project, seemed to be unaware of the knowledge center. Young people were the most frequent users; many of them were enthusiastic about the opportunities to learn computer skills and to obtain information about jobs. Relatively well-off farmers also benefited from the agricultural and veterinary information. The *Economist*'s conclusion was that "rural ICTs appear particularly useful to the literate, to the wealthier and to the younger—those, in other words who sit at the top of the socio-economic hierarchy."

So what lessons can be drawn from the initiatives that have been taken to extend the benefits of ICTs and Internet connectivity, in particular to the rural poor in India? Kenneth Keniston, Andrew Mellon Professor of Human

Development at the Massachusetts Institute of Technology and director of the MIT program in India, provides a set of "lessons from India" in his book *IT Experience in India: Bridging the Digital Divide*, which is based on his field research on "grassroots ICT projects" in India.[75]

Keniston and his group of experts in India from different disciplines were concerned with the effects on the social structure as well as the economic well-being of the whole community. Another research project from a very different source, the World Economic Forum, reached some of the same conclusions. The World Economic Forum is an organization of the world's wealthiest corporations, which encourages private-public sector partnerships to "improve the state of the world." Under the motto "entrepreneurship in the global public interest," it implements initiatives focusing on various global issues. At its annual meeting in 2004 it launched the "IT Access for Everyone (ITAFE) initiative," which evolved into an investigation of fifty major ICT projects around the globe with a view to identifying conditions of success (in terms of the objectives of each project).[76] Two dozen of these were selected for a more in-depth analysis. This is one of a few efforts to draw "key lessons" from a cross-national database, albeit from a corporate perspective.

The lesson considered most important in both studies was what ITAFE called the necessity for "rigorous, structured, grass roots research of end-users needs." The Swaminathan Foundation spent a great deal of time in advance ascertaining local needs and how ICTs might meet these needs before it began to develop databases with appropriate information. Local content in the local language is essential for this purpose. Second, in order to develop and maintain networks of useful information, close relationships with relevant institutions and agencies are necessary. For example, an ICT project would benefit from a special relationship with a technological institute for developing appropriate software applications and for ongoing technical support; with a hospital as a source of health information and even medical diagnostics; and with an agricultural extension service for agricultural information. Strong relationships with various levels of government are also beneficial, but, according to the ITAFE study, the most successful projects have built business models that did not rely solely on ongoing governmental support. In fact, reliance on any other single source is also risky, whether it is a nongovernmental organization, a foundation, or a private sector venture. Third, both studies, from very different perspectives, emphasize the importance of long-term realistic planning for funding that will lead eventually to "economic sustainability." This objective involves not only a balance of financial support but also some means of generating income. Various technological innovations from the IT sector in India have helped to reduce costs and to compensate for infrastructure deficiencies. For example, the Indian Institute of Technology in Chennai has pioneered the development of Wireless in Local Loop (WLL) technology, which significantly reduces the cost of expanding telephone services in rural areas and makes possible information systems where there is no electricity supply and cable is not practical.

Fourth, ICTs should be considered just one element of a larger development strategy that considers a broad array of technologies, old and new. Sometimes cheaper, older technologies like radio or television can communicate information as well but with less cost, so information technologies should be used only when they are the most effective means of meeting the needs of a community. A few mobile telephones in a village would be cheaper than establishing and maintaining an information center, and the economic impact could be greater. Dramatic stories and photographs abound in the media of poor women in Bangladesh villages and the jungles of the Congo not only using cell phones but also generating income by renting out usage on them. The lesson here is the critical importance of applying cost-effective criteria to all aspects of an ICT project proposal and its implementation.

The final lesson is that special planning and effort is necessary for ICT projects to reach and benefit the less privileged segments of a community, the "bottom of the pyramid producers and consumers," in the words of the ITAFE report. This imperative is echoed by yet another field researcher of rural technology projects in India, Aditya Dev Sood, who warns that every aspect of the design and implementation of rural ICT projects must be aimed at enabling and including the rural non-elite in order to prevent the projects from becoming "exclusivist elitist information centers," benefiting only the "semi-elite landowning groups."[77]

The jury is still out on these experiments in India. The evidence suggests that ICTs can meet needs and improve the lives of some of the poorest and most isolated people in the world—but only if the projects are integrated into larger development programs and both the design and implementation incorporate lessons suggested by previous efforts and evaluations of those efforts. There are also positive consequences of "wiring a village," beyond the specific kinds of information that are provided and the number of people who use them. One significant potential impact is an improvement in the quality of education. Students have access to a virtual library that provides far greater resources than would be available to a rural school. (This is assuming that the local language condition is met.) Computer resources can help teachers develop and update their curriculum. But most important, a connection to the world beyond the village can make the village a more acceptable place for good teachers, who otherwise might seek to escape its isolation.

ICTs and Development

Is the digital divide bridgeable? According to one theory of technological diffusion, the gap will never close because those with greater material resources and the knowledge to use new technologies will always stay ahead, with late adopters lagging and nonadopters marginalized.[78] This model may be particularly applicable to digital technologies, which are more difficult to use than, for example, radio and television, and they change rapidly, requiring a continuous flow of additional expenditures and new learning to keep up. It has even been argued that "efforts to bridge the digital divide will have the effect of locking developing countries into a new form of dependency on the West," trapping them in an increasing complexity of hardware and software that is "designed by developed country entities for developed country conditions."[79] This argument reflects a view that digital technologies are simply one more instrument for the powerful to maintain control over the powerless.

The debate between the optimists and the pessimists regarding ICTs for development helps to define the range of possible effects of these technologies—the possibilities and the limitations—and thereby provides a sounder basis for policy choices.

Although the initial euphoria over the capacity of ICTs to improve the fate of nations and the lives of individuals everywhere has subsided, the idea of universal access to ICTs still underlies many international initiatives, such as the World Economic Forum's "IT Access for Everyone" initiative. The pessimists' warnings continue to be an essential guard against unrealistic expectations, as well as against unanticipated negative consequences.

Optimists point to new economic and professional opportunities for developing countries, their firms, and their citizens when they are connected to global communication and information systems. Although some people obviously benefit more than others, a larger segment of the population will be better off than before, at least in some respects. One of the most important benefits is access to a far broader and more current knowledge base. University libraries tend to have sparse and outdated collections of books and few journal subscriptions, and there are few public libraries. It is now technically feasible for university libraries in developing countries to have immediate access to journals and other valuable research materials. Although the cost of electronic journal subscriptions remains a barrier, special rates could mitigate this problem. And what is freely available on the Internet still represents a larger store of current information than most libraries in many developing countries possess.

The Internet also provides more educational opportunities for more people with the proliferation of distance education programs. The Virtual University of the Monterrey Institute of Technology in Mexico, for example, offers courses on twenty-five or thirty campuses in Mexico and by satellite to every country in Latin America, enrolling thousands of degree and nondegree students each year. The African Virtual University, headquartered in Nairobi, Kenya, works in collaboration with African universities and universities worldwide to provide "world class quality" online degree programs and resources in twenty-seven African countries. Resources include a digital library to help compensate for the scarcity of scientific journals in the region's libraries.[80]

The Internet not only provides access to knowledge, information, and expertise, but it is also a medium of communication. The Internet has great potential to enhance communication and collaboration between scholars in developing countries and their colleagues elsewhere. Previous research has demonstrated how marginalized scholars in the developing countries can be because of the time, cost, and difficulty of communicating with colleagues abroad. By the time a scholar learns about a conference, it might be over; at least the deadline for submitting a proposal is likely to be past. When a scholar does manage to attend a conference, he or she is less likely to be able to follow up on contacts.[81] With the Internet, papers can easily be exchanged, and even collaborations are possible.

For ICTs to advance development objectives, however, access to them must expand beyond academic institutions and business firms. The market-driven spread of cybercafes and their variants (well over 4,200 in the world as of 2007) has extended the benefits of e-mail and access to the Internet to thousands of people who cannot afford their own computer and connectivity.[82] In addition, many governments in developing countries have implemented policies establishing public access centers in rural areas, as discussed above, and elsewhere. The United Nations Conference on Trade and Development, in a recent assessment of the digital divide, found much more significant gains in Internet usage in developing countries than in the number of personal computers. The conclusion was that gains in usage may be attributable to a great extent to policy initiatives such as community telecenters and public access points—good news. But a pessimist might point out the tremendous advantages to having broadband on a home computer rather than sporadic access to a dial-up Internet host in a public place.

Modern information and communication technologies have a global reach, but there is highly unequal access to their benefits. Obviously, levels of income explain much of the variation in ICT diffusion—but not everything. One of the most critical factors influencing the spread of ICTs and their distributional effects is government policy. Government initiatives and financial support help to build networking infrastructure and provide facilities for broad public access. Government policies determine the educational levels of their citizens, from basic literacy to technical training. Governments also establish regulatory structures that determine who can develop, operate, and use the technologies and under what conditions, that is, the role or the market. Market pressures provide powerful incentives for the development and spread of ICTs but primarily to places and people with purchasing power. But it is individuals who decide to buy the products and how they want to use them. The cheaper the products and the easier to use, the more accessible they will be to more people. It is the interaction of all these factors that will shape the impact of ICTs on development.

Conclusion

With their capacity to compress space, time, and transaction costs, new information and communication technologies have facilitated the spectacular growth of transnational economic activities that is transforming the world economy. That transformation is ongoing and without a fixed trajectory. The globalizing processes that are occurring in trade, production, and finance are the product of technological innovation, market forces, political change, and consumer choices—combining and mutually reinforcing each other. The interaction of these forces is shaping the current and future impact of the new technologies and the economic changes they help to bring about. Inherent in these economic changes and globalizing processes are opposing tendencies and contradictory effects.

The information revolution has improved the capacity of firms to organize and manage production at a distance and the flexibility to disperse various aspects of production across different national locations. The internationalization of production, with the development of global sourcing and supply chains, provides new opportunities for small- and medium-sized enterprises and developing countries to become integrated into the global economy. A new worldwide division of labor has evolved with a significant shift in the location of manufacturing from the developed to the developing countries. An unprecedented number of states and firms have become involved in global trade and production networks, and there is a wider spread of competition.

But the intensification of the competition makes it even more difficult for many countries to participate in the global economy, and there are domestic as well as global distributive effects. When production can be shifted relatively easily to a country with lower wages, it puts downward pressure on wages and working conditions. The relative power of labor is further diminished by the

trend toward subcontracting out parts of the production process, a practice that
blurs responsibility for working conditions. Trade and the internationalization
of production both create and destroy jobs.

The impact of new information and communication technologies, and the
economic changes they have facilitated, is mixed, dynamic, and contingent.
The diffusion of these technologies creates new possibilities for states and
their citizens, but unequal access creates new patterns of exclusion and inclusion.[83] The case of India illustrates both realities. A flourishing IT sector
is giving India a niche in the global economy and is expanding professional
and economic opportunities for increasing numbers of the middle class, especially in urban areas. But the vast majority of the population remains un-
touched by the IT revolution in India, and the levels of poverty and illiter-
acy have changed only a little since it began a decade ago. The lessons of
rural ICT for development projects suggest that these technologies, judi-
ciously used as part of larger development strategies, could enhance the well-
being of many who are marginalized, but there are many reasons for skepticism. The debate between the optimists and the pessimists over the
distributional effects of ICTs is part of the larger set of debates over economic
globalization. These debates serve as a reminder that there are a range of possible effects, which choices of individuals, as well as corporations and governments, will determine.

Notes

1. David Held, Anthony McGrew, David Goldblatt, and Jonathan Perraton, eds.,
Global Transformations: Politics, Economics, and Culture (Stanford, Calif.: Stanford
University Press, 1999), 2.

2. Anthony McGrew, "The Logics of Globalization," in *Global Political Economy*,
ed. John Ravenhill (New York: Oxford University Press, 2005), 209.

3. In current dollars. World Trade Organization (WTO), *World Trade Report 2005*
(Geneva: Author, 2005), xxiii; John T. Rourke, *International Politics on the World
Stage*, 10th ed. (New York: McGraw-Hill, 2005), 384.

4. Joseph M. Grieco and G. John Ikenberry, *State Power and World Markets: The
International Political Economy* (New York: W. W. Norton, 2003), 6.

5. Charles Kegley, with Eugene R. Wittkopf, *World Politics: Trends and Transformation*, 10th ed. (Belmont, Calif.: Thomson Wadsworth, 2006), 284–85; Michael
Mazarr, *Global Trends 2005* (London: Palgrave, 1999).

6. Held et al., *Global Transformations*, 176.

7. Held et al., *Global Transformations*, 172.

8. World Trade Organization, "Recent Trends in World Trade," June 11, 2004, at
www.wto.org/english/news_e/pres04pr378_e.htm (accessed July 18, 2005), 1.

9. Peter Dicken, *Global Shift: Transforming the World Economy*, 3rd ed. (New York: Guilford Press, 1998), 42.

10. WTO, *World Trade Report 2005*, 3; Kegley and Wittkopf, *World Politics*, 287.

11. Ronald J. Deibert, "Network Power," in *Global Political Economy*, ed. Richard Stubbs and Geoffrey R. D. Underhill, 2nd ed. (Toronto: Oxford University Press, 2000), 200.

12. An MNC is a company that "produces goods or markets its services in more than one country" (Held et al., *Global Transformations*, 237).

13. Michael Clancy, *Sweating the Swoosh: Nike, the Globalization of Sneakers, and the Question of Sweatshop Labor* (Washington, D.C.: Georgetown University, 2000), 4; Nike home page, at www.nikebiz.com.

14. Information on Wal-Mart taken from a PBS *Frontline* program, "Is Wal-Mart Good for America?" which was based on interviews with both scholars and Wal-Mart executives. Interviews can be found at www.pbs.org/wgbh/pages/frontline/shows/walmart (accessed August 21, 2005).

15. PBS *Frontline*, "Is Wal-Mart Good for America?"

16. Gary Gereffi, "The Organization of Buyer-Driven Global Commodity Chains," in *Commodity Chains and Global Capitalism*, ed. Gary Gereffi and Miguel Korzeniewicz (Westport, Conn.: Praeger, 1993), 25; Held et al., *Global Transformations*, 257.

17. United Nations Conference on Trade and Development (UNCTAD), *World Investment Report 2004: The Shift toward Services* (New York: United Nations, 2004), 19; Held et al., *Global Transformations*, 245.

18. Bank for International Settlements, *International Banking and Financial Market Developments* (Geneva: BIS, 2003); McGrew, "The Logics of Globalization," 213.

19. Bank for International Settlements, *75th Annual Report* (Geneva: BIS, 2005), 80–81. Averages are for the month of April each year.

20. Thomas D. Lairson and David Skidmore, *International Political Economy*, 3rd ed. (Belmont, Calif.: Wadsworth, 2003), 105.

21. Peter Dicken, *Global Shift: Reshaping the Global Economic Map of the 21st Century*, 4th ed. (New York: Guilford Press, 2003), 439.

22. *Economist*, "Survey of Online Finance," May 20, 2000, 5.

23. Dicken, *Global Shift*, 443.

24. Lairson and Skidmore, *International Political Economy*, 109.

25. FOREX.com, home page, at www.forex.com.

26. Dicken, *Global Shift*, 454.

27. Susan Roberts, "Fictitious Capital, Fictitious Spaces: The Geography of Offshore Financial Flows," in *Money, Power, and Space*, ed. Nigel Thrift, Stuart Corbridge, and Ron Martin (Oxford: Blackwell, 1994), 92. Quoted in Dicken, *Global Shift*, 466.

28. Lairson and Skidmore, *International Political Economy*, 112.

29. Randall Germaine, *The International Organization of Credit* (Cambridge, UK: Cambridge University Press, 1997), 164; Held et al., *Global Transformations*, 215, 234.

30. Charles Kindleberger, *Manias, Panics, and Crashes: A History of Financial Crises* (New York: Basic Books, 1988).

31. *Economist*, "Outsourcing to India: Back Office to the World," May 5, 2001, 59.

32. Saritha Rai, "Software Success Has India Worried," *New York Times*, February 3, 2003, C7.

33. UNCTAD, *World Investment Report 2004*, 28.

34. Michael Kanellos, "Offshoring: The Reality behind the Politics," at http://news.zdnet.com/2100-9589_22_5766212.html (accessed July 21, 2005).

35. WTO, *World Trade Report 2005*, tab. 2, 278.

36. Robert Gilpin, *Global Political Economy: Understanding the International Economic Order* (Princeton, N.J.: Princeton University Press, 2001), 3.

37. Dicken, *Global Shift*, 89.

38. Dicken, *Global Shift*, 335.

39. Dicken, *Global Shift*, 494.

40. PBS *Frontline*, "Is Wal-Mart Good for America?" (see also Edna Bonacich interview for this *Frontline* program, at www.pbs.org/wgbh/pages/frontline/shows/walmart/interviews/bonacich.html [accessed August 21, 2005]); and Dicken, *Global Shift*, 495–96.

41. Held et al., *Global Transformations*, 429.

42. Held et al., *Global Transformations*, 17, 429.

43. UNCTAD, *World Investment Report 1995: Transnational Corporations and Competitiveness* (New York: United Nations , 1995), 2; UNCTAD, *World Investment Report 2001: Promoting Linkages* (New York: United Nations, 2001), 47; and UNCTAD, *World Investment Report 2004*, 8.

44. WTO, *World Trade Report 2005*, 1, 2.

45. Held et al., *Global Transformations*, 246.

46. Dicken, *Global Shift*, 438.

47. Held et al., *Global Transformations*, 427.

48. Held et al., *Global Transformations*, 215–16.

49. McGrew, "The Logics of Globalization," 209.

50. Held et al., *Global Transformations*, 440–41.

51. Held et al., *Global Transformations*, 429.

52. Dicken, *Global Shift*, 565.

53. WTO, "World Trade 2004, Prospects for 2005," press release, April 14, 2005, at www.wto.org/english/news_e/pres05_e/pr401_e.htm (accessed September 8, 2005).

54. Kegley and Wittkopf, *World Politics*, 287.

55. UNCTAD, *World Investment Report 2004*, 11, 19.

56. United Nations Development Programme (UNDP), *Human Development Report 2005*, at http://hdr.undp.org/reports/global/2005/pdf/HDR05_complete.pdf, 117 (accessed September 10, 2005); Dicken, *Global Shift*, 48, 60.

57. UNDP, *Human Development Report 2005*, 34–35.

58. Kegley and Wittkopf, *World Politics*, 209.

59. This information on the role of market gatekeepers is taken from UNDP, *Human Development Report 2005*, 142–43.

60. UNDP, *Human Development Report 2005*, 118, 139.

61. UNDP, *Human Development Report 2005*, 127.

62. Held et al., *Global Transformations*, 27.

63. Ashfaq Ishaq, "On the Global Digital Divide," *Finance and Development* 38, no. 3 (September 2001) , at www.imf.org/external/pubs/ft/fandd/2001/09/ishaq.htm (accessed October 9, 2005).

64. International Telecommunication Union (ITU), *World Telecommunication Development Report, 2003: Access Indicators for the Information Society* (Geneva: Author, 2003), 3, 5.

65. Statistics from 2005 taken from Internet World Stats, "Internet Usage Statistics: The Big Picture," at www.internetworldstats.com/stats.htm (accessed June 30, 2007). Nua statistics are from Nua Internet Surveys, "How Many Online?" November 1998, at www.nua.ie/surveys/analysis/graphs_charts/1998graphs/location.html (accessed October 10, 2005). This information is no longer available on the site above, which has been moved to http://nuasoft.com.

66. Nanette S. Levinson and Anne-Claire Hervy, "Bridging Knowledge Gaps: Communication, Digital Divides, and Development" (paper presented at the annual meeting of the International Studies Association, Portland, Ore., February 26, 2003).

67. World Summit on the Information Society, "Declaration of Principles: Building the Information Society: A Global Challenge in the New Millennium," December 12, 2003, at http://itu.int/wsis/docs/geneva/official/dop.html (accessed September 6, 2007).

68. Sam Howe Verhovek, "Bill Gates Turns Skeptical on Digital Solutions," *New York Times*, November 3, 2000, A18.

69. *Forbes*, "India Software Exports Seen Growing 32 pct in yr to March 2006," September 2, 2006, at www.forbes.com/technology/feeds/afx/2006/02/09/afx2512585.html (accessed July 10, 2007).

70. Azim Premji, BBC news, January 23, 2001.

71. Celia W. Dugger, "Connecting Rural India to the World," *New York Times*, May 28, 2000, A1.

72. Indian Institute of Management in Ahmedabad, "An Evaluation of Gyandoot," at www1.worldbank.org/publicsector/bnpp/Gyandoot.PDF (accessed October 17, 2005), 27.

73. V. Balaji, K. G. Rajamohan, R. Rajasekara Pandy, and S. Senthilkumaran, "Toward a Knowledge System for Sustainable Food Security: The Information Village Experiment in Pondicherry," in *IT Experience in India: Bridging the Digital Divide*, ed. Kenneth Keniston and Deepak Kumar (New Delhi: Sage, 2004); Dugger, "Connecting Rural India to the World"; and the M. S. Swaminathan Research Foundation website, "Measures of Impact of Science and Technology in India: Agriculture and Rural Development," 2007, at www.mssrf.org/studies/measures_impact.pdf (accessed October 3, 2007).

74. *Economist*, "Behind the Digital Divide," March 12–16, 2005, 22.

75. Kenneth Keniston and Deepak Kumar, "The Four Digital Divides," in *IT Experience in India: Bridging the Digital Divide*, ed. Kenneth Keniston and Deepak Kumar

(New Delhi: Sage, 2004), 21–34. Also, two articles can be accessed from his Web page, "Grassroots ICT Projects in India: Some Preliminary Hypotheses," 2002, and "IT for the Common Man: Lessons from India," 2002, at http://stuff.mit.edu/people/kken/FILES/pubs.htm (accessed October 18, 2005).

76. World Economic Forum, "IT Access for Everyone: Global Benchmarking Study," Geneva, January 2005, at www.weforum.org/pdf/Initiatives/Global_Digital_Inclusion_Benchmarking_Study_Jan05.pdf (accessed October 10, 2005), 28.

77. Aditya Dev Sood, "How to Wire Rural India: A Survey of the Problems and Possibilities of Digital Development," Center for Knowledge Societies, Bangalore, India, at www.cks.in/html/cks_pdfs/how_to_wire_rural_india.pdf (accessed October 20, 2005).

78. Jan A. G. van Dijk, *The Deepening Divide: Inequality in the Information Society* (Thousand Oaks, Calif.: Sage, 2005), 65–68; Pippa Norris, *The Digital Divide: Civic Engagement, Information Poverty, and the Internet Worldwide* (New York: Cambridge University Press, 2001), 30–33.

79. Robert Hunter Wade, "Bridging the Digital Divide: New Route to Development or New Form of Dependence," *Global Governance* 8, no. 4 (October–December 2002): 443.

80. World Bank, *World Bank Development Report 1998/1999: Knowledge for Development* (Washington, D.C.: Author, 1999), 55; African Virtual University, "About the AVU," at www.avu.org (accessed September 7, 2007); *Technology Review*, "Lessons e-Learned: We Have the Technology to Reinvent Teaching, Says MIT's Distance-Learning Guru, but Do We Have the Will?" July 31, 2001, at www.technologyreview.com/articles/01/07/wo_leo073101.asp (accessed October 22, 2005).

81. For this discussion on conferences, see Richard L. Merritt and Elizabeth C. Hanson, *Science, Politics, and International Conferences: A Functional Analysis of the Moscow Political Science Congress* (Boulder, Colo.: Lynne Rienner Publishers, 1989).

82. Cybercafes, "Database," at www.cybercafe.com (accessed July 10, 2007).

83. Held et al., *Global Transformations*, 58.

CHAPTER SIX

↗

Global Communication
and the Nation-State

As we interconnect ourselves many of the values of a nation-state will give way to those of both larger and smaller communities.

—Nicholas Negroponte[1]

The stage of world politics is becoming so crowded that it is sometimes difficult to see who the main characters are. The stars are supposed to be the ones who have the most lines and provide the most action. But occasionally minor characters lurking in the background, or even previously invisible ones, leap to the center of the stage or simply assume a more important role. Chapter 4 indicated how new information and communication technologies are empowering individuals and groups, an array of nonstate actors, to play a more significant role in world politics. This chapter explores the impact of this expanded cast of characters and their new roles on the actors that have occupied the center of the stage for more than three and one-half centuries—nation-states.

The concept of the nation-state is an amalgam of two different concepts. The state is a physical legal and political concept designating a body of people occupying a defined territory under one central government. The central government has exclusive power to make laws and enforce them in that territory, that is, sovereignty. A monopoly of the legitimate use of force in its territory enables the state to maintain internal order and to protect the territory and citizens therein against external threats. While it is generally agreed that the nation is a more subjective, psychological, cultural concept—and much attention has been given to efforts to define it—the precise meaning remains

179

contentious. In one way or another a nation is generally defined as a group of people with a common sense of identity, based on one or more of the following: language, religion, race, culture, and history. John Rourke adds the condition that the group should also share a desire to be politically separate, self-governing—either as an autonomous entity within a state or as a separate state.[2] At the other extreme, a nation has been defined simply as a group of people who feel they are a nation.[3] In any case, a nation-state can be defined as a group of people within a defined territory under one central, sovereign government, where the people feel a sense of common identity with each other and allegiance to the government.

States have been the principal actors in the international political system since the Treaty of Westphalia in 1648, although this form of political organization obviously resulted from a long process that both preceded and followed this event. The "sentiment of solidarity" that characterizes the nation was not attached to the state until later.[4] Benedict Anderson, who famously described the nation as an "imagined community" (because the members would probably never know most of their fellow members), dates this phenomenon from the end of the eighteenth century.[5] Just how and to what extent new information and communication technologies are affecting the nation-state—its centrality in the international system, its sovereignty, and its relationship to its citizens—is a highly controversial issue and the focus of this chapter.

The Debate

Jessica Mathews argues that a fundamental "power shift" is occurring in the international system, a redistribution of power among states, transnational corporations, and transnational organizations.[6] Similarly, J. P. Singh argues that "the locus of authority, order, and legitimacy are shifting away from the state toward pluralism and actor advocacy."[7] Transnational corporations have greater mobility and flexibility in their strategies and policies than do territorially bound states. They can evade taxes, as well as environmental and other regulations, by their choice of investment opportunities. These choices have profound effects on the distribution of the world's wealth. As indicated in chapter 4, the new information and communication technologies, with their ability to compress time and space and to reduce transaction costs, have facilitated the spectacular growth of all kinds of transnational economic activities. The web of resulting economic relationships and the enmeshment of national economies affect the autonomy of states and their ability to pursue preferred policies. Their autonomy is also limited by the numerous agreements they have entered into and international organizations they have joined.

The new technologies have also enabled individuals and groups to play a more important role in world politics by connecting those with common objectives and providing sources of information, as well as the means for mobilizing and coordinating actions. The array of nonstate actors that establish transnational networks in order to play a role in the international arena is diverse and not easily categorized. Transnational advocacy groups, such as the Committee to Ban Land Mines, mobilize across national borders to support or oppose specific policies and to advocate broader social and political changes. Dissidents seeking domestic political change—autonomy, independence, regime change, or reform—organize internationally to gain support for their cause and exert pressure on their government. The Free Tibet Movement, Tamil groups, and various Chinese groups are among the multitude of examples that could be mentioned. Other subnational groups organize transnationally in order to strengthen the bonds of ethnic, religious, or cultural community. And there is the dark side of globalization—terrorists, criminal syndicates, drug cartels, and smugglers, to name a few examples of a very different type of transnational network.

Joshua Goldstein and Jon Pevehouse sum up the view that the growth in numbers and influence of nonstate actors constitutes a challenge to the nation-state: "By empowering substate and transnational actors, information technology is undermining the centrality of states themselves in world affairs."[8] New information and communication technologies (ICTs) potentially expand the scope of all nonstate actors' activities and enhance their organizational and operational capabilities. By making more information more accessible to more people and by facilitating the formation of networks, they increase the capacity of nonstate actors to challenge the actions and policies of states. At the same time these "technologies without boundaries" weaken the control of states over the flow of information and cultural products across their borders, thus eroding their sovereignty and threatening their cultural integrity, in the view of some analysts.[9]

At the individual level, these technologies pose another challenge to the geographically fixed state system by reducing the importance of proximity for the development of communities. "Although the new technologies are a powerful globalizing force," Mathews contends, "they can also have the opposite effect, amplifying political and social fragmentation by enabling more and more identities and interests scattered around the globe to coalesce and thrive."[10] New communication technologies have contributed to the growth of multiple affiliations and associations outside the nation-state and have generated new forms of organizing and networking across national boundaries. For example, they not only connect distant groups with common or compatible political objectives, but also the Internet in particular helps to strengthen the ties that bind geographically dispersed members of ethnic communities to each other and to their homeland. The diffusion of satellite television links together audiences speaking the same language, creating "geolinguistic regions," and forging new ties of identity. Robin Cohen, a scholar of global diasporas, sees a consequent trend toward the "deterritorialization of social identities."[11]

Finally, the massive flow of cultural products across national boundaries threatens the cultural integrity of nation-states. The influx of these products threatens to overwhelm the local cultures and to erode the common sense of identity that is attached to the nation-state. In his book on the information revolution and state power, Monroe Price asserts, "Globalization means that the potential of the media to buttress the identity of the state and its inhabitants is altered. Globalization means that the cultural bonds and loyalties that seemed once to be within the control of the state are now less so."[12]

The idea that power and authority are shifting away from the nation-state has been disputed vigorously, notably by Stephen Krasner.[13] He does not deny that the impact of economic globalization and the growth in numbers and influence of transnational organizations pose challenges to the nation-state or that their ability to control transborder movements has become more difficult. His main argument is that states have always been challenged from within and without, and today they are in many ways better able to respond and adapt than in the past. One reason that many observers see the decline of sovereignty, he insists, is that they have an exaggerated view of what sovereignty actually meant historically. Other scholars have pointed to the advantages that ICTs provide to governments that enhance their power. A highly developed information and communication infrastructure contributes to economic growth and competitiveness in the global economy. Military applications of new ICTs dramatically improve intelligence capabilities and organizational effectiveness in warfare, and they generate an array of computer-based "smart" weapons and delivery systems.

Robert O. Keohane and Joseph S. Nye contest the "new conventional wisdom" that the information revolution has a leveling effect of reducing the power of large states, while enhancing that of small states and nonstate actors.[14] Technological change takes place in the context of an existing power structure, these international relations scholars contend. The holders of power have a clear advantage because they are likely to make the rules that distribute the benefits and also to possess the resources to develop and use the new technologies. At the systemic level Keohane and Nye claim that those who see the nation-state being eclipsed by transnational organizations and financial markets fail to understand that institutions tend to persist, and loyalties are not easily changed. Others go a step further to claim that the new ICTs actually reinforce and strengthen existing power structures, both domestically and internationally. For example, Paul Heyer writes, "It is the rich and powerful nations like the U.S. which can afford to exploit this technology to its limits, who in the guise of making it available to others, extend their information empire."[15] On the domestic front, television provides a powerful tool for generating patriotic emotions and mobilizing support for government policy. And advanced surveillance technologies allow governments to monitor more effectively their populations to identify violators of the law or suspected threats to national security. Joanna Neuman argues that throughout history new media technologies have challenged leaders only until they figured out how to adapt to the innovations and thus to maintain their control.[16]

This controversy is about the impact of the information revolution on the way human beings organize and identify themselves and how that defines political power and community in the world. How do more porous borders affect the capacity of governments to maintain the allegiance and loyalty of their citizens? How and to what extent have the new ICTs empowered individuals and groups to participate in world politics, to influence political outcomes, and to effect political change? What is the impact of massive transnational flows of cultural products on indigenous cultures?

The rest of this chapter addresses these issues by focusing on the following topics. The first considers the role of ICTs in bringing about regime change. China is an obvious case study, given the degree to which its leaders attempt to control the flow of communication, the size of the population, and the growing importance of that country in world politics. The second topic explains how the new technologies are contributing to the growth of nongovernmental organizations (NGOs) and transnational activist networks, increasing their capacity to act in the international arena. Transnational activists have as their major purpose political change. The next topic looks at transnational ethnic communities, which are formed for a variety of reasons, most often not explicitly political. But they have profound implications for individual, group, and national identity. Immigrants from India and their descendants in the United States are examined to illustrate some of these points. Some ethnic groups do form transnational networks for the purpose of achieving political goals, for example, the Sri Lankan Tamil and Tibetan networks working for greater autonomy. The impact of the Internet and Arab-language satellite television on conceptions of Arab and Muslim identity is also considered. Finally, the impact of the new media on national culture is considered by examining new patterns in the massive transnational flows of cultural products, focusing on popular culture.

Global Technologies, State Control, and Political Change

Information and ideas have always ignored political boundaries. Technologies as old as the printing press have facilitated this flow, sometimes producing tumultuous political consequences. What is different today is the volume of information that circulates around the planet, the rapidity with which ideas spread, and the number of transmission channels for this traffic. For these reasons national boundaries are more porous, more easily penetrated than ever before in history. For governments with democratic political systems, these technological developments add to the diversity of information sources available to their citizens, which can complicate the development of policy consensus and support. These technologies pose a more serious challenge to "closed regimes," governments that maintain their power in part by their control over information.

The expansive properties of the new ICTs have generated much discussion about their potential for opening up and democratizing authoritarian regimes. The Internet in particular has been a focus of attention, as it poses most sharply the "dictator's dilemma." Internet connectivity is necessary for recognition as a major power and important for economic growth, which is essential to political stability. But the Internet also increases the cost and difficulty of controlling information and provides a tool for protest and anti-regime activities. Authoritarian governments have confronted this dilemma in different ways. The most extreme way of escaping the political effects of the Internet is to avoid all Internet connectivity with the rest of the world. North Korea, for example, has a minimal presence on the Internet, and the Web pages of its official agency are hosted by the agency's bureau in Japan.[17] Some governments have restricted Internet access to a small number of political and business elites and to politically trustworthy individuals and organizations.[18] Other governments have employed a variety of tools to limit any serious political challenge. Indeed, some scholars contend that not only have these countermeasures been effective for that purpose but also the Internet in many respects has enhanced the strength and control of these governments.[19]

Containing the Web in China

The debate over the democratizing potential of the Internet has frequently focused on China, an authoritarian government with the second largest number of Internet users in the world but also with multiple strategies for restricting the circulation of information deemed antithetical to the interests of the state. An analysis of some of these strategies and some of the users' countermeasures reveals an ongoing struggle in which the government has the upper hand in the short term, but the long-term effects of even highly regulated Internet use are more uncertain and controversial.

The Communist Party of China has attempted to control the flow of information on the Internet with an array of technical, legal, political, and psychological approaches. The basic infrastructure of the system restricts all international Internet connections to nine state-controlled backbone networks. A second tier of proliferating access networks, essentially Internet service providers (ISPs), may be private, but they must operate through the backbone networks in order to be licensed and to make international connections.[20] This infrastructure has provided the basis for what is often called the "Great Firewall of China." It also provides the technical basis for implementing the numerous legal restrictions that have accumulated, most notably blocks on sites hosted abroad that are considered politically sensitive. These include CNN, the BBC, and the *New York Times*. Content designated as illegal in various regulations includes pornography, rumor, slander, and information that endangers state secrecy or security, harms the honor or interests of the state, or preaches superstitious beliefs.[21] E-mail to certain sites abroad can also be blocked. Control over the gateways to the global Internet means that an ISP or an Internet cafe can be in effect shut down.

An extensive and layered monitoring system facilitates the enforcement of these regulations. The Ministry of Public Security has computer supervision and monitoring units in every provincial capital and in most large cities.[22] ISPs and Internet content providers (ICPs) (websites, forums, chat rooms, and blogs), and Internet cafes must be registered as well as licensed. Government regulations consider them responsible for preventing the flow of prohibited content. Some employ monitors known as "big mammas" to delete prohibited content, and others install software that deletes certain key terms. Monitors are required to keep personal details of users. Failure to comply with rules or to report infractions is subject to a severe penalty and the possibility of closure. Periodically there is a sweep to detect Internet cafes that have not registered or have allowed prohibited activity. In the last three months of 2004, for example, 12,575 cybercafes were closed.[23] An example of a more subtle approach, aimed specifically at the curious and resourceful young crowd, is the student-run Internet monitoring group pioneered by Shanghai Normal University. According to a *New York Times* report, as many as five hundred student volunteers monitor the university's Internet forums. They introduce politically correct themes for discussion, steer negative conversations into more acceptable directions, and report offensive material to the school's webmaster for deletion.[24]

In addition to regulating the content that Chinese citizens can access, the government also floods the Internet with its own content. In 2001, more than three thousand government departments had sites on the Web, constituting almost one-tenth of all mainland sites.[25] This activity serves two kinds of purposes. One is to provide government services online (e-government) and to improve government administrative efficiency. Online services provide information, forms, and, in some cases, interactive communication with officials. The Internet infrastructure also facilitates communication with and administrative control over provincial and local officials, providing the basis for greater transparency and accountability. The other kind of government activity on the Web is directed at diluting or countering politically unacceptable information or to advance the government's political agenda. It sets up special websites to convey its perspective on events.

In such an enormous country with so many users (123 million at the end of 2006),[26] much of the effectiveness of regulation and control rests with the willingness of individual users, as well as the ISPs, ICPs, and Internet cafes, to police themselves. The ubiquity (and stealth) of monitors, combined with the fear of punishment if caught, undoubtedly keeps much of the information that the government considers subversive off the Internet in China. Assisting the government in this effort are several U.S. companies. Cisco and Sun Microsystems have sold the Chinese government hardware and filtering systems used to block access to prohibited sites.[27] Microsoft has agreed to block access within China to individual blogs if the government so requests and to censor their content. Google aroused much controversy in the United States when it agreed to set up a separate politically correct search engine according to Chinese standards, which blocks access to content the government regards as controversial. The often-cited example is the phrase "Tiananmen Square," which takes the Chinese user to information about and pictures of a tourist site, while anywhere else in the world users learn about the 1989 protests at this site and the bloody crackdown that followed.[28] These companies defend their cooperation with the government's censorship policies with the argument that they must comply with local laws to do business there, and their involvement in China ultimately does more to open up the country and to expand freedoms than to stifle them.[29]

The Political Impact of the Internet in China

All the above suggests that China has what is probably the most sophisticated Internet monitoring and censorship system in the world. The political leaders even appear to have dealt successfully with the "dictator's dilemma," or to put it in colloquial terms, they are managing "to have their cake and eat it, too." The Communist Party is benefiting enormously from the wide diffusion of the Internet, successfully guiding the development of the Internet to promote its interests and priorities. It gives them access to global market information and to Internet-based supply chains, allowing the country to become a major economic power. Domestically, it fuels a dynamic economy with soaring growth rates. Economic prosperity enhances the image of the government abroad and its legitimacy at home. The Internet has the potential to improve the efficiency and accountability of the government. At the same time the government has managed to contain any serious threats to the regime. Indeed, the Internet even assists the government in tracking down dissidents.[30]

It is, therefore, not surprising that most scholars, including the more optimistic ones, are cautious in assessing the impact of the Internet on the fate of the regime or the transition to democracy in China, especially in the short term. There is general agreement that it will not have a revolutionary impact, that is, it does not immediately threaten Communist Party rule. The combination of deterrent punishment and proactive strategies has been successful thus far in minimizing the subversive potential of the Internet while using it as a powerful tool to modernize and strengthen the regime. Most websites that challenge the regime are located abroad.[31] Further, hundreds of government-based websites are designed to explain and justify official policies, while other perspectives might be less accessible. The Internet even provides a forum for fostering nationalism—for example, chat rooms filled with nationalist sentiment after NATO accidentally bombed the Chinese embassy in Belgrade and following the downing of a U.S. Navy reconnaissance plane in China in 2001.[32]

But, as one observer has noted, "total control of today's vast, borderless, redundant cyber-architecture is not possible."[33] The resourcefulness and determination of Internet users in China make the task of controlling Internet content extremely difficult and costly for the government. The use of proxy servers for reaching blocked sites is one of the most common ways to circumvent barriers. The proxy server is an intermediate site that the user can access, which will forward a request to the blocked site. Obviously, the government's monitors are ever vigilant to detect these proxy sites in order to block them as well, while proxy site addresses change in response in a game of cat and mouse. Information from banned sites, such as a *New York Times* article, is often cut and pasted onto sites that are accessible, especially sites abroad. Another common practice is for the user to obtain a Web-based e-mail address under an assumed name, although Internet cafes are required to maintain personal information of users.

Guobin Yang has provided some detail on the ways the Internet is actually used by the population on the basis of his empirical study in China. From February 2000 to July 2001 he immersed himself in the country's "emerging Internet culture," participating and interacting with other users and keeping extensive records of his observations. He was impressed by the popularity and abundance of chat rooms, newsgroups and bulletin boards, and weblogs. The official Chinese news agency, Xinhua, reported that in 2006 the number of weblog sites was thirty-seven million, with the number expected to double by the end of that year.[34] Yang estimated that there are thousands of active bulletin boards that post information on a variety of topics; many become forums for discussion.[35]

Yang's research found that the Internet is increasingly used for personal expression and public discussion in China. By facilitating social interaction the Internet has encouraged the creation of more social organizations and new kinds of associational forms in "virtual communities." A small number of advocacy groups, particularly groups concerned about the environment, are increasingly connecting with their counterparts in transnational networks. Chinese citizens also interact with individuals and groups in the Chinese diaspora, who often provide very different perspectives on issues. Chinese abroad, as well as human rights and other transnational organizations, are often instrumental in assisting Internet users in China in circumventing government controls.

The Internet provides powerful communication channels through which ideas and information can spread and citizens can mobilize more easily—and occasionally influence policy.[36] Even with censorship, Chinese citizens have access through the Internet to far more information sources, including sources in many other countries, than were available prior to the 1990s. Although it takes some ingenuity and determination to circumvent the blocked sites, it takes just one individual to put a piece of prohibited information into circulation through e-mail and the host of bulletin boards. Information from the Internet spreads well beyond computer users. The growing number of cellular telephones, combined with the Internet, increases the speed and expands the scope of information flows, which diffuse out to the larger public.

Examples abound of information that the government tried to suppress making its way to and through the Internet and to the broader public. The outbreak of the SARS flulike epidemic in 2003 is one notable example. There were no reports in the official news media; the government apparently wished to prevent the news of the outbreak and the spread of the disease from reaching the Chinese population and the rest of the world. But information on SARS immediately began circulating through e-mails and other Internet-based communications, and pressure increased both within and outside China for the government to respond to the crisis.[37] Punishment for some of those who circulated this information did not have enough deterrent effect to stop the flow of this information. After watching the minister of health declare on television that the situation was not serious, one courageous doctor e-mailed a letter to the New York Times, which confirmed to the world what was happening. Under such scrutiny and pressure, the government began to take action to contain the spread of the disease. The minister of health and the mayor of Beijing were held responsible for concealing the facts and were removed.

After Nicholas D. Kristof, the Chinese-speaking New York Times journalist, spent some time experimenting with the Internet in China in 2006, he concluded that this was not the police state that its leaders would like it to be, that "the Communist Party is crumbling, and its monopoly on power will follow."[38] In view of the benefits that the party gains from the Internet and the effectiveness of the multiple strategies used to contain the subversive effects, the downfall of the regime would appear to be unlikely in the near future. But in the long run, Nina Hachigian predicts, "the Internet has the potential to aid those who would challenge the CCP. . . . Control over information will slowly shift from the state to networked citizens."[39] Even if the Internet is not precipitating political ferment or prompting a mass democratic movement, it is bringing about profound political change that could lead in several directions, one of which is a transition to a more democratic political system.

Transnational Politics

In 1994 an article in the journal Foreign Affairs noted that an "associational revolution" was occurring at the global level, which "may prove to be as significant to the latter twentieth century as the rise of the nation-state. . . . The proliferation of these groups may be permanently altering the relationship between states and citizens."[40] The author, Lester M. Salamon, described a "global third sector," a massive array of private organizations that were not corporations but "pursuing public purposes outside the formal apparatus of the state." He attributed the explosive rise in the number of these organizations in large part to growing popular frustration with the limitations of governments in addressing such problems as development and environmental degradation. Another important aspect of his explanation for the growth in "third-sector organizing" was the revolution in communications during the 1970s and 1980s—fiber-optic cable, computers, fax, and satellite television.

The "Associational Revolution"

Since Salamon published that article, the growth of this third sector has been even more dramatic, and new developments in information and communication technologies have played an even more critical role. This third sector—between the corporate world and the system of sovereign states—now encompasses a far more diverse array of actors, with different organizational structures, purposes, strategies, and tactics but united in the conviction that "politics across borders is no longer the sole domain of the representatives of sovereign states."[41] The new ICTs connect not only governments and markets but also societies—more quickly, cheaply, and effectively than in the past.

One indicator of growth in this third sector is the increase in the number of nongovernmental organizations (NGOs) that have been given a consultative status in the Economic and Social Council (ECOSOC) of the United Nations (UN). As specified in the UN Charter and subsequent ECOSOC resolutions, the purpose of this arrangement is twofold: to allow ECOSOC to obtain the benefits of expertise in areas the NGOs can provide and "to enable international, regional, subregional and national organizations that represent important elements of public opinion to express their views."[42] Two years after the United Nations was established there were forty NGOs with consultative status. By 1995 there were 886, and in 2005 there were 2,719, triple the number ten years earlier.[43] Because the eligibility requirements for consultative status in ECOSOC are very restrictive, these numbers represent only a very small fraction of the total NGOs and an even smaller percentage of the growing number of transnational "associations." To be eligible for UN consultative status, an organization must have, for example, a headquarters, a "democratic constitution," a "representative structure," and "transparent decision-making processes."

UN world conferences have provided NGOs with opportunities to participate in international negotiations on important global issues. In the three decades since the UN began holding large-scale world conferences, the number of NGOs attending and the variety of ways they were allowed to participate have increased dramatically.[44] Since the Stockholm Conference on Human Environment in 1972, NGOs have monitored the preparatory sessions, which establish the agenda and draft proposals, and the proceedings themselves, with varying degrees of involvement. A persistent feature of every global conference has been a parallel NGO forum with a separate agenda with lectures, workshops, and much discussion. The forum provides information about the issues and the daily developments at the conference. Some NGOs focused on lobbying governments and intergovernmental organizations at the conference, and sessions are scheduled for the purpose of developing and coordinating strategies. Other NGOs are more interested in building connections with other NGOs to plan less conventional forms of action.

Elisabeth Jay Friedman, Kathryn Hochstetler, and Ann Marie Clark, who analyzed NGO participation in the UN world conferences of the 1990s, concluded that their study "offers partial support for the view of NGOs as regular and consistent influences on states in world politics."[45] At the conferences they kept pushing the limits of participation and gained considerable success. Whereas at the earlier conferences in the 1970s governments could ignore NGOs, they became increasingly visible, vocal, and effective with each passing conference. By 1996 at the Habitat conference governments were putting NGOs on drafting committees and allowing summit time for presentation of positions.[46] Sometimes one or more governments would support an NGO position or greater NGO access, which helped to legitimize and encourage broader NGO participation. NGOs helped to put new issues on the agenda. For example, the women's NGOs managed to get gender issues on the agenda of all the conferences. NGOs also lobbied for stronger commitments by states and stronger institutions for implementing agreements. Even when they lost debates, the authors claim, NGOs expanded the parameters of the debate and put governments on the defensive. On this basis the authors maintain that "these conferences have offered a platform for sustained, peaceful challenge to the monopolization of global affairs by states."[47]

New information and communication technologies have played an important role in the efforts of NGOs to become more involved in decision making at the UN world conferences. Information about the conferences—from the UN, governments, and alternative sources—and the issues to be deliberated, can be diffused more quickly and more widely before, during, and after the event. NGO representatives can be much more confident and better prepared to engage government officials. Online forums broaden the discussion of issues, positions, and strategies. One NGO, the Association for Progressive Communications (APC), was the primary Internet service provider for the UN conferences between 1990 and 1996. The APC is actually a network of networks, consisting of nonprofit Internet providers serving NGOs in 133 countries. The APC posted and disseminated documentation during the preparatory process and the conference itself, ensuring the widest possible access to information about the conference. It also managed an online discussion forum and facilities at the conference for electronic communication with NGOs that could not attend. One of the major benefits of these conferences for NGOs was the opportunity for networking, a process that multiplied linkages among diverse groupings, which were continued over the Internet, and facilitated action in other venues.

The New Transnational Activists

New information and communication technologies have not only contributed to the growth in numbers and influence of formal nongovernmental organizations with headquarters and constitutions, but they have also enabled new organizational forms of transnational activism to emerge and flourish. A number of scholars have distinguished between the political activism of more formally structured NGOs and "the new transnational activism."[48] What W. Lance Bennett calls "first-generation transnational activism" involves issue specific, NGO-led coalitions (e.g., labor, environment, and human rights), aimed at national and international institutions for the purpose of achieving specific policy goals.[49] Their campaigns are centrally organized, usually around prominent leaders, and they tend to use conventional political tactics such as lobbying and negotiation. In contrast, the "second-generation transnational activists" are broad coalitions of diverse and geographically dispersed groups (and especially networks) advocating multiple issues and multiple goals. They are more inclined to use confrontational and direct action tactics, such as protest demonstrations.

The new transnational activists have also been more experimental with the new digital technologies and have skillfully adapted them to serve their organizational and programmatic needs.[50] Digital communication channels—e-mail, websites, and cellular telephones—facilitate information exchange and collective action on a sustained basis across great distances among multitudes of individuals and groups with a variety of goals. The Internet in many respects becomes the organizational structure linking diverse groups together into broad networks, building coalitions at minimal financial cost. These characteristics of the Internet broaden the number and range of people who can participate in any given campaign. Inclusive of such diversity, these broad networks have a very loose identity, which allows both formal and informal groups with very different identities to work together.

As an example of groups with very different identities and goals joining together in collective action coordinated through the Internet, Bennett cites the North American Fair Trade Coffee Campaign, conducted by a coalition of three organizations with little in common and very different concerns.[51] The broad network Global Exchange was concerned about the threat of agribusiness to the livelihood of small-scale coffee farmers and also the negative environmental consequences—massive deforestation and pesticide pollution—of replacing their traditional shade-grown farming techniques with "sun cultivation" techniques. Their main objective was to ensure that the vast majority of smallholder coffee farmers in the world would be able to stay in business and to earn a living wage from their coffee sales. The Audubon Society joined the campaign out of concern for the migrating songbirds that were disappearing with the trees as sun cultivation replaced shade-grown techniques. The Organic Consumers Association joined the campaign as a way of promoting sustainable farming techniques in poor countries. Among the coalition's first targets was the highly visible Starbucks, which eventually gave in to their demands for a commitment to offer Fair Trade Certified Coffee. According to Global Exchange's website, over one hundred other companies have made a similar commitment. But the campaign continued.

The Fair Trade Coffee Campaign was part of a larger fair trade movement that led to the creation in 1997 of the Fair Trade Labeling Organizations International (FLO). This is an umbrella organization that coordinates the work of national organizations that certify, market, and promote fair trade coffee in seventeen different countries. It also connects through partnerships and contractual relationships the small farmer cooperatives with fair trade importers, roasters, and retailers. While the FLO negotiates and works with the coffee companies, its various national organizations maintain links to activist organizations that seek not only to educate the public but also to conduct aggressive campaigns to change the behavior of coffee companies. These activist organizations are a part of broad networks that are linked by websites and e-mail to multiple activist groups.

Web networks are continuously refigured as campaigns shift focus and change players.[52] Global Exchange had formerly been a hub of the Nike Sweatshop campaign but left it after providing enough negative publicity to prompt President Phil Knight to promise to assume more responsibility for bad labor conditions in his subcontracted factories. Other organizations wanted to see a more effective monitoring system for labor standards, and the campaign continued with student activist organizations as the main hubs. The loose collective identity of many activist networks provides a flexibility that allows individuals, groups, and even networks to move from one issue to another.

Both campaigns were also part of a larger, evolving antiglobalization movement or, the label preferred by the participants and some analysts, the "global justice" movement. Concerns about negative effects of globalization grew in the latter part of the 1990s. Mark Lichbach has identified nineteen "campaigns for global justice" against various multilateral economic institutions between January 1994 and November 1999.[53] The mounting backlash against globalization received little media attention until the dramatic protests against the World Trade Organization ministerial meeting in Seattle in 1999. This meeting, which was to begin another round of negotiations to further liberalize global trade, was confronted by about fifty thousand demonstrators from five hundred different protest groups. This "event coalition" consisted of organized labor, established NGOs, and social movement organizations representing an array of diverse causes, notably the environment, peace, human rights, and economic justice.[54] The WTO served as a common target, a symbol for globalization. The size and intensity of the protests, the colorful costumes (sea turtles, monarch butterflies, etc.), and, especially, the crackdowns by a surprised police force hit the television screens and the front pages of newspapers around the world.

Known thereafter as the "Battle of Seattle," the protests disrupted the meeting and exacerbated the tensions that already existed among the member states, thus contributing to their failure to reach agreement. Although there were plenty of arrests, police attempts to quell the protests by arresting the ringleaders were thwarted by the decentralized structure of the protest networks. The street protests themselves were coordinated largely by cell phones. One group, the Direct Action Network, had set up prior to the meeting a communication network consisting of a combination of mobile devices, such as laptops, wireless handheld computers, and cell phones. When the FBI managed to shut down the network they simply bought more cell phones.[55]

Planning and preparations for this event took place over the previous year and included national and international organizations. The Internet was the key to the long-distance mobilization, organization, and coordination of the diverse collection of groups that converged in Seattle. Websites and e-mail communication spread the word of the planned protest, and there was both online and offline instruction on nonviolent protest, communication, and collective strategy and tactics. Although there was relatively little international participation in Seattle, there was a much broader involvement in the planning process on the Internet. For example, information about local conditions and effects of globalization from various local and transnational activist groups provided useful input. Even more significant were the number of protest demonstrations against the WTO around the world that were designed to coincide with the event in Seattle. Mark Lichbach identified more than two dozen in the United States and more than sixty abroad, including a dozen in developing countries.[56] These protests were not organized by the Seattle coalition. Information about them was transmitted almost entirely through activist networks on the Internet. And antiglobalization and global

justice protests have been repeated at major meetings of multinational economic organizations subsequently.

Global justice has been a highly effective organizing frame because it "facilitates the condensation of many distinct targets in the same protest campaign," and the WTO was a particularly convenient "condensing symbol."[57]
Sidney Tarrow, an authority on social movements who has turned his attention to transnational activists, explains the effectiveness of the antiglobalization and global justice theme in terms of its "frame-bridging capacity."
This broad frame brings together advocates of multiple diverse causes, including but going well beyond labor issues, human rights, environmental
concerns, debt relief, peace, and the rights of indigenous peoples. The global
justice frame also facilitates the transnationalization of local activist movements, bridging global and local levels of activism. This process of global
framing of local movements has become both easier and more rapid with the
greater availability of electronic communication.[58]

The transnationalization of local protest is dramatically illustrated by the
rise to international prominence of a small group of indigenous peasants
from the impoverished state of Chiapas in southern Mexico. On New Year's
Day 1994 about 2,500 lightly armed soldiers suddenly emerged out of the
rainforest, declared themselves the Zapatista Army of National Liberation
(EZLN), captured San Cristobal de las Casas and several other towns, and
declared war on the Mexican president and army. They "proclaimed themselves the product of a 500-year struggle of the poor and dispossessed" and
issued a declaration (Declaración de la Selva Lancandona) that demanded
"work, land, housing, food, health care, education, independence, liberty,
democracy, justice, and peace."[59] The Mexican army's heavy-handed coun-
terattacks added drama to the rebellion. The Zapatistas became almost immediately an international cause celebre. Within the first week more than
140 NGOs sent representatives to Chiapas to help a cause that was not very
sharply defined, and the rebellion received extensive national and international media coverage. Then, even more remarkably, over the following
months and years the Zapatistas "galvanized one of the world's first Internet
solidarity networks."[60]

The trajectory of the Zapatistas presents two puzzles. How was it that this
obscure, previously clandestine group managed to gain sudden international
fame, and how did they manage to elicit and maintain over the long term
widespread international support from NGOs? The timing of the rebellion,
namely, the day that the North American Free Trade Agreement (NAFTA)
came into effect, helped to generate international interest at the outset. The
potential harm of cheap U.S. imports to the livelihood of the poor farmers in

this region, so heavily dependent upon corn, provided a compelling argument for the opponents of free trade, although this connection was not emphasized by the Zapatistas at the beginning. A second reason for the catapult to fame was the spectacular nature of the seizure of San Cristóbal and the newsworthiness of this event and its masked spokesman, who called himself Subcomandante Marcos.

The progressive Mexican newspaper *La Jornada* initially took up the cause and became a kind of unofficial press agency for the Zapatistas.[61] As an early source of information about the rebellion, the newspaper's sympathetic portrayal of the movement helped to produce a positive response among the Mexican public and to generate interest in the foreign press. From the earliest days *La Jornada* published most of the Zapatista communiqués, which were then translated and reprinted on the e-mail and Listservs of foreign supporters. Later communiqués and updates on the movement appeared on the newspaper's website. These communiqués and reports made it onto Listservs and other websites in different languages constructed by supporters abroad. One of the earliest Listservs to circulate information about the Zapatistas was already in place from the year before, set up by a group of academics and activists at Oakland University in Michigan who were concerned about the Mexican government's amendment to the constitution to abolish communal ownership of land in the Indian regions. Another important early supporter was an economics professor at the University of Texas, Harry Cleaver, who circulated information on his Listserv and on his website to various progressive groups, some of which set up their own websites and Listservs dedicated to the Zapatistas. Yet another was the ¡Ya Basta! website established soon after the rebellion by Justin Paulson, a computer systems administrator at Swarthmore College.[62]

Remarkably, support for the Zapatistas did not become a passing fad but, in fact, expanded to become a transnational solidarity network. Part of the explanation lies in the steady stream of new material—communiqués, manifestos, and other kinds of statements—that Marcos provided for the movement's electronic supporters to maintain their awareness and interest. He received visitors in Chiapas and occasionally organized large transnational assemblies on social issues. More important, according to Clifford Bob, were Marcos's public relations and strategic skills, especially his ability to adapt and to frame the movement for both Mexican and international audiences. After the dramatic seizure of San Cristóbal, the movement shifted away from the use of violent tactics, in part because they were opposed by some of the early supporters. The way the movement and its goals were framed was also reoriented, as Marcos keenly and quickly observed what themes resonated best with the various audiences. What evolved over the first year was an ideological orientation that emphasized two key struggles, deftly related, the struggle for indigenous rights and against neoliberal globalization.

The initial declarations and demands listed a number of grievances, which included but did not emphasize NAFTA or globalization. In response to a question from the press on the first day, however, Marcos happened to state that NAFTA was a "death sentence" for the indigenous people.[63] After observing the attention this "passing response" received in the media and from the transnational anti-NAFTA network and other NGOs, the Zapatistas began to emphasize the disastrous impact of neoliberal economic policies. Similarly, the indigenous rights frame, barely visible at the beginning, became increasingly salient as national and international indigenous groups, as well as human rights groups, responded enthusiastically to that appeal. Further, Marcos skillfully integrated the two struggles, posing the Zapatistas as "champions of 'difference' in an age of globalized homogeneity."[64] By framing the grievances of one group of Indians in one region of one country as part of a global struggle, "the Zapatistas became a key inspiration and symbol for the global justice movement."[65]

The case of the Zapatistas demonstrates how the Internet provides a bridge (with two-way traffic) connecting local and global (or transnational) movements. It provides the physical means of building coalitions across great distances, connecting local groups with international allies and enabling them to frame their claims in global terms. For transnational networks, the incorporation of local movement organizations broadens participation and gives specificity to globally framed campaigns. Internet-enabled political mobilization is shaping and enlarging the repertoire of political action by expanding the possibilities for interconnection across time, space, and issues.[66]

The Internet has contributed to the growth of all kinds of transnational organizations, and to the connections among them, by facilitating communication, information exchange, and coordination of activities. The new transnational activist networks in particular—loose alliances of diverse groups with different agendas—have flourished in this Internet-mediated environment. Fewer resources are required, as the Internet serves to some extent as an organizing mechanism, reducing the need for headquarters, regional offices, and staff. Coalition formation and collective action is cheaper and accessible to more groups at every level, local, national, and transnational. Online communication and mobilization continue and expand the effects of face-to-face encounters; the two forms supplement and mutually reinforce each other. The NGO forums at UN conferences provided networking opportunities that were continued online subsequently to organize and coordinate future collective action. The Zapatistas enhanced their role in the global justice movement by holding large assemblies on global issues, bringing to Chiapas individuals and groups who were attracted on the basis of online communication. Summing up what is new about transnational activism, Tarrow explains that "there is more of it, that it involves a broader spectrum of ordinary people and elites, and that it extends to a wider range of domestic and international concerns."[67]

Transnational Ethnic Networks

Although states are the basic political units of the international system, cultural boundaries (ethnic, linguistic, and religious) have never coincided neatly with political boundaries. Colonial powers drew lines either arbitrarily or in accordance with their own interests when defining new states, leaving behind a patchwork of ethnicities. Most of the world's religions long ago spread well beyond their place of origin, with the result that religious beliefs are widely shared across national borders. War, political oppression, and lack of opportunity motivate many people every year to seek a better life in another country. New ICTs, especially the Internet and satellite television, provide new opportunities for groups that share cultural similarities but are geographically dispersed to connect, communicate, and strengthen (or even develop) a sense of common identity.

Migration-Based Networks

The number of people living outside their country of birth in 2002 was estimated to be 175 million, double the number in 1975. Almost one in every ten persons living in the developed countries is a migrant.[68] The Organisation for Economic Co-operation and Development (OECD) has developed a comparable database on international migrants for its thirty member states, which indicates the percentage of foreign-born persons in the population of each country in 2003. The data show that 10 percent were foreign born in the total populations of Belgium, France, Greece, and Ireland. The figure is 12 percent for the United States, approximately the same as for Austria, Sweden, and Germany. Almost 20 percent of Canada's population is foreign born. Diasporic ethnic communities are expanding across the globe.[69]

Immigrants have always maintained a psychological connection with their homeland, but today culturally based satellite television channels, ethnic-based websites, and e-mail communication can maintain and strengthen these ties in ways not previously possible. Ironically, Paul Adams and Rina Ghose note, these "place transcending" technologies can strengthen ethnic ties, which means ties to a particular place.[70] Not long ago expensive telephone calls with poor reception or letters that took one to two weeks by airmail were typically the main alternatives for keeping in touch with the friends and relatives back home. News from the home country was scarce; newspapers were hard to find and no longer news by the time they arrived. Today e-mail is quick, cheap, and widely available through cybercafes, even for those who do not own computers. Newspapers from around the world are available on the Internet, often in local languages, as are many radio and television channels. A profusion of websites convey current news and information about not only many countries but also subgroups based on ethnicity and interests. Satellite television channels are created for the purpose of keeping the diaspora informed and interested in the home country.

Ethnic-based websites serve many purposes, all of which have the effect of strengthening a sense of ethnic or subethnic identity. They are increasingly being used by individuals and groups, who are separated from their country of origin and widely dispersed, "to re-create a sense of virtual community through a rediscovery of their commonality."[71] The Internet not only helps to maintain the connection with the homeland, but it also is used to foster ethnic solidarity in the new place of residence. Being a stranger in a strange land is painful, difficult, and often lonely. Typically and historically, immigrants have formed organizations and networks to provide support and assistance to their newest compatriots. But these communities were most likely to emerge in cities with high concentrations of a particular group. Local-level organizations are still very important, but most of these also find a virtual presence on the Web. Locally oriented ethnic websites organize and publicize festivals and programs, and other related activities. Some websites are strictly commercial, selling clothing and other cultural items, but they, too, help to maintain attachment to the homeland. Finally, many ethnic-based websites are used to foster communication and linkages across national borders, to create transnational ethnic communities.

More, better, faster communication facilitates and even encourages continued involvement in the home country's life and politics. Publicity and support for various charitable causes in the home country are a common feature among ethnic associations and websites. Disasters, such as the tsunami that struck South and Southeast Asia in December 2004, activate many existing charitable groups and give rise to others. Aid to the country of origin is provided in many forms at all levels. One example of a transnational endeavor is the "Digital Diaspora Networks" project, sponsored by the United Nations Information and Communication Technologies Task Force. Three diaspora networks have been launched—for Africa, the

Caribbean, and Latin America. The stated purpose is to "bring together qualified members of the diaspora—high-tech professionals, entrepreneurs, and business leaders—into a network with their counterparts in order to promote ICT-for-development initiatives in their homeland."[72] All these examples have focused on the Internet, but e-mail, especially Listservs, and Voice over Internet technology, combine to magnify the potential for immigrants to maintain communication with their country of origin.

Economic globalization facilitates diasporic investment in the home economy, a much more feasible endeavor when oversight is easier and new technologies speed the flow of money across borders. Indeed, Robin Cohen suggests that immigrants are in a uniquely advantageous position to benefit from economic globalization with their knowledge of and ability to bridge the two cultures.[73] The diasporas have played a particularly important role in the economic transitions of home countries from closed to open economies. With the collapse of communism in 1989 the diaspora from Eastern Europe began to establish business linkages with their countries of origin. Since the Chinese economy began to move in the direction of capitalism, expatriate Chinese have played a crucial role in transforming the Chinese economy. In the world of investment banking in the United States, for example, Chinese-born, Western-educated bankers are becoming "the new power brokers" in closing deals for U.S. firms in China. Because they possess the most sought-after skills, combining their backgrounds in China and Wall Street, every major investment bank in the United States now has a Chinese-born (and well-paid) star banker. The chief executive of Morgan Stanley China explained, "When you're engaged in high-level negotiations, it's the nuances that are important."[74]

Immigrants from India to the United States provide an excellent case to illustrate the creative use of the Internet for all these purposes. They have demonstrated, according to the communication scholar Ananda Mitra, a "strong commitment to mobilizing the Internet for building community."[75] This is a very large group, as India has been the number 3 source country since 1996, and it is scattered across the United States and on every continent. The variety and complexity of the thousands of relevant Internet sites reflect the diversity of the population in India. Paul C. Adams and Rina Ghose have delineated and analyzed three main types of websites used by non-resident Indians (NRIs) to remain in touch with Indian and subethnic cultures.[76]

The first category consists of nodal sites in India—news or multipurpose sites designed to provide access to many specialized sites for both residents of India and NRIs. Specialized sites cover the arts, business, computers, cul-

ture, education, entertainment, family, government, news, reference, regional interests, science, and sports.[77] Many sites serve as platforms for debate and discussion on both practical issues and cultural values. Others provide services, such as online shopping, chat rooms, daily astrological
readings, and especially matrimonial services. One touching example is
www.flowers2india.com, which will deliver flowers to loved ones back home
in one to three hours and even has a reminder service to ensure that special
dates are remembered.

A second category also consists of nodal sites in India that serve a similar
purpose in providing access to specialized links and general news, but they are
designed for NRIs from a particular state or subethnic group. These sites are
often in the language of that particular state. They provide links to regional
newspapers with local news in the local language and to specialized sites with
information and services. In addition to such services as online shopping for
cultural products from a particular region, there are sites that link directly to
nongovernmental organizations engaged in addressing local issues.

The third category consists of websites constructed in the United States.
Generally, they are important extensions of local and regional NRI voluntary
associations in the United States, which are engaged in organizing and pub-
licizing activities of interest to NRIs. In the aggregate these associations and
websites "promote the perpetuation of cultures associated with the various
immigration streams and encourage the development of NRI and sub-ethnic
identities."[78] They also help with the task of redefining new identities in the
new place, facilitating adjustment and assimilation with information and assistance. Many of these sites are constructed by local and regional organizations of subethnic groups. For example, www.prabasi.org (*prabasi* in Bengali
means one who lives in a foreign land) is the site for Bengalis in the San
Francisco Bay area. Others are dedicated to NRIs with special interests from
cooking to religion or in particular professions. For example, the Silicon Valley Indian Professionals Association (www.sipa.org) connects fifty thousand
Indian American technology professionals to further their professional development and to "function as a bridge between US and India for cross border career and business opportunities."[79] Finally, one of the most important
uses of the Internet is in facilitating marriage arrangements. Adams and
Ghose found eighty-eight thousand members of one matrimonial site alone
and estimated that a full count would number in the hundreds of thousands.
The result is a "proliferation of extended families that are split between two
or more continents."[80]

The case of India also illustrates how satellite television serves to
strengthen a sense of cultural identity at the transnational as well as regional,

national, and subnational levels. The state broadcaster, Doordarshan, launched DD India in 1995 with the stated mission "to build bridges of communication with Indians living abroad and to show-case the real India, its cultures, its values, its tradition, its modernity, its diversity, its unity, its agony and its ecstasy." DD India's mission statement describes the channel as "a complete India-centric channel giving an insight into the Culture and Traditions of India."[81] For India's largest private broadcaster, Zee TV, it was the lure of markets abroad that provided the motivation to reach out to diasporic communities. Zee TV claimed in 2006 an estimated reach of 225 million viewers in over eighty countries, including the United States, Canada, Europe, Africa, the Middle East, Southeast Asia, Australia, and New Zealand.[82] In contrast to DD India, Zee markets itself as a South Asian ethnic channel outside India, especially in the Gulf and Europe, where different South Asian ethnicities are more integrated. Broadcasts are in Urdu (for the Pakistanis), Bengali, and Tamil as well as Hindi.[83]

Ethnonationalist Networks
The multiplicity of communication channels also makes it easier for immigrants to participate in the politics of their former homeland in a variety of ways, as they are more fully informed of current events there. This involvement might be in the form of financial contributions and moral support for particular parties or causes or more direct forms of political participation. Sidney Tarrow claims that immigrants are increasingly supporting candidates for office back home, lobbying home governments, and trying to retain home-country voting rights.[84] A broader and more assertive form of political action mobilizes members of a particular ethnic group through transnational networks into a focused campaign to undermine the home government or bring about significant political change there. This kind of political action has a long history, but the new ICTs improve communication with the population of the home country, facilitate the formation of networks abroad, and expand the scope of their activities.

Sarah Wayland calls these transnational ethnic networks that are politically motivated "ethnonationalist networks" and emphasizes their importance as nonstate actors in world politics.[85] She focuses on the Sri Lankan Tamils to illustrate a particular type of transnational ethnic network—one that campaigns for greater autonomy or independence for a subethnic group within a particular country. The Tamils in Sri Lanka are ethnically related to Tamils in the southern state of Tamil Nadu, so most Tamil websites are oriented toward the larger diaspora of Indian Tamils with little or no attention to the Sri Lankan Tamil struggle. But there is a collection of websites that is playing an important role in the Tamil struggle for a homeland on the island of Sri Lanka, reinforcing the interpersonal network and offline activities of the diaspora in three ways.[86] The websites provide information for the Tamil diaspora with daily accounts of developments in the civil war in Sri Lanka. More broadly, they mobilize sentiment for the Tamil cause, strengthen a sense of Tamil identity, and organize activities—demonstrations and lobbying—that spread awareness of the Tamil struggle. All this increased awareness mobilizes fundraising. Wayland maintains that these funds have helped to prolong the insurgency against the Sri Lankan government.[87]

Some ethnic campaigns generate strong support beyond their own communities because they manage to frame their issues in larger terms, as did the Zapatistas. Exiles who were forced to flee an authoritarian regime are sometimes able to garner the support of human rights and other international groups or otherwise capture the imagination of the general public. Such is the case of the Tibetan diaspora's campaign to gain greater autonomy or independence for Tibet in China. A study by Michael Chase and James Mulvenon identified six main Tibetan NGOs and an extensive network of international advocacy organizations dedicated to that cause. These include Students for a Free Tibet, the International Campaign for Tibet, the International Tibet Independence Movement, the Tibet Support Group, the Tibet Fund, the Committee of 100 for Tibet, Tibet Environmental Watch, the Tibetan Plateau Project, the Tibet Justice Center, Tibet House, and the Tibetan Center for Human Rights and Democracy.[88] Their numerous websites provide news of relevant developments in Tibet and China, mobilize support, coordinate various global campaigns, and raise funds. The sites are densely linked to each other and to extensive information about Tibetan culture.

Both of these "ethnonationalist networks" represent a class of nonstate actors who "use the transnational arena to influence national politics in their homelands."[89] It is notable that, although the political goal was the same in both cases, namely, autonomy or independence, the Tibetans have been much more successful in mobilizing support beyond their own community than the Sri Lankan Tamils. One reason for this difference lies in the nature of the targeted regimes and of the challengers opposing them. Although Sri Lanka's treatment of its Tamil minority has been deplorable, it is a democratic government by most traditional criteria, while certain widely publicized practices of the Tamil insurgents, especially the use of female suicide bombers, have clouded their public image. In contrast, it is the perpetually smiling Dalai Lama, committed to nonviolence, who represents the cause of Tibet, which is ruled by an authoritarian Communist government.

Arab and Muslim Identity and the New Media

A considerable body of scholarship suggests that the new media are giving coherence and vitality to emerging conceptions of Arab and Muslim identity. Chapter 4 indicated how the growing number of Pan-Arab satellite channels provided alternative interpretations of events during the war in Iraq, which were more culturally resonant than those in the Western media. Although there was considerable variation in the reporting, certain prominent frames, such as "Arab humiliation," helped to create a sense of Arab solidarity.[90] Elsewhere in the chapter the use of the Internet by Islamist extremists and others intent upon using terrorist tactics to achieve their goals was discussed. Accustomed to identifying Al Jazeera and the Arab media more generally as anti-American, emotional, and extremist, many Americans would be surprised to learn how broad the range of both political and religious views is in the new media.

Marc Lynch explains how Pan-Arab satellite television, particularly Al Jazeera, is creating a "new Arab public sphere . . . constituting a new Arab identity explicitly independent of and often critical of Arab states and the official Arab order." He defines a public sphere in terms of "active arguments before an audience about issues of shared concern." What makes it new is the proliferation of political talk shows, which "transform the satellite television stations into a genuinely unprecedented carrier of public argument."[91] Lynch points out that satellites did not make this development inevitable; they merely created the physical basis for this public sphere. It was only when Al Jazeera oriented its programming "toward political argument about Arab issues defined by an Arab identity," and when vast audiences responded to this approach, that it became a reality.[92] Particularly significant is the fact that the popularity of this format prompted other stations to emulate it. Widening the public sphere, and linking expatriate communities to the Arab world itself, newspapers that are published in London and aimed at a Pan-Arab audience are also read on satellite TV news broadcasts.[93]

Lynch provides voluminous examples to illustrate the broad range of views that Al Jazeera includes in its programming, in keeping with its motto, "The opinion and the other opinion." Also critically important for the public sphere concept is the interactive aspect of the call-in shows. Participants come from the diaspora in Europe as well as countries throughout the Middle East. The topics discussed in the talk shows have been overwhelmingly Arab or Arab-Islamic concerns. Three topics have dominated: Palestine, Iraq, and political reform. Consensus reigns on the first, but there was more ambiguity and uncertainty than would be expected on the second. What Lynch finds most positive about the new Arab public sphere is the consistent and emphatic attention given to the need for political change in the Arab world.

Dale F. Eickelman and Jon W. Anderson and the contributors to their edited volume see an emerging *Muslim* public sphere, situated outside of formal state control and facilitated by the diffusion of the new media.[94] The Internet, with its global reach and capacity to incorporate and spread information from diverse sources, has expanded the domain of Muslim discourse. Islamic texts, questions, answers, discussions, and multiple interpretations circulate widely through the Internet, broadening access to religious texts and diverse views just as the printing press did almost five hundred years earlier. Thus, the Internet has become "an arena for alternative expressions and interpretations of Islam . . . a world of competing voices, multiple authorities, and problematic legitimacies."[95] Although the more extremist voices are certainly the loudest and they seem to Western eyes and ears to dominate this arena, there is diversity and dialogue. That discourse, combined with rising educational levels, is transforming Middle Eastern politics.[96]

Culture, Identity, and the New Media

Cultural diffusion has always occurred—in some times and places more than others—and the more powerful countries have dominated the process historically. What is different today is not only the volume of ideas, images, information, and cultural products crossing national boundaries but also the speed with which they spread and the redundancy of media and modes for transmitting them. Platforms for transmitting images, music, and programs have multiplied, and the digital revolution facilitates moving from one transmission mode to another. Although governments can pass laws to limit the amount of "foreign" media input in the schedules of their own domestic stations, the number of satellite channels, which are more difficult to control, has proliferated and they now cover most of the planet. Music, films, sermons, and programs can be recorded in multiple copies in one place and widely distributed across national boundaries through audiocassettes, videocassettes, compact discs, DVDs, and iPods. The Internet provides yet another platform for transmitting cultural products. Digital technology enables transfer from one medium and form of delivery to another. Whereas in the past, the vast majority of transnational cultural interactions were elite to elite, the global reach of new communication technologies spreads ideas, images, information,

and cultural products across broad segments of societies. There is no historical precedent for the volume, scope, and speed of these global cultural flows.[97]

Cultural globalization is the term commonly given to this phenomenon,
and it is as fraught with controversy as the concept of globalization itself. The
first issue is the extent to which it is actually occurring. Part of the answer
lies in the infrastructures for producing and distributing cultural products.
Another part lies in the patterns of reception and use of these products. The
second issue concerns the political impact of increased and accelerated international cultural flows. More specifically, is the "centrality of national cultures, national identities, and their institutions" challenged by cultural globalization, as Held et al. suggest?[98]

As indicated in chapter 3, the patterns of production, distribution, and
consumption of cultural products are more complex than the term "cultural
globalization" implies. New technologies, in combination with widespread
policy shifts toward deregulation and privatization, are multiplying the channels for transmitting cultural products almost everywhere in the world. Two
contradictory tendencies flow from this conjuncture of technology and policy change. Global conglomerates have formed that dominate the production and distribution of media products, concentrating economic power in
the cultural industries. At the same time there has been a burgeoning of entrepreneurial activity at the regional, national, and even local levels, creating new media channels, networks, production centers, and export markets.

Massive changes have been occurring in the structure of the media industries since the 1980s. Previously, most radio and television systems, with the
significant exception of the United States, were partly or fully owned by the
state. Broadcasting, except for the shortwave international stations, was limited to domestic audiences by state regulations and the technical scarcity of
electromagnetic frequencies. The development of satellite and digital technologies in the 1970s reduced the physical limitations on transcontinental
communication, and the new opportunities they made available created
pressures on governments to reduce restrictions, end their monopolies, and
open the door to both domestic and foreign private companies.

Although most states continue to own or support broadcasting systems today, the overall balance has shifted from public to private ownership. In the
wake of changes in regulatory policies, corporate mergers and alliances have
proliferated, creating global conglomerates that are both vertically and hori-
zontally integrated—that is, they control substantial amounts of both production and distribution not only within a single medium but also across different media. Mergers of producers of cultural products, telecommunications
corporations, and computer and software firms have also increased.[99] In

search of efficiencies and economies of scale, these corporations expand abroad through subsidiaries, purchase of ownership, or partial equity in local companies, licensing, and coproduction arrangements. About ten megacorporations dominate the transmission of popular culture today, and the majority of these are based in the United States.[100]

The Globalization of American Popular Culture

The United States' leading role in the export of entertainment fare goes back to the earliest days of Hollywood films. U.S. companies' share of the world film market continues to grow, having doubled between 1990 and 2004.[101] Hollywood films are shown in at least 150 countries, and the most widely viewed are the highly promoted, expensive "blockbusters." Ten films, just 0.02 percent of the world's total, accounted for 25 percent of the global box office revenues in 2005, and all but one were produced by U.S. studios. The international market accounted for 58 percent of the revenues from the top ten, a clear indication of the dependence of Hollywood on foreign box offices.[102] Three films were well above the rest in earning power: *Harry Potter and the Goblet of Fire*, *Star Wars: Episode 3*, and *The Chronicles of Narnia*. Reporting these figures, the industry journal *Screen Digest* attributed the success of the top three to their "universal appeal." It is not clear whether that appeal rests on the power of myth, the elaborate productions, or simply the amount of publicity.

The advent of television presented new opportunities for U.S. exports, as major film studios also became television production companies. It took almost twenty years, however, for these companies to realize fully their advantages and for a global market in television programs to develop. Television spread slowly, as the use of the technology requires the purchase of a piece of equipment, a big expense for much of the world's population. Further, many state-owned media systems, especially in the newly independent countries, saw television as a state-building and development tool. With scarce frequencies and a commitment to those purposes, there was little inclination to import television programming. The market for U.S. television exports in Western Europe began to grow from the early 1970s, but there remained a strong commitment to "public service broadcasting" until the next decade.

The proliferation of new television channels and stations in the 1980s stimulated the demand for programming. Because of the large U.S. market, films and television programs could be sold at much lower cost than they could be produced in countries with smaller markets or more newly established television systems. Besides this cost advantage, U.S. firms benefited earlier than most others from the wave of deregulation that encouraged the surge in cross-media and cross-border mergers and helped to create global markets and distribution networks. When various sectors operate within a single corporate structure, synergies among them amplify profits and expand market share. For example, in 2003 the motion picture industry worldwide generated $21.3 billion in revenues in theaters but more than twice that amount, $55 billion, in the form of licensing, videos, and DVDs.[103] These figures vastly underestimate the audience, as they do not include illegal duplications.

U.S. dominance in the film sector ensures a stronghold in television schedules around the world, as films constitute a substantial portion of the programming in most countries, and there are cable and satellite channels devoted exclusively to films. Sound tracks from films become musical recording exports. The United States is the largest exporter of film and television programming by far, but even more remarkable is the balance (or the lack thereof) in the flow of cultural products into the United States from the rest of the world. The share of foreign films in the U.S. market is less than 7 percent. Reliable statistics on the current global flow of television programming are not available at this point. They are extremely difficult to calculate due to the volume and diversity of ways television is transmitted, and the complexity of ownership and programming arrangements (described below). There is some indication of the imbalance with Europe in a UNESCO study that shows the United States clearly dominating the flow of television programs with Europe between 1995 and 2000. The proportion of the flow from the European Union to North America averaged about 6 percent of the value of North American exports to the European Union.[104] In sum, there is strong evidence to support the argument that there is a global media system dominated by a few media giants headquartered in wealthy countries, primarily the United States. But that is not the whole picture.

Countervailing Tendencies: Regional, National, and Local

The globalization of media conglomerates has, paradoxically, encouraged the growth of regional, national, and local media industries, as well as a revival of cultural nationalism in many parts of the world. Initially, satellite technologies brought mostly U.S. television programs in English. The introduction of foreign channels into an increasingly deregulated media environment was a catalyst for growth in the domestic media industries of many countries. The process of expanding across national boundaries generally requires arrangements and even collaboration with national governments and their domestic enterprises. These linkages intensified interconnectivity among television industries and, significantly, spread worldwide the advertising-driven, profit-oriented business model of U.S. commercial television.[105] Many domestic entrepreneurs soon realized the potential competitive advantage of locally produced programs in the local language, and private channels oriented to the domestic market began to emerge. The existence of indigenous competition, catering to local tastes and interests, prompted many multinational media corporations to adapt their formats, programming, and language accordingly. Local firms were created to fill these needs for adaptation. In the effort to maximize participation in the local market, global corporations established an array of arrangements, including coproduction, licensing, joint ventures, and subsidiaries.

The complex interaction of the global with the local is well illustrated in the phenomenal growth of exports in television formats, that is, "programming ideas that are adapted and produced domestically."[106] There are several reasons for the popularity of formats. First, they can more easily evade most restrictions on foreign programming that might exist, such as quotas or bans on subtitles. Second, television formats have exceptional economic value, as they appeal to a large audience, they cost less than canned programs, and there is a track record of their success elsewhere. A growing body of research has demonstrated that audiences prefer domestic and regional content to foreign programs.[107] Local performers, language, accents, jokes, and political and social context generally have broader appeal, but domestic industries often cannot afford the cost of programming from scratch. Local productions of imported formats provide a good economic compromise. There is also a low-risk benefit to imported television formats. If local adaptations of *Who Wants to Be a Millionaire?* have succeeded in more than seventy countries, there should be a high probability of success with another local adaptation.

Finally, Silvio Waisbord argues that formats are popular because they can be "customized to domestic cultures. . . . Television is simultaneously global and national, shaped by the globalization of media economics and the pull of local and national cultures."[108]

Examples of this growing practice of selling and licensing formats abound. It was Viacom's MTV that pioneered the model on a large scale, as discussed in chapter 3. Another example is the children's program *Sesame Street*, which now appears in more than 120 countries. Initially, most of the programs were the American version dubbed or subtitled, and they tended to appear on the cable or niche channels with small audiences, but twenty-five countries have now developed coproductions. France and India are two countries that have made extensive modifications of the U.S. version in order to accommodate cultural differences and to resonate better with the audience. Besides substituting more appropriate scenery and characters (determined by psychologists and children's focus groups), the producers worked on the tone and implicit cultural values. The director of the French coproduction explained, "We had to adapt it to keep 'Sesame street' values and ours, finding a way to make it work with French issues. . . . We had a feeling that it was a little bit sweet, too nice."[109] In the Indian coproduction, Big Bird is replaced by a seven-foot lion named Boombah, who speaks Hindi but is learning the fifteen other official languages of India. Aiming at a different segment of the population, the Walt Disney Company is licensing *Desperate Housewives* for three different coproduced versions in Latin America, and possibly more. The director of the Argentine version explained that the narrative of the story remained the same but that "we are Latins, and we have to communicate as Latins. We touch more, kiss more and cry more, and our version has to reflect that."[110] The different coproductions are designed not only to adapt to a "Latin" audience but also to account for linguistic and cultural differences within Latin America.

The pattern of U.S. television exports to Latin America is similar to that in many other countries. In the early days of television, imported programming from the United States provided a cost-saving alternative to local productions for new national networks. Programs were typically broadcast in English with subtitles. Over time, more indigenous programming was produced, and U.S. imports—although still a substantial part of the schedule— are having a harder time getting prime-time slots on mainstream channels. In Latin America, telenovelas brought bigger audiences and came to monopolize prime time all over the region, while American programs tended to migrate to cable channels operated by the main Hollywood studios.[111] According to the industry journal *Broadcasting and Cable's TV International*, U.S. programming no longer dominates the mass-audience market in Europe because audiences prefer that their dramas and comedies have a local flavor.[112] Although the flow is still mostly one way from the United States to Europe, there was a drop in the number of hours of American programming exported to the five largest markets in Europe between 2000 and 2002.[113]

Many countries, especially those with small domestic markets, remain heavily dependent on U.S. films and television programming, but the international circulation of media products has become more complex. Dynamic regional markets for media production and exchange are emerging. Export success sometimes comes to unexpected places. In 2005 South Korea appeared to be the "pop culture leader of Asia," spreading its culture abroad through television dramas, films, and popular music.[114] Concerned about Japanese and Chinese cultural imports, the South Korean government implemented, with a substantial budget increase, a five-year plan to build up the domestic entertainment industries and to encourage exports. South Korean dramas and music soon began to edge out American and Japanese exports to Taiwan, and so began a Korean wave that swept over Asia and beyond. In China, South Korean dramas are sold and pirated everywhere, and copies are even smuggled into North Korea. Clothing and hairstyles of South Korean stars are imitated in other Asian countries, and tourists flock to the places where their favorite dramas are filmed.

Three Australian scholars, John Sinclair, Elizabeth Jacka, and Stuart Cunningham, see a new pattern in global television in the growth of "geolinguistic regional markets" for media production and exchange, each dominated by one or more centers. These regional markets are defined not merely by geography but also by cultural and linguistic similarities, and they have "their own internal dynamics as well as their global ties."[115] Typically, a cultural product gains popularity in a substantially large national market, then it begins to export abroad to countries that share the language or have a minority that does. The multiplicity of satellite and cable channels makes it feasible to broadcast even where only a minority speak the language. This is the pattern the export of Mexican telenovelas has followed—to other countries in Latin America, to Spain, and especially to the Spanish-speaking population of the United States. Similarly, Brazil's telenovelas gained international success by first expanding its domestic market with exports to Portugal. Once a niche in the international market was established, Brazil not only developed a worldwide export market in telenovelas, dubbed in many languages, but also in other forms of entertainment programming. Out of this expanding trade two major media conglomerates based in Latin America have arisen, Mexico's Televisa and Brazil's Globo. India is a major center for film production and, in fact, produces more films most years than any other country, including the United States. In 2005, India's 1,041 films topped not only the United States but also the entire European Union.[116] Videocassettes, DVDs, and niche television channels have increased the export markets for these films.

The multiplicity of satellite and cable channels provides many more opportunities for exporting niche programming than in the more restrictive era of nationally regulated terrestrial broadcasting. Channels and programming designed for relatively small segments of the population can be economically feasible. This technological and political change has encouraged the growth of transnational channels serving immigrant and diaspora communities, where there is a high concentration of a particular ethnic group. These initiatives have important economic consequences, creating non-Western, regional centers of production and distribution of media products. Besides Mexico and Brazil in Latin America, other examples are Hong Kong and Taiwan, which have been centers for the Chinese-speaking populations of Asia, and India, serving an expanding South Asian diaspora in Europe, the Middle East, and the United States. As suggested above, the cultural implications of geolinguistic regional markets are as important, if not more so, as the economic benefits.

Conclusion

Global information and communication technologies pose difficult challenges to nation-states, which are defined in terms of territorial boundaries. Looking into the future, David Elkins anticipates that territorial states will suffer "a significant reduction in autonomy or sovereignty because territorial organizations cannot control non-territorial forces. . . . Individuals, ethnic communities, and virtual communities will experience enhanced autonomy because states will not be able to control the transmissions their populations receive in this way."[117]

The case of the Internet in China casts some doubt on that assertion and demonstrates that authoritarian governments are, in fact, able to exert significant control over incoming electronic information through an array of technical, legal, political, and psychological approaches. China thus far has been able to use the Internet to advance economic and political objectives while containing potential subversive threats from this expansive technology, a situation likely to continue in the short term. But "containing" the Internet is costly and only partially effective, as many determined Internet users develop skills and techniques to circumvent the barriers imposed by the government. Sympathetic Internet users abroad, especially in the Chinese diaspora, facilitate these efforts. There is no centralized counterstrategy but rather the response of a multitude of autonomous Internet actors resisting state control. Increased and improved communication has encouraged the growth of new kinds of communities for personal expression and exchange of information. Over the long term, control over information, a key to any authoritarian government's control, might shift to China's networked citizens.[118] The Internet generates political change but not necessarily more democratic institutions. Political institutions must be deliberately created. The same could be said regarding satellite television in the Middle East.

Once a government connects to the Internet, its actions become more visible to the rest of the world, however stringent the restrictions. Chinese and Farsi are among the ten most widely used languages on blogs worldwide, even though both China and Iran are among the "worst enemies of Internet freedom," according to Reporters without Borders.[119] Human rights abuses and protests are more difficult to hide. When demonstrations led by Buddhist monks broke out in Myanmar, one of the world's most closed societies, the military government initially hesitated to crack down on the demonstrators, as it had done in 1988. Although the government soon cut off access to the Internet and cell phones and also cracked down on the demonstrators, the actions of the government had already attracted worldwide attention. The Internet can facilitate not only evolutionary political change but also revolutionary change.

In the international arena, the state, or rather the government that operates in the name of the state, has the exclusive authority to represent and to make decisions on behalf of the people within its territory. But new ICTs have contributed to the growth of multiple affiliations and associations outside the nation-state and have empowered them to exert influence in international politics more effectively than in the past. The Internet in particular facilitates communication, information exchange, and collective action across great distances. New forms of organizing and networking across national boundaries have evolved, expanding the arena of political action beyond the nation-state and thus changing the nature of world politics.

The growth of transnational ethnic and subethnic networks poses a challenge to national identities. E-mail, ethnic-based websites, and culturally based satellite channels sustain immigrant identities and ties with the country of origin. In addition, these technologies provide opportunities to consolidate a diaspora in order to preserve a culture, strengthen a sense of common identity, or pursue political objectives. Diasporas become international political actors when they engage in political action, as in the case of the Tamils seeking support for a separate homeland in Sri Lanka.[120] The Internet and satellite television are mobilizing transnational identities in the Middle East, providing forums for discussion, dialogue, and argumentation over political and religious issues of common interest. A "public sphere" is emerging, which is independent of and often critical of Arab states.[121] This public sphere can evolve in a number of directions, only one of which is to encourage more liberal, pluralist politics in the region. Another direction is all too visible. The Internet is also being used to diffuse a very one-sided, extremist form of Islam and to carry out very destructive acts, as indicated in the previous chapter. It is also notable that this public sphere consists of overlapping transnational identities, not only Arab and Muslim but also a host of other ethnic and religious identities. In sum, what is occurring today, according to Robin Cohen, is "an increasing proliferation of subnational and transnational identities that cannot easily be contained in the nation-state system."[122]

The emergence of international media corporations with expansive strategies is diffusing more cultural products across national boundaries to more people, more rapidly than ever before in history. The fact that a few corporations based in Europe and especially the United States dominate the production and distribution of these products poses a challenge to national identities, values, and cultures. But the challenge is not a simple one of a few megacorporations eroding national cultures and imposing a U.S. version.

One source of resistance to this process comes from the consumers. Scholars who have investigated "media effects" have found that audiences are far more active and resistant to messages from the media than earlier mass communication research had claimed.[123]

Television programs, for example, may be globally distributed, but they are selected, understood, and interpreted within a preexisting cultural framework. Further, audiences tend to prefer programming that is resonant with their culture. Local entrepreneurs have emerged to respond to those preferences. To compete, international corporations have been forced to adapt their products to accommodate local tastes and to collaborate with indigenous programmers, scriptwriters, and performers through a variety of arrangements, including joint ventures, coproductions, and licensing. The growth in exports of television formats, essentially an idea or template for a program that is circulated in many countries but adapted and produced appropriately in each, suggests a local-global interaction pattern best described as "hybridization." National (and subnational) cultures are not being eroded by the influx of Western programming, but they are being altered. Indeed, satellite channels and the Internet are even preserving the cultures of dispersed expatriates, émigrés, and their children who are growing up in very different cultures.

Although Europe and the United States continue to dominate the global media landscape, there is enormous entrepreneurial activity occurring elsewhere at the national, regional, and local levels. Given the wider range of choices in news and entertainment today, the volume of programming that flows from the United States to the rest of the world may be less significant than the lack of exposure that most Americans have to the cultural products of other countries. The small percentage of films and television programming that is imported is viewed by very narrow segments of the population. Foreign films, for example, constitute less than 1 percent of the U.S. film market today.[124] The most profound cultural influence from the United States comes from the spread of its profit-oriented, entertainment-focused model for television as a medium.

This chapter has explored the impact of new information and communication technologies on national sovereignty, identity, and culture. They challenge the political control of states by vastly increasing the costs—technical, economic, and political—of controlling information that flows across national borders. The actions of governments are more transparent. Individuals and groups are empowered to act in the international arena by their access to more information and by their expanded communications capacity. The growth of transnational activist groups challenges the exclusive prerogative of the state to act on the world political stage. The expansion of transnational ethnic networks challenges the exclusive hold of states on the identity and loyalty of their citizens. The global flow of cultural products is changing the ways that national cultures are transmitted and reproduced, the context in which officials govern, and the relationship between states and their citizens. The direction of this change is contingent upon the interaction of forces to be discussed in the next chapter.

Notes

1. Nicholas Negroponte, *Being Digital* (New York: Alfred A. Knopf, 1996), 7.

2. John T. Rourke, *International Politics on the World Stage* (New York: McGraw-Hill, 2005), 100.

3. Rupert Emerson, cited in Sheila L. Croucher, *Globalization and Belonging: The Politics of Identity in a Changing World* (Lanham, Md.: Rowman & Littlefield, 2004), 86.

4. A term used by Max Weber, quoted in Croucher, *Globalization and Belonging*, 86.

5. This famous phrase comes from the title of Benedict Anderson's book, *Imagined Communities: Reflections on the Origins and Spread of Nationalism* (London: Verso, 1991).

6. Jessica T. Mathews, "Power Shift," *Foreign Affairs* 76, no. 1 (January/February 1997): 50.

7. J. P. Singh, "Introduction: Information Technologies and the Changing Scope of Global Power and Governance," in *Information Technologies and Global Politics: The Changing Scope of Power and Governance*, ed. James N. Rosenau and J. P. Singh (Albany: State University of New York Press, 2002), 2.

8. Joshua S. Goldstein and Jon C. Pevehouse, *International Relations*, 7th ed. (New York: Pearson Longman, 2006), 400.

9. The quoted phrase is from the title of Ithiel de Sola Pool, *Technologies without Boundaries* (Cambridge, Mass.: Harvard University Press, 1990).

10. Mathews, "Power Shift," 52.

11. Robin Cohen, *Global Diasporas: An Introduction* (Seattle: University of Washington Press, 1997), 173–75.

12. Monroe E. Price, *Media and Sovereignty: The Global Information Revolution and Its Challenge to State Power* (Cambridge, Mass.: MIT Press, 2002), 26.

13. Stephen D. Krasner, "Sovereignty," *Foreign Policy* (January/February 2001): 20–29.

14. Robert O. Keohane and Joseph S. Nye, "Power and Interdependence in the Information Age," *Foreign Affairs* 77, no. 5 (September/October 1998): 87–88.

15. Paul Heyer, *Communications and History: Theories of Media, Knowledge, and Civilization* (Westport, Conn.: Greenwood Press, 1988), 121.

16. Joanna Neuman, *Lights, Camera, War: Is Media Technology Driving International Politics?* (New York: St. Martin's Press, 1996).

17. BBC News, "Country Profile: North Korea," at http://news.bbc.co.uk/2/hi/asia-pacific/country_profiles/1131421.stm (accessed June 26, 2006).

18. Shanthi Kalathil and Taylor C. Boas, *Open Networks, Closed Regimes: The Impact of the Internet on Authoritarian Rule* (Washington, D.C.: Carnegie Endowment for International Peace, 2003), 142.

19. See, for example, Kalathil and Boas, *Open Networks*; and Tamara Renee Shie, "The Tangled Web: Does the Internet Offer Promise or Peril for the Chinese Communist Party?" *Journal of Contemporary China* 13, no. 4 (August 2004): 523–40.

20. Shie, "The Tangled Web," 531; Kalathil and Boas, *Open Networks*, 21.

21. Shie, "The Tangled Web," 532. Taken from article 15 of the "measures for the Administration of Internet Information Services."

22. Nina Hachigian, "China's Cyber-Strategy," *Foreign Affairs* 80, no. 2 (March/April 2001): 126.

23. "News Track," *Communications of the ACM* 48, no. 4 (April 2005): 9.

24. Howard French, "As Chinese Students Go Online, Little Sister Is Watching," *New York Times*, May 9, 2006, 3.

25. Hachigian, "China's Cyber-Strategy," 124.

26. Central Intelligence Agency, *The World Factbook 2007*, at www.cia.gov/library/publications/the-world-factbook/index.html (accessed July 10, 2007).

27. Chandler Clay, Zhang Dan, Eugenia Levenson, and Joan L. Levinstein, "Inside the Great Firewall of China," *Fortune* 153, no. 4 (March 6, 2006): 148.

28. Clay et al., "Inside the Great Firewall of China," 148–49.

29. Rebecca MacKinnon, "China's Internet: Let a Thousand Filters Bloom," *YaleGlobal Online*, June 28, 2005, http://yaleglobal.yale.edu/display.article?id=5928 (accessed August 28, 2007).

30. Shie, "The Tangled Web," 538.

31. Yongnian Zheng and Guoguang Wu, "Information Technology, Public Space, and Collective Action in China," *Comparative Political Studies* 38, no. 5 (June 2005): 528.

32. Shie, "The Tangled Web," 537.

33. Hachigian, "China's Cyber-Strategy," 127.

34. Reuters, "China Expected to Have 50 Million Bloggers on the Internet by 2007," *Financial Post* (Canada), May 11, 2006, 3.

35. Guobin Yang, "The Internet and Civil Society in China: A Preliminary Assessment," *Journal of Contemporary China* 12, no. 36 (August 2003): 453–75.

36. Hachigian, "China's Cyber-Strategy," 130.

37. This account is taken from Yongnian and Guoguang, "Information Technology," 528–29.

38. Nicholas D. Kristof, "In China It's ******* vs. Netizens," *New York Times*, June 20, 2006, 17.

39. Hachigian, "China's Cyber-Strategy," 127, 130.

40. Lester M. Salamon, "The Rise of the Nonprofit Sector," *Foreign Affairs* 73, no. 4 (July/August 1994): 109, 114.

41. Ronald J. Deibert, *Parchment, Printing, and Hypermedia: Communication in World Order Transformation* (New York: Columbia University Press, 1997), 206.

42. UN Charter, "Principles Governing the Nature of the Consultative Arrangements," at www.un.org/esa/coordination/ngo/Resolution_1996_31/Part_2.htm (accessed July 11, 2006).

43. UN Charter, "Consultative Status with ESOSOC," at www.un.org/esa/coordination/ngo/about.htm (accessed July 11, 2006).

44. Elisabeth Jay Friedman, Kathryn Hochstetler, and Ann Marie Clark, *Sovereignty, Democracy, and Global Civil Society: State-Society Relations at UN World Conferences* (Albany: State University of New York Press, 2005), 159.

45. Friedman, Hochstetler, and Clark, *Sovereignty, Democracy, and Global Civil Society*, 160.

46. Friedman, Hochstetler, and Clark, *Sovereignty, Democracy, and Global Civil Society*, 159.

47. Friedman, Hochstetler, and Clark, *Sovereignty, Democracy, and Global Civil Society*, 4.

48. See, for example, W. Lance Bennett, "Social Movements beyond Borders: Understanding Two Eras of Transnational Activism," in *Transnational Protest and Global Activism*, ed. Donatella Della Porta and Sidney Tarrow (Lanham, Md.: Rowman & Littlefield, 2005); Wilma de Jong, Martin Shaw, and Neil Stammers, eds., *Global Activism, Global Media* (Ann Arbor, Mich.: Pluto Press, 2005); Sidney Tarrow, *The New Transnational Activism* (New York: Cambridge University Press, 2005).

49. Bennett, "Social Movements beyond Borders."

50. The use of digital communication by the new transnational activists has been discussed most extensively by W. Lance Bennett in several articles. See, for example, "Social Movements beyond Borders"; "New Media Power and Global Activism," in *Transnational Protest and Global Activism*, ed. Donatella Della Porta and Sidney Tarrow (Lanham, Md.: Rowman & Littlefield, 2005), 203–26; "Communicating Global Activism: Strengths and Vulnerabilities of Networked Politics," *Information, Communication and Society* 6, no. 2 (2003): 143–68; and "New Media Power: The Internet and Global Activism," in *Contesting Media Power: Alternative Media in a Networked World*, ed. Nicholas Couldry and J. Curran (Lanham, Md.: Rowman & Littlefield, 2003).

51. Bennett, "New Media Power," 29–30. See also Global Exchange, "Frequently Asked Questions about Fair Trade Coffee," at www.globalexchange.org/campaigns/fairtrade/coffee/coffeeFAQ.html.pf (accessed July 16, 2006); David Iozzi, "The Sustainable Coffee Activist Network," at http://depts.washington.edu/ccce/assets/documents/DavidIozzi/IozziAnalysis.pdf (accessed July 16, 2006).

52. Bennett, "Communicating Global Activism," 148, 152.

53. Mark Irving Lichbach, "Global Order and Local Resistance: Structure, Culture, and Rationality in the Battle of Seattle," at http://depts.washington.edu/wtohist/Research/documents/Lichbach.pdf (accessed July 18, 2006).

54. Lichbach, "Global Order and Local Resistance," 9.

55. Andrew Chadwick, *Internet Politics: States, Citizens, and New Communication Technologies* (New York: Oxford University Press, 2006), 127.

56. Lichbach, "Global Order and Local Resistance," 14–15.

57. Tarrow, *The New Transnational Activism*, 73–74.

58. Tarrow, *The New Transnational Activism*, 60, and see chap. 7 on "Shifting the Scale of Contention."

59. Clifford Bob, *The Marketing of Rebellion: Insurgents, Media, and International Activism* (New York: Cambridge University Press, 2005), 117–18. The quote is from the declaration, which is cited in Bob.

60. Bob, *The Marketing of Rebellion*, 118.

61. Tarrow, *The New Transnational Activism*, 114. Unless otherwise indicated, the rest of the information in the following three paragraphs comes from Bob's account in chap. 4 of *The Marketing of Rebellion*.

62. Bob, *The Marketing of Rebellion*, 132.

63. Cited by Bob, *The Marketing of Rebellion*, 157.

64. Bob, *The Marketing of Rebellion*, 177.

65. Bob, *The Marketing of Rebellion*, 158.

66. Chadwick, *Internet Politics*, 142–43.

67. Tarrow, *The New Transnational Activism*, 4.

68. United Nations Department of Economic and Social Affairs, Population Division, *International Migration 2002* (New York: United Nations, 2002).

69. Ananda Mitra, "Virtual Commonality: Looking for India on the Internet," in *Virtual Culture: Identity and Communication in Cybersociety*, ed. Steven G. Jones (Thousand Oaks, Calif.: Sage, 1997), 57.

70. Paul C. Adams and Rina Ghose, "India.com: The Construction of a Space Between," *Progress in Human Geography* 27, no. 4 (2003): 415.

71. Mitra, "Virtual Commonality," 58.

72. United Nations Information and Communication Technologies Task Force, "Digital Diaspora Networks," at http://unicttaskforce.org/stakeholders/ddn.html (accessed July 29, 2006).

73. Robin Cohen, *Global Diasporas: An Introduction* (Seattle: University of Washington Press, 1997), 161.

74. David Barboza, "The New Power Brokers," *New York Times*, July 7, 2005, C1.

75. Ananda Mitra, "Creating Immigrant Identities in Cybernetic Space: Examples from a Non-Resident Indian Website," *Media, Culture, and Society* 27, no. 3 (2005): 381.

76. Adams and Ghose, "India.com," 421–30, esp. 422 for diagram. Information on the Internet in India comes from this article unless indicated otherwise.

77. Adams and Ghose, "India.com," 426.

78. Adams and Ghose, "India.com," 428.

79. Silicon Valley Indian Professionals Association, "About," at www.sipa.org/about.php (accessed July 30, 2006).

80. Adams and Ghose, "India.com," 430.

81. Doordarshan, "DD India," at www.ddindia.gov.in/About+DD/DD+India (accessed September 10, 2006).

82. Zee Network, home page, at www.zeetelevision.com/ (accessed September 10, 2006).

83. David Page and William Crawley, *Satellites over South Asia: Broadcasting, Culture and the Public Interest* (New Delhi: Sage, 2001), 133.

84. Tarrow, *The New Transnational Activism*, 52.

85. Sarah Wayland, "Ethnonationalist Networks and Transnational Opportunities: The Sri Lankan Tamil Diaspora," *Review of International Studies* 30 (2004): 405–26.

86. Wayland, "Ethnonationalist Networks," 418. Note the insurgent group, Liberation Tigers of Tamil Eelam, known by its acronym LTTE or Tamil Tigers, is the primary group behind the struggle for an independent homeland.

87. Wayland, "Ethnonationalist Networks," 406.

88. Michael Chase and James Mulvenon, *You've Got Dissent: Chinese Dissident Use of the Internet and Beijing's Counter-Strategies* (Santa Monica, Calif.: Rand Corporation, 2002), 14.

89. Wayland, "Ethnonationalist Networks," 425.

90. Hussein Amin, "'Watching the War' in the Arab World," *Transnational Broadcasting Studies Journal* (Spring/Summer 2003), at www.tbsjournal.com/Archives/Spring03/amin.html (accessed January 14, 2006).

91. Marc Lynch, *Voices of the New Arab Public: Iraq, Al-Jazeera, and Middle East Politics Today* (New York: Columbia University Press, 2006), 32, 54.

92. Lynch, *Voices of the New Arab Public*, 33.

93. Lynch, *Voices of the New Arab Public*, 49; Jon B. Alterman, "The Information Revolution and the Middle East," in *The Future Security Environment in the Middle East*, ed. Dan Byman and Nora Bensahel (Washington, D.C.: Rand Corporation, 2004), 230–31.

94. Dale F. Eickelman and Jon W. Anderson, "Redefining the Muslim Publics," in *New Media in the Muslim World: The Emerging Public Sphere*, ed. Dale F. Eickelman and Jon W. Anderson (Bloomington: Indiana University Press, 1999).

95. Jon Anderson, "The Internet and Islam's New Interpreters," in *New Media in the Muslim World: The Emerging Public Sphere*, ed. Dale F. Eickelman and Jon W. Anderson (Bloomington: Indiana University Press, 1999), 49, 42.

96. Dale F. Eickelman, "Communication and Control in the Middle East: Publication and Its Discontents," in *New Media in the Muslim World: The Emerging Public Sphere*, ed. Dale F. Eickelman and Jon W. Anderson (Bloomington: Indiana University Press, 1999), 38.

97. David Held, Anthony McGrew, David Goldblatt, and Jonathan Perraton, eds., *Global Transformations: Politics, Economics, and Culture* (Stanford, Calif.: Stanford University Press, 1999), 327.

98. Held et al., *Global Transformations*, 327.

99. Held et al., *Global Transformations*, 347.

100. Daya Kishan Thussu, *International Communication: Continuity and Change* (London: Arnold, 2000), 127–28. The exact number varies because of mergers and splits.

101. Akbar Marvasti and E. Ray Canterberry, "Cultural and Other Barriers to Motion Pictures Trade," *Economic Inquiry* 43, no. 1 (January 2005): 39.

102. "World Film Production/Distribution: Global Production Total Soars as Local Films Gain Market Share," *Screen Digest* 417 (June 2006): 205; InfoTrac OneFile, Thomson Gale, University of Connecticut (accessed August 16, 2006).

103. United Nations Educational, Scientific and Cultural Organization (UNESCO), *International Flows of Selected Cultural Goods and Services, 1994–2003: Defining and Capturing the Flows of Global Cultural Trade* (Montreal: UNESCO Institute for Statistics, 2005), 47.

104. UNESCO, *International Flows*, 48.

105. Silvio Waisbord, "McTV: Understanding the Global Popularity of Television Formats," *Television and New Media* 5, no. 4 (November 2004): 359; Thussu, *International Communication*, 167.

106. Waisbord, "McTV," 357. This excellent article provides the explanations here for the popularity of television formats.

107. Waisbord, "McTV," 369; Colin Hoskins, Stuart McFayden, and Adama Finn, *Global Television and Film* (New York: Oxford University Press, 1998).

108. Waisbord, "McTV," 360.

109. Doreen Carvajal, "Sesame Street Goes Global: Let's All Count the Revenue," *New York Times*, December 12, 2005, C8.

110. Larry Rohter, "How Do You Say 'Desperate' in Spanish?" *New York Times*, August 13, 2006, 22.

111. Rohter, "How Do You Say 'Desperate' in Spanish?" 22.

112. Georgina Higham, "U.S. Programming Losing Its Grip on Europe's Prime-Time Audiences," *Broadcasting and Cable's TV International* 11, no. 6 (March 14, 2003): 1.

113. *Economist*, "Anti-Americanism and Television," April 3, 2003, 59.

114. Norimitsu Onishi, "Roll Over, Godzilla: Korea Rules: Seoul's Pop Culture Takes Asia by Storm," *New York Times*, June 28, 2005, 3.

115. John Sinclair, Elizabeth Jacka, and Stuart Cunningham, eds., *New Patterns in Global Television: Peripheral Vision* (New York: Oxford University Press, 1995), 5.

116. "World Film Production/Distribution," 210.

117. David Elkins, "Globalization, Telecommunication, and Virtual Ethnic Communities," *International Political Science Review* 18, no. 2 (April 1997): 148.

118. Hachigian, "China's Cyber-Strategy," 129.

119. Technorati, "The State of the Live Web," April 2007, at http://technorati.com/weblog/2007/04/328.html (accessed September 30, 2007); Anna Johnson, "Bloggers in Mideast Transforming Political, Social Dialogue but Authorities Hitting Back," Associate Press Financial Wire, February 9, 2007.

120. Wayland, "Ethnonationalist Networks," 410.

121. Lynch, *Voices of the New Arab Public*, 54.

122. Cohen, *Global Diasporas*, 175.

123. Annabelle Sreberny-Mohammadi, "The Global and the Local in International Communications," in *Mass Media in Society*, ed. James Curran and Michael Gurevitch (New York: Arnold, 1996), 181.

124. Marvasti and Canterberry, "Cultural and Other Barriers," 39.

CHAPTER SEVEN

⤻

Issues and Choices

> There is nothing inevitable about this story: it is the composite of thousands of decisions which could have been decided otherwise.
>
> —Margaret E. Keck and Kathryn Sikkink[1]

History is full of inventions that served very different purposes from those that inspired their creation. Typically, there are optimists who hail a new technology for its potential benefits to humankind and pessimists who warn against the potential negative effects. Others emphasize the instrumental nature of technology and the importance of social forces and structures in determining its impact. The controversies that accompany the emergence of new technologies serve a useful purpose in identifying a range of possible effects, which may indeed be both positive and negative. The preceding chapters demonstrate the multiple and even contradictory effects of the major new information and communication technologies (ICTs) that provide the context for world politics today.

More people today have access to more diverse sources of information (and entertainment) than ever before, as well as a greater capacity to influence national and international agendas. Common interests and concerns are more easily shared across national boundaries, and the organization of collective action, even across great distances, is more feasible. The conduct of international relations is a more public affair, and leaders are under greater scrutiny from more sources. The information revolution has facilitated spectacular growth in transnational economic activities, transforming the world economy and bringing unprecedented prosperity to some states, enterprises, and individuals.

Yet, the tools that connect and inform can also exacerbate international conflict by bringing opposing values and lifestyles into direct contact with each other. They can broaden the scope of a conflict. The rapid spread of an image from a digital camera to the Internet to satellite television can turn a minor local incident into a global-scale crisis. The same technologies that facilitate the organization of human rights activists also enhance the organizational and operational capabilities of terrorists. The same technologies that empower people to challenge their leaders also provide those leaders with more effective tools of surveillance, communication, and persuasion. The same technologies that offer an escalator from poverty for some leave others at the margins of the global economy.

With such contradictory evidence, how can the impact of the information revolution on world politics be assessed? The story of the evolution of global communication recounted here has demonstrated how the impact and direction of new technologies are shaped by the interaction of four sets of influences: the properties of the technology; political structures, institutions, and policies; economic structures and market forces; and the social uses of the technology. The printing press provided an early example of the interaction of these influences. The intrinsic properties of the movable type technology, that is, the capacity to reproduce text quickly and cheaply, held the potential for greatly expanding the existing body of knowledge, advancing scholarly exchange, and encouraging commercial activity. These positive effects were limited by the social reality of a largely illiterate European population and by the constraints that some political and religious authorities tried to impose on the production and distribution of printed materials. But the determination of Protestant reformers to spread their ideas converged with the profit motives of booksellers and peddlers to increase greatly the volume of print in circulation in vernacular languages and to encourage further the growth of literacy. In areas where the political structures were more favorable to the expansion of reading material and the reading public, the proliferation of printing presses served to stimulate the growth of literacy and economic prosperity.

Figure 7.1 illustrates how the interaction of the four sets of influences shapes the impact and direction of communication technologies. The properties of a technology, as developed by scientists, engineers, and inventors, define the range of possibilities for its development and applications. Either government policies or market forces (or some combination of these) will control its development and limit access to the technology.

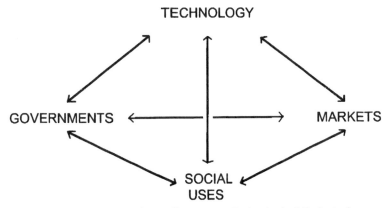

Figure 7.1. Four Interacting Influences on Technological Trajectories

Government policies influence market behavior, and commercial interests may attempt to influence government policies. Users decide how and to what extent they want to use the technology, and this response can influence development indirectly by creating consumer demand on markets or governments or directly by prompting the developers to recognize new technological possibilities.

Control, Access, and Purpose

Issues of control, access, and purpose have been vigorously contested throughout the development of communication technologies. With the electric telegraph, the first global communication system, the issue was international control. The vast majority of submarine cables that provided the infrastructure was owned, managed, and monitored by British companies, which posed security risks for all other countries that relied on the cables. The search for alternatives that would eliminate this vulnerability and overcome the limitations of the electric telegraph led to the wireless telegraph, radio telephony, and eventually broadcasting. The development of the wireless telegraph, then radio, posed an additional philosophical problem— should the airwaves be controlled at all? Were they a common resource? Who should decide on access and for what purpose? As the free-for-all use of the airwaves increased competition at the international and national levels, interference undermined the utility of the technology until there was an agreement on the allocation of wavelengths for different purposes and an international organization to implement it.

With the invention of broadcasting, governments were forced to make choices that would determine the structure and form of radio and television broadcasting in their respective countries. These choices reflected political preferences, cultural values, and assumptions about the purposes that broadcasting ought to serve. The most important issue concerned the relative merits of private versus public control over the broadcasting institutions. In most countries television was incorporated into the institutional structures that had been established for radio and was placed under the same regulatory control. Consequently, the initial decisions about radio set the pattern for television.

The power of both media to mold attitudes and shape opinions was clearly apparent. Viewing the radio primarily as an instrument of socialization and political mobilization, some governments, especially those in newly independent countries, sought to exercise direct control by establishing a state monopoly funded from tax revenues. The Soviet Union and fascist Germany were extreme versions of this model; they maintained firm control over both the institutional structure and the content. The United States, where laissez-faire views prevailed, followed the opposite approach. Stations were privately owned, financed by advertising, and only minimally regulated by government. The government did not control broadcasting, but neither did it support it in any significant financial way. The development of television, like radio, was market driven. Radio in Latin America tended to follow a similar pattern. In Europe a tradition of noncommercial public service broadcast systems developed, such as the BBC, funded by the government, often through license fees paid by owners of radio sets. A philosophical commitment to the "public interest" rather than private, commercial interests, underlay this difference with emphasis on the educational role of the medium.

The choices that governments made on the issue of public versus private control and access were based on assumptions about the purposes that broadcasting should serve, and these assumptions influenced the content of programming. Where private broadcasting predominated, primarily commercial criteria determined program content, heavily orienting it toward entertainment. Where governments controlled or set standards for programming, they typically attempted to serve certain political or social objectives. Many governments initially emphasized the role of radio and television as media for education, information, and the transmission of values. The tension between these basic objectives and audience demands for entertainment was often resolved in favor of the latter. An emphasis on entertainment was especially likely when the broadcasting system began to rely more on commercial sponsors, who sought as large an audience as possible—potential consumers of their products. Both public and private models have restricted access and choice—in different ways. Government monopolies limited stations and channels, and some forms also influenced program content. In the commercial model, as exemplified by the United States, programming was determined by market values, which favored certain kinds of programming over others. Most states eventually developed some mixture of public and commercial systems, but the lure of revenues has introduced increasing amounts of advertising into most systems.

Technological constraints and government policies limited the reach and expansion of broadcasting until the last decade of the twentieth century. Except for international shortwave broadcasting and some trade in taped programs, most systems served primarily domestic audiences. Television and radio were dominated by broadcasting monopolies in Europe and much of the rest of the world and by three commercial networks in the United States. Similarly, telecommunications were territorially organized as government monopolies or government-protected monopolies (as with AT&T). The telephone did not become an affordable means of international communication until the latter part of the twentieth century. The development and diffusion of satellite and fiber-optic cable networks removed the technical constraints on international communication just as a widespread political trend toward privatization, deregulation, and liberalization in trade was emerging. One result was a proliferation of private channels at the domestic and international levels and a general shift in the broadcasting media from the public to the private sector. Another result was the formation of enormous transnational conglomerates that control production and distribution in the entertainment, news, and information industries.

The development of communication satellites raised a new set of issues regarding control and access. To gain maximum advantages from the technology, a global satellite system was necessary. But who would own and manage the system, and how would the benefits be distributed? What would the role of the private sector be? The choice was an intergovernmental consortium, Intelsat, which operated as a commercial cooperative. As the leader in the technology, the United States had the largest ownership share and the loudest voice and provided most of the technology for the launching, but it was a more multilateral arrangement than the telegraph networks that the British had dominated. In 2001 Intelsat became a private company, which officially was committed to nondiscriminatory access. Fiber-optic cables were private sector ventures from the beginning.

The Internet began as a government-sponsored project in the United States and in the majority of other countries it has connected. The initial network systems typically linked academic and research institutions, then expanded to provide access to a larger public. Governments had to decide whether to invest the funds required to establish enough long-distance backbone networks to meet growing demand for services or whether to turn this task over to the private sector. Whether to remain the sole Internet service provider or to open those services up to the private sector posed another basic choice. In any case, a government can retain a "chokehold" over the international connection. Government-controlled networks can be blocked and filtered. As the case of China illustrates, savvy and determined users can evade these controls, but certain policy choices do limit access.

Economic constraints on access to the benefits of the Internet are as significant as the political ones. Establishing network connections is costly, especially if an institution or country is starting from scratch. The management of computer networks requires extremely advanced technical skills. Computer hardware is expensive, and the software takes training to learn. Thus, the argument goes, those who are the most disadvantaged and the most in need of the benefits of the new technology are the least likely to have access to it. Since those individuals, groups, and nations that are most likely to enjoy the benefits are already the most privileged, the others will fall even farther behind. The now ubiquitous term, "digital divide," conveys the idea of what is perceived by many to be a widening gap if significant action is not taken. What action should be taken by whom is a hotly contested issue in the scholarly literature and policy papers at national and international levels.

At the global level there are no regulations or controls over the Internet. There has to be a way, however, to ensure that any computer on the network can find and pass along data to any other computer—an addressing system and some entity to manage it. From 1968 to 1998 this task was coordinated largely by Jon Postel, an American engineer acting under the auspices of the Defense Department. In 1998 a nonprofit organization called the Internet Corporation for Assigned Names and Numbers (ICANN) was created in a Memorandum of Understanding with the Department of Commerce, which oversees its work. ICANN controls only one aspect of the Internet, the assignment of domain names such as dot com, and it has the responsibility to ensure that they match a single Internet address.

Although this is a technical matter, it became a highly controversial international issue and a focus of attention during two years of United Nations–sponsored talks that culminated in the meeting of the World Summit on the Information Society in November 2005. Because the Internet is an international resource, in which the majority of users are now outside the United States, there was concern about the United States retaining the exclusive control over the Internet's core infrastructure. Numerous alternatives were proposed for sharing that authority or ceding it to an intergovernmental organization that would also set policies for running the Internet. The outcome was the continuation of ICANN's management but the beginning of a process of weaning it away from the U.S. government's oversight and giving it more autonomy as a corporation in the private sector. A new organization was also created, the Internet Governance Forum, which would bring together all the "stakeholders" in the Internet, from consumer groups to governments to private business. The forum was authorized to take up any Internet issue from spam to security to multilingualism, but it has no oversight or policymaking functions.[2]

The intrinsic properties of the Internet—decentralized design structure, easy access, transmission speed, and global reach—pose a distinctive set of issues regarding control, access, and purpose. The designers envisaged and developed a network with no center point of control that could be subject to failure, a structural characteristic that hampers control. There are technical, political, and economic limits to access, as indicated above, but these are not intrinsic to the technology. It is a technology that gives the individual a considerable amount of control in determining how it is used and for what purpose. Unlike traditional mass media, the user can be a producer as well as a consumer. The power that the Internet gives to individuals to convey information and to express ideas quickly to a large audience is historically unprecedented. It is also a force multiplier, which gives influence to individuals and groups disproportionate to their size and resources.

But unlimited access and limited controls make the Internet available for a wide range of purposes. Jeffrey Ayres warns that, in the "cyberdiffusion of contentious politics" (that is, the rapid dissemination of information, protest ideas, and tactics through the Internet), lies the danger that unreliable and unverifiable information may generate repeated "global electronic riots."[3] The difficulty of verifying information on the Internet can even encourage video hoaxes, perpetrated for sheer entertainment or for more insidious purposes. A video of an American being beheaded in Iraq that appeared on a militant website and subsequently on Arab television was the creative staging effort of an American in his own living room using fake blood.[4] Even more serious is the fact the Internet provides the same opportunities for perpetrators of violence as for human rights activists. A recent National Intelligence Estimate on Global Terrorism concluded that "the radicalization process is occurring more quickly, more widely and more anonymously in the Internet age, raising the likelihood of surprise attacks by unknown groups whose members and supporters may be difficult to pinpoint."[5] Gladys Ganley alludes to the dangers of the dark side of the Internet in her book, *The Exploding Political Power of Personal Media*, warning that "power to the people can mean, not just freedom, but also that nobody is in charge anymore, with as yet incalculable political consequences."[6]

Prosperity, National Sovereignty, and Democracy

The historical uniqueness of the current information environment has been amply demonstrated throughout this book. What is truly novel and important is the collective impact of many new technologies. It is not merely the reduction in time and cost for communicating over great distances but also the sheer number and variety of channels of communication and sources of information. The fact that digital technology allows all kinds of data, images, and information to be easily and quickly transmitted from one medium to another accelerates and expands the diffusion process. These expansive technologies are transforming relationships and patterns of behavior at every level on a global scale. They have contributed to the growth of transnational linkages and have generated new forms of organizing and networking across national boundaries. The information revolution is affecting every dimension of world politics.

The impact is perhaps most obvious in the economic realm, where new ICTs provide the infrastructure for a global economy, facilitating transnational economic activities and new forms of transnational and global economic organization.[7] Economic globalization is an ongoing process, the product of technological innovations combining with the widespread adoption of liberalization policies, market forces, and consumer choices. The economic impact of these technologies is mixed, dynamic, and contingent upon choices made by governments, corporations, and individuals. Decisions on these matters are influenced by millions of individuals—how and when they decide to use the technologies. This influence decreases when economic power is centralized in a few large conglomerates or an enterprise with a monopoly in a product or service. Governments make the policies that determine the nature and scope of economic power. People (in democracies) elect the officials who make these policies.

The distributional effects of the new ICTs are a major issue of contention and part of the larger debate over economic globalization. These technologies have improved the capacity of companies to operate at a distance and with greater flexibility. One result is the growth of global production and distribution networks and a concentration of economic power in large multinational corporations. Another trend is the dispersal of production across an unprecedented number of countries, which has provided new opportunities for small- and medium-sized businesses and for some developing countries to become important players in the global economy. The impact upon labor is mixed, as jobs are both created and destroyed. Further, subcontracting and, more generally, the fragmentation of production lead to loss of accountability and a blurring of responsibility for labor conditions. Unequal access to the new ICTs puts much of the world's population at a disadvantage in the highly competitive global economy.

Another aspect of the ICT and economic globalization debate concerns the impact on the power and authority of the nation-state, a controversy that spans all the issue areas covered in this book. States are now enmeshed in trade, production, and financial networks that reduce their autonomy in domestic and foreign economic policy decisions or, at least, change the costs and benefits of certain policy choices.[8] Interest rates cannot be changed without considering the implications for foreign investment. There are costs to imposing regulatory mechanisms in a world of intense competition. Control over monetary affairs is threatened by the enormous volume of currency exchanged in global markets. States bargain with large, mobile multinational corporations, which distribute wealth and technology and have the advantage of being transnational in character.

To claim that the power of states is eroding, however, would underestimate how much the politics and policies of states still matter. Liberalization policies opened up national borders to trade and investment, and reduced controls over the flow of capital. Governments created the World Trade Organization in which they make decisions to further reduce barriers to trade. Other intergovernmental organizations constrain the decision-making authority of states, but governments decide to join them and agree or disagree with the decisions. Governments still legislate to control who can invest within their borders and on what terms. Multinationals can evade stringent controls by doing business in countries with a more favorable environment, and this flexibility enhances their bargaining power. This does not mean that governments have lost control but that the costs and benefits of control strategies have changed.[9]

Similarly, the context for making foreign policy, conducting diplomacy, and waging war has been transformed by the new ICTs—with contradictory implications for the power of states. In some respects these technologies strengthen the hands of states. Communication with other world leaders is much quicker and easier. More sources of intelligence are available, and sophisticated surveillance capabilities enable governments to monitor the actions and words of people at home and abroad. There are new ways to mobilize domestic support. But faster communication means accelerated decision making, which is further complicated by information overload and a more transparent environment that raises the stakes and magnifies failure. And the same technologies that provide more effective tools of communication and persuasion for governments also empower those who wish to challenge them.

The empowerment of nonstate actors to participate more assertively in world politics has created a new international political environment. The growth in numbers and assertiveness of nonstate actors challenges the exclusive prerogative of states as actors in world politics. Governments continue to control the international agenda and decision making, but new ICTs enhance the capacity of individuals and groups to influence that agenda and those decisions. The Internet in particular facilitates communication and collective action among multitudes of individuals and diverse groups, bridging the local and global levels of action. Governments must contend with domestic groups allied with counterparts in other countries and sometimes with other governments to mobilize public support or diffuse opposition.

The conduct of war itself has been radically changed by the new ICTs, again in contradictory ways. Networks of sensors, satellites, and computer-guided weapons further augment the military superiority of the most technologically advanced states, providing "an omniscient view of the battlefield" and vastly improved command, control, and intelligence capabilities. At the same time, cell phones and the Internet enhance the operational capabilities of insurgents using guerilla tactics and terrorist networks, enabling small groups to plan and coordinate operations over long distances. These transnational networks, thus empowered, challenge the military advantage of states and cannot be confronted effectively by any single state.

Public diplomacy—in peace and war—has become more important even as it has become more difficult in a more competitive media environment. Western news sources no longer have a monopoly on international news. Government leaders, because of their privileged access, can still flood their domestic media and dominate the way that events are interpreted, but appealing to multiple publics with different cultural values is more difficult. And there are alternative sources of information and interpretation from the Internet and satellite and cable television channels. In a world of abundant and diverse information sources, political and military struggles become contests over credibility and the ability to manage the way the situation is represented to multiple publics.

The new information environment clearly affects the state's capacity to control the flow of information across its borders. Even for democratic countries, the abundant sources of information potentially complicate the task of framing events and mobilizing support for policies. For those governments that manage to stay in power in part by controlling the flow of information, the challenge is more serious. In a globalizing economy, connectivity to the Internet is essential for economic growth, which is necessary to maintain political stability. China has thus far managed to extract maximum economic use from the Internet while restricting incoming information that is perceived to be threatening to the social and political order. The cost of this control is extremely high, however, involving an array of technical, legal, and political strategies that make the task of circumventing controls much more difficult.

The new ICTs are also affecting the cultural bonds and loyalties that once seemed to be within the control of the state.[10] They are fueling a dramatic expansion in transnational ethnic networks at a time when the number of foreign born in most of the developed countries is increasing. These networks are created for a variety of purposes. Some seek to mobilize transnational campaigns for political change in the government they have left behind. Most networks are designed mainly to sustain links with the home country and to promote ethnic solidarity in the new country. Ethnically based television channels, the Internet, e-mail, and online newspapers all help to maintain a psychological connection with the country of origin and encourage participation in its political, economic, and social life.

These new media may also be forming political identities that are not linked to any territory, a more direct challenge to the geographically fixed state system.[11] The Internet and satellite television can encourage a sense of solidarity and even identity within a geolinguistic region, consisting of several countries where language and culture are shared. Notably, some scholars claim that these new media are giving coherence and vitality to conceptions of Arab and Muslim identity.[12] Kurdish media have helped to bring coherence to the concept of Kurdish nationhood.[13] What seems to be emerging is a world of more complex loyalties and multilayered identities, posing new challenges for the nation-state.[14]

A more direct challenge to national identities and cultures may come from the flood of media products across national boundaries. The new communication technologies, together with widespread policy shifts toward deregulation and privatization, have created an entirely new global media environment. Western, primarily U.S., media conglomerates now dominate the export markets of the entertainment, news, and information industries. But the combination of technological innovation and policy change has also generated an enormous amount of entrepreneurial activity at the local, national, and regional levels, which the general tendency of audiences to prefer indigenous programming has further encouraged. The net result of these two trends has been a third trend toward various forms of hybrid programming, which adapt Western ideas and formats to local tastes, presumably altering the national culture in the process. But the most important cultural impact may be the spread of an advertising-based "American model" of television, which emphasizes entertainment.

Although the spread of ideas and images enriches human experience, this model makes cultural products merely an economic good, things to be bought and sold.[15]

Who is learning what from whom about what in this international flow of media products? How does this knowledge, attained consciously or unconsciously, shape the attitudes and values of societies and ultimately their relations with each other? The power of the media to bring the distant near and to make the foreign familiar can have both negative and positive consequences in international relations. It can encourage ethnocentricity, stereotypes, prejudices, and fear—and even provoke conflict. But joy and grief can sometimes be shared with strangers in remote places. The new ICTs and the media products they transmit are profoundly affecting the ways in which people and societies perceive each other and the world. The asymmetrical flow of media products from the United States to the rest of the world has concerned scholars and policy makers since the Third World demands in the 1970s for a New World Information Order. This unbalanced flow may be just as detrimental to the United States, which needs to know more about the world it seeks to lead.

In sum, the new communication technologies have not eroded the power of the state, but they have changed significantly the context in which that power is exercised. Economies are more closely linked, changing the costs and benefits of different national policies.[16] Governments still have some control over the flow of information across borders, but the cost—economic and political—is high. National and local cultures persist, albeit in hybrid form. The empowerment of nonstate actors to participate more assertively in world politics has created a new context for foreign policymaking, diplomacy, and war.

The information revolution enhances the ability of ordinary individuals to monitor international events as they occur, as well as the responses of governments to those events. The diversity of sources that are widely available can expose individuals to interpretations of these events other than the "official" ones and thus enable them to exercise their own judgment regarding the most appropriate policies. This abundance of information has the potential for richer public debate. Now that individuals can more easily mobilize support across national boundaries, they can more effectively put issues on national and international agendas and exert pressure for preferred policies. The new media environment is democratizing insofar as it widens public access to information, increases governmental accountability, and encourages political participation. Never before have the tools for communicating and learning been so numerous and so widely dispersed.

One picture of globalization conveys the idea of powerful, impersonal forces—technologies, markets, and states—controlling the fates of individuals and of the new ICTs as enablers of these processes. Contemporary technological optimists, on the other hand, view the new ICTs as a source of individual empowerment. This book argues that inherent in each of these new technologies, as in their antecedents, is a set of distinct characteristics that determine the range of possible effects. The trajectory of each technology is open ended and indeterminate because it is the net effect of choices made by individuals, groups, enterprises, and governments. These choices are, of course, constrained by existing structures of power and wealth, but ultimately they are ours.

Notes

1. Margaret E. Keck and Kathryn Sikkink, *Activists beyond Borders: Advocacy Networks in International Politics* (Ithaca, N.Y.: Cornell University Press, 1998), 213.

2. Victoria Shannon, "A Compromise of Sorts on Internet control," *New York Times*, November 16, 2005, C2; Victoria Shannon, "U.S. Loosens Its Control over Web Address Manager," *New York Times*, September 30, 2006, C4.

3. Jeffrey M. Ayres, "From the Streets to the Internet: The Cyber-Diffusion of Contention," *Annals of the American Academy of Political and Social Science* 566 (November 1999): 132–43.

4. Associated Press, "American Admits Beheading Was a Hoax," *New York Times*, August 8, 2004, 20.

5. National Intelligence Estimate, "Declassified Key Judgments of the National Intelligence Estimate," from "Trends in Global Terrorism: Implications for the United States," April 4, 2006, at www.dni.gov/press_releases/Declassified_NIE_Key _Judgments.pdf (accessed December 1, 2006).

6. Gladys D. Ganley, *The Exploding Political Power of Personal Media* (Norwood, N.J.: Ablex, 1992), 10.

7. Anthony McGrew, "The Logics of Globalization," in *Global Political Economy*, ed. John Ravenhill (New York: Oxford University Press, 2005), 222.

8. David Held, Anthony McGrew, David Goldblatt, and Jonathan Perraton, eds., *Global Transformations: Politics, Economics, and Culture* (Stanford, Calif.: Stanford University Press, 1999), 441.

9. Held et al., *Global Transformations*, 371, 440, 441, 443.

10. Monroe E. Price, *Media and Sovereignty: The Global Information Revolution and Its Challenge to State Power* (Cambridge, Mass.: MIT Press, 2002), 26.

11. Jessica T. Mathews, "Power Shift," *Foreign Affairs* 76, no. 1 (January/February 1997): 62.

12. Marc Lynch, *Voices of the New Arab Public: Iraq, Al-Jazeera, and Middle East Politics Today* (New York: Columbia University Press, 2006), 54.

13. Philip Seib, "Hegemonic No More: Western Media, the Rise of Al-Jazeera, and the Influence of Diverse Voices," *International Studies Review* 7, no. 4 (December 2005): 608.

14. David Held, "Culture and Political Community: National, Global, and Cosmopolitan," in *Conceiving Cosmopolitanism: Theory, Context, and Practice*, ed. Steven Vertovec and Robin Cohen (New York: Oxford University Press, 2002), 54.

15. United Nations Development Programme, *Human Development Report 1999* (New York: Oxford University Press, 1999), 33.

16. The idea that economic globalization has not eroded the state but rather changed the way power is exercised and altered the costs and benefits of policy choices is a theme in Held et al., *Global Transformations*, 371.

Bibliography

Abbate, Janet. *Inventing the Internet*. Cambridge, Mass.: MIT Press, 1999.

Abramson, Albert. "The Invention of Television." In *Television: An International History*, edited by Anthony Smith, 13–34. New York: Oxford University Press, 1995.

Adams, J. M. "Development of the Anglo-Indian Telegraph." *Engineering and Science Education Journal* (August 1997): 140–48.

Adams, Paul C., and Rina Ghose. "India.com: The Construction of a Space Between." *Progress in Human Geography* 27, no. 4 (2003): 415–37.

African Virtual University. "About the AVU," at www.avu.org (accessed September 7, 2007).

Allied Media Corp. "Al Jazeera TV Viewer Demographic," at www.allied-media .com/aljazeera/JAZdemog.html (accessed September 21, 2007).

Alterman, Jon. B. "The Information Revolution and the Middle East." In *The Future Security Environment in the Middle East*, edited by Dan Byman and Nora Bensahel, 224–51. Washington, D.C.: Rand Corporation, 2004.

Amin, Hussein. "'Watching the War' in the Arab World." *Transnational Broadcasting Studies Journal* (Spring/Summer 2003), at www.tbsjournal.com/Archives/Spring03/ amin.html (accessed January 14, 2006).

Ancker, Clinton J., III, and Michael D. Burke. "Asymmetric Warfare." *Military Review* (July–August 2003): 18–22.

Anderson, Benedict. *Imagined Communities: Reflections on the Origins and Spread of Nationalism*. New York: Verso, 1991.

Anderson, Jon. "The Internet and Islam's New Interpreters." In *New Media in the Muslim World: The Emerging Public Sphere*, edited by Dale F. Eickelman and Jon W. Anderson, 41–56. Bloomington: Indiana University Press, 1999.

Andrews, Edmund. "68 Nations Agree to Widen Markets in Communications." *New York Times*, February 16, 1997, A1.

Andrus, D. Calvin. "The Wiki and the Blog: Toward a Complex Adaptive Intelligence Community." September 10, 2005, at http://papers.ssrn.com/sol3/papers.cfm?abstract_id=755904#PaperDownload (accessed June 22, 2007).

Arquilla, John, and David Ronfeldt. *Networks and Netwars: The Future of Terror, Crime, and Militancy*. Santa Monica, Calif.: Rand Corporation, 2001.

Associated Press. "American Admits Beheading Was a Hoax." *New York Times*, August 8, 2004.

Avery, Robert K. *Public Service Broadcasting in a Multichannel Environment*. New York: Longman, 1993.

Ayres, Jeffrey M. "From the Streets to the Internet: The Cyber-Diffusion of Contention." *Annals of the American Academy of Political and Social Science* 566 (November 1999): 132–43.

Balaji, V., K. G. Rajamohan, R. Rajasekara Pandy, and S. Senthilkumaran. "Toward a Knowledge System for Sustainable Food Security: The Information Village Experiment in Pondicherry." In *IT Experience in India: Bridging the Digital Divide*, edited by Kenneth Keniston and Deepak Kumar, 37–47. New Delhi: Sage, 2004.

Bank for International Settlements. *International Banking and Financial Market Developments*. Geneva: BIS, 2003.

———. *75th Annual Report*. Geneva: BIS, 2005.

Bannan, Karen J. "Continental Drift." *Internet World* 7, no. 5 (March 1, 2001): 64–66.

Barboza, David. "The New Power Brokers." *New York Times*, July 7, 2005, C1.

Barnouw, Eric, ed. *International Encyclopedia of Communications*. New York: Oxford University Press, 1989.

BBC News. "Country Profile: North Korea," at http://news.bbc.co.uk/2/hi/asia-pacific/country_profiles/1131421.stm (accessed June 26, 2006).

Bearak, Barry. "Many, Many in India Want to Be a Millionaire." *New York Times*, August 30, 2000, A1.

Becker, Elizabeth. "The American Portrayal of a War of Liberation Is Faltering across the Arab World." *New York Times*, April 5, 2003, B10.

———. "Hearts and Minds: In the War on Terrorism, a Battle to Shape Opinion." *New York Times*, November 11, 2001, A1.

Belson, Ken. "New Undersea Cable Projects Face Some Old Problems." *New York Times*, May 10, 2004, C4.

Benjamin, Daniel. "Changes seen in Al-Qaeda Structure." Interview on Morning Edition, National Public Radio news transcript, November 23, 2005.

Bennett, W. Lance. "Communicating Global Activism: Strengths and Vulnerabilities of Networked Politics." *Information, Communication, and Society* 6, no. 2 (2003): 143–68.

———. "New Media Power and Global Activism." In *Transnational Protest and Global Activism*, edited by Donatella Della Porta and Sidney Tarrow, 203–26. Lanham, Md.: Rowman & Littlefield, 2005.

———. "New Media Power: The Internet and Global Activism." In *Contesting Media Power: Alternative Media in a Networked World*, edited by Nicholas Couldry and J. Curran, 17–37. Lanham, Md.: Rowman & Littlefield, 2003.

———. "The News about Foreign Policy." In *Taken by Storm: The Media, Public Opinion, and U.S. Foreign Policy in the Gulf War*, edited by W. Lance Bennett and David L. Paletz, 12–43. Chicago: University of Chicago Press, 1994.

———. "Social Movements beyond Borders: Understanding Two Eras of Transnational Activism." In *Transnational Protest and Global Activism*, edited by Donatella Della Porta and Sidney Tarrow, 203–26. Lanham, Md.: Rowman & Littlefield, 2005.

———. "Toward a Theory of Press-State Relations in the United States." *Journal of Communication* 40, no. 2 (Spring 1990): 103–25.

Bennett, W. Lance, and Jarol B. Manheim. "Taking the Public by Storm: Information, Cuing, and the Democratic Process in the Gulf Conflict." *Political Communication* 10, no. 4 (October–December 1993): 331–52.

Berkowitz, Bruce. *The New Face of War: How War Will Be Fought in the 21st Century.* New York: Free Press, 2003.

Berwanger, Dietrich. "The Third World." In *Television: An International History*, edited by Anthony Smith, 309–30. New York: Oxford University Press, 1995.

Best, Samuel J., Brian Chmielewski, and Brian S. Krueger. "Selective Exposure to Online Foreign News during the Conflict with Iraq." *Harvard International Journal of Press/Politics* 10, no. 4 (2005): 53–65.

Bob, Clifford. *The Marketing of Rebellion: Insurgents, Media, and International Activism.* New York: Cambridge University Press, 2005.

Boddy, William. "The Beginnings of American Television." In *Television: An International History*, edited by Anthony Smith, 35–61. New York: Oxford University Press, 1995.

Boyd, Douglas. *Broadcasting in the Arab World: A Survey of the Electronic Media in the Middle East.* 2nd ed. Ames: Iowa State University Press, 1993.

Brown, Jeffrey. "Opposing Views on Planting Stories." *NewsHour with Jim Lehrer*, December 12, 2005, at www.pbs.org/newshour/bb/middle_east/july-dec05/media_12-02.html (accessed December 5, 2005).

Brown, Robin. "Information Technology and the Transformation of Diplomacy." *Knowledge, Technology, and Policy* 18, no. 2 (Summer 2004): 14–29.

———. "Spinning the War: Political Communications, Information Operations, and Public Diplomacy in the War on Terrorism." In *War and the Media*, edited by Daya Kishan Thussu and Des Freedman, 87–100. Thousand Oaks, Calif.: Sage, 2003.

Bumiller, Elisabeth. "Even Critics of War Say the White House Spun It with Skill." *New York Times*, April 20, 2003, B14.

Burkhart, Grey E., and Seymour E. Goodman. "The Internet Gains Acceptance in the Persian Gulf." *Communications of the ACM* 41, no. 3 (March 1998): 19–25.

Burkhart, Grey E., Seymour E. Goodman, Arun Mehta, and Larry Press. "The Internet in India: Better Times Ahead?" *Communications of the ACM* 41, no. 11 (November 1998): 21–26.

Bush, George W. "President Says Saddam Hussein Must Leave Iraq within 48 Hours." Office of the Press Secretary, March 17, 2003, at www.whitehouse.gov/news/releases/2003/03/20030317-7.html (accessed January 5, 2006).

———. Transcript. *New York Times*, September 12, 2001, A4.

Carvajal, Doreen. "Sesame Street Goes Global: Let's All Count the Revenue." *New York Times*, December 12, 2005, C8.

Castells, Manuel. *The Rise of the Network Society. The Information Age: Economy, Society, and Culture*. Cambridge, Mass.: Blackwell, 2000.

Central Intelligence Agency. *The World Factbook 2007*, at www.cia.gov/library/publications/the-world-factbook/index.html (accessed July 10, 2007).

Chadwick, Andrew. *Internet Politics: States, Citizens, and New Communication Technologies*. New York: Oxford University Press, 2006.

Chase, Michael, and James Mulvenon. *You've Got Dissent: Chinese Dissident Use of the Internet and Beijing's Counter-Strategies*. Santa Monica, Calif.: Rand Corporation, 2002.

Clancy, Michael. *Sweating the Swoosh: Nike, the Globalization of Sneakers, and the Question of Sweatshop Labor*. Washington, D.C.: Georgetown University, 2000.

Clay, Chandler, Zhang Dan, Eugenia Levenson, and Joan L. Levinstein. "Inside the Great Firewall of China." *Fortune* 153, no. 4 (March 6, 2006): 148–55.

Cohen, Robin. *Global Diasporas: An Introduction*. Seattle: University of Washington Press, 1997.

Cortese, Amy. "Media Talk: U.S. Reaches Out to Younger Readers, in Arabic." *New York Times*, February 17, 2003, C7.

Croucher, Sheila L. *Globalization and Belonging: The Politics of Identity in a Changing World*. Lanham, Md.: Rowman & Littlefield, 2004.

Cybercafes. "Database," at www.cybercafe.com (accessed July 10, 2007).

Dao, James, and Andrew C. Revkin. "A Revolution in Warfare." *New York Times*, April 16, 2002, D1.

Dao, James, and Eric Schmitt. "Hearts and Minds: Pentagon Readies Efforts to Sway Sentiment Abroad." *New York Times*, February 19, 2002, A1.

Defense Science Board Task Force. *Strategic Communication*. Washington, D.C.: Office of Under Secretary of Defense, 2004, at www.acq.osd.mil/dsb/reports/2004-09-Strategic_Communication.pdf (accessed December 5, 2005).

Deibert, Ronald J. "Network Power." In *Global Political Economy*, edited by Richard Stubbs and Geoffrey R. D. Underhill, 198–207. 2nd ed. Toronto: Oxford University Press, 2000.

———. *Parchment, Printing, and Hypermedia: Communication in World Order Transformation*. New York: Columbia University Press, 1997.

de Jong, Wilma, Martin Shaw, and Neil Stammers, eds. *Global Activism, Global Media*. Ann Arbor, Mich.: Pluto Press, 2005.

Dicken, Peter. *Global Shift: Reshaping the Global Economic Map of the 21st Century*. 4th ed. New York: Guilford Press, 2003.

———. *Global Shift: Transforming the World Economy*. 3rd ed. New York: Guilford Press, 1998.

Dizard, Wilson P., Jr. *Meganet: How the Global Communications Network Will Connect Everyone on Earth*. Boulder, Colo.: Westview Press, 1997.

Djerejian, Edward P. "Changing Minds, Winning Peace: A New Strategic Direction for U.S. Diplomacy in the Arab and Muslim World." Report of the Advisory Group on Public Diplomacy for the Arab and Muslim World, submitted to the Committee on Appropriations, U.S. House of Representatives, October 1, 2003.

Doordarshan. "DD India," at www.ddindia.gov.in/About+DD/DD+India (accessed September 10, 2006).

Douglas, Susan J. *Inventing American Broadcasting: 1889–1922*. Baltimore: Johns Hopkins University Press, 1987.

Downey, John, and Graham Murdock. "The Counter-Revolution in Military Affairs: The Globalization of Guerilla Warfare." In *War and the Media*, edited by Daya Kishan Thussu and Des Freedman, 70–86. Thousand Oaks, Calif.: Sage, 2003.

Dudley, Leonard M. *The Word and the Sword: How Techniques of Information and Violence Have Shaped Our World*. Cambridge, Mass.: Blackwell, 1991.

Dugger, Celia W. "Connecting Rural India to the World." *New York Times*, May 28, 2000, A1.

Economist. "All That Jazeera," June 21, 2003.

———. "Anti-Americanism and Television," April 3, 2003, 59.

———. "Behind the Digital Divide," March 12–16, 2005.

———. "Island in the Sun," September 5, 2002.

———. "Murdoch's Twinkler," July 26, 2003.

———. "Outsourcing to India: Back Office to the World," May 5, 2001.

———. "Survey: New Media," April 20, 2006, at www.economist.com/surveys/display story.cfm?story_id=6794172 (accessed June 19, 2007).

———. "Survey of Online Finance," May 20, 2000, 5.

———. "Survey of Telecoms Convergence," October 14, 2006.

———. "Survey of the Internet Society," January 25, 2003, 3.

———. "Survey: Television," April 11, 2002.

———. "A World of Connections: A Special Report on Telecoms," April 28, 2007.

Eedle, Paul. "Terrorism.com." *Guardian*, July 17, 2002, 4(G2).

Eickelman, Dale F. "Communication and Control in the Middle East: Publication and Its Discontents." In *New Media in the Muslim World: The Emerging Public Sphere*, edited by Dale F. Eickelman and Jon W. Anderson, 29–40. Bloomington: Indiana University Press, 1999.

Eickelman, Dale F., and Jon W. Anderson. "Redefining the Muslim Publics." In *New Media in the Muslim World: The Emerging Public Sphere*, edited by Dale F. Eickelman and Jon W. Anderson, 1–18. Bloomington: Indiana University Press, 1999.

Eisenstein, Elizabeth. *The Printing Press as Agent of Change: Communications and Cultural Transformations in Early Modern Europe*. New York: Cambridge University Press, 1979.

Elkins, David. "Globalization, Telecommunication, and Virtual Ethnic Communities." *International Political Science Review* 18, no. 2 (April 1997): 138–52.

El-Nawawy, Mohammed, and A. Iskandar. *Al Jazeera: How the Free Arab News Network Scooped the World and Changed the Middle East*. Boulder, Colo.: Westview Press, 2002.

El-Nawawy, Mohammed, and Leo A. Gher. "Al Jazeera: Bridging the East-West Gap through Public Discourse and Media Diplomacy." *TBS Journal*, no. 10 (Spring/ Summer 2003), at www.tbsjournal.com/ (accessed December 15, 2005).

Encyclopaedia Britannica Online. "Telephone and Telephone System," at www.britannica.com/eb/article-9110260/telephone-and-telephone-system (accessed August 12, 1999).

Entman, Robert. *Projections of Power: Framing News, Public Opinion, and U.S. Foreign Policy*. Chicago: University of Chicago Press, 2004.

Fackler, Martin. "Chasing the iPhone." *New York Times*, July 2, 2007, C1.

Febvre, Lucien, and Henri-Jean Martin. *The Coming of the Book: The Impact of Printing, 1450–1800*. Translated by David Gerard. Atlantic Highlands, N.J.: Humanities Press, 1976.

Finel, Bernard I., and Kristen Lord. *Peace and Conflict in the Age of Transparency*. New York: Palgrave, 2000.

Forbes. "India Software Exports Seen Growing 32 pct in yr to March 2006." September 2, 2006, at www.forbes.com/technology/feeds/afx/2006/02/09/afx2512585.html (accessed July 10, 2007).

French, Howard. "As Chinese Students Go Online, Little Sister Is Watching." *New York Times*, May 9, 2006, 3.

Friedman, Elizabeth J., Kathryn Hochstetler, and Ann Marie Clark. *Sovereignty, Democracy, and Global Civil Society: State-Society Relations at UN World Conferences*. Albany: State University of New York Press, 2005.

Friedman, Thomas L. "Barney and Baghdad." *New York Times*, October 18, 2006, A23.

Galloway, Jonathan F. *The Politics and Technology of Satellite Communications*. Lexington, Mass.: Lexington Books, 1972.

Ganley, Gladys D. *The Exploding Political Power of Personal Media*. Norwood, N.J.: Ablex, 1992.

Ganley, Oswald H., and Gladys D. Ganley. *To Inform or to Control? The New Communications Networks*. 2nd ed. Norwood, N.J.: Ablex, 1989.

Gereffi, Gary. "The Organization of Buyer-Driven Global Commodity Chains." In *Commodity Chains and Global Capitalism*, edited by Gary Gereffi and Miguel Korzeniewicz, chap. 5. Westport, Conn.: Praeger, 1993.

Germaine, Randall. *The International Organization of Credit*. Cambridge, UK: Cambridge University Press, 1997.

Gibney, Frank. "Score One for AOLTW." *Time*, December 25, 2000.

Gillespie, Andrew, and Kevin Robins. "Geographical Inequalities: The Spatial Bias of the New Communications Technologies." *Journal of Communication* 39, no. 3 (Summer 1989): 7–18.

Gilpin, Robert. *Global Political Economy: Understanding the International Economic Order*. Princeton, N.J.: Princeton University Press, 2001.

Global Exchange. "Frequently Asked Questions about Fair Trade Coffee," at www.globalexchange.org/campaigns/fairtrade/coffee/coffeeFAQ.html.pf (accessed July 16, 2006).

Global Information Infrastructure Commission. *Building the Global Information Economy*. Washington, D.C.: Center for Strategic and Information Studies, 1998.

Goldstein, Joshua S., and Jon C. Pevehouse. *International Relations*. 7th ed. New York: Pearson Longman, 2006.

Goodman, S. E., L. I. Press, S. R. Ruth, and A. M. Rutkowski. "The Global Diffusion of the Internet: Patterns and Problems." *Communications of the ACM* 37, no. 8 (August 1994): 27–32.

Gore, Al. Speech to the International Telecommunications Union, Argentina, March 21, 1994.

Gowing, Nik. "Real-Time Television Coverage of Armed Conflicts and Diplomatic Crises: Does It Pressure or Distort Foreign Policy Decisions?" Working Paper 94-1. Cambridge, Mass.: Joan Shorenstein Center on the Press, Politics, and Public Policy, 1994.

Grazia, Victoria de. "The Selling of America, Bush Style." *New York Times*, August 25, 2002, 4(4).

Grieco, Joseph M., and G. John Ikenberry. *State Power and World Markets: The International Political Economy*. New York: W. W. Norton, 2003.

Gunther, Marc. "MTV's Passage to India." *Fortune*, August 9, 2004.

Hachigian, Nina. "China's Cyber-Strategy." *Foreign Affairs* 80, no. 2 (March/April 2001): 118–33.

Hafner, Katie, and Matthew Lyon. *Where Wizards Stay Up Late: The Origins of the Internet*. New York: Simon and Schuster, 1996.

Hale, Julian. *Radio Power: Propaganda and International Broadcasting*. Philadelphia: Temple University Press, 1975.

Hanley, Delinda C. "Al Jazeera English: The Brave New Channel They Don't Want You to See." *Washington Report on Middle East Affairs* 87554917 26, no. 7 (September/October 2007): 24.

Harmon, Amy. "Technology: Improved Tools Turn Journalists into a Quick Strike Force." *New York Times*, March 24, 2003, C1.

Haykel, Bernard. "Changes Seen in Al-Qaeda Structure." Interview on Morning Edition, National Public Radio news transcript, November 23, 2005.

Headrick, Daniel R. *The Invisible Weapon: Telecommunications and International Politics, 1851–1945*. New York: Oxford University Press, 1991.

———. *The Tentacles of Progress: Technology Transfer in the Age of Imperialism, 1850–1940*. New York: Oxford University Press, 1988.

Held, David. "Culture and Political Community: National, Global, and Cosmopolitan." In *Conceiving Cosmopolitanism: Theory, Context, and Practice*, edited by Steven Vertovec and Robin Cohen, 48–58. New York: Oxford University Press, 2002.

Held, David, and Anthony McGrew, eds. *The Global Transformation Reader: An Introduction to the Globalization Debate*. Cambridge, UK: Polity Press, 2000.

Held, David, Anthony McGrew, David Goldblatt, and Jonathan Perraton, eds. *Global Transformations: Politics, Economics, and Culture*. Stanford, Calif.: Stanford University Press, 1999.

Herman, Edward S., and Noam Chomsky. *Manufacturing Consent: The Political Economy of the Mass Media*. New York: Pantheon, 2002.

Heyer, Paul. *Communications and History: Theories of Media, Knowledge, and Civilization*. Westport, Conn.: Greenwood Press, 1988.

Higham, Georgina. "U.S. Programming Losing Its Grip on Europe's Prime-Time Audiences." *Broadcasting and Cable's TV International* 11, no. 6 (March 14, 2003): 1.

Holbrooke, Richard. National Commission on Terrorist Attacks upon the United States. *The 9/11 Commission Report*. New York: W. W. Norton, 2004.

Hoskins, Colin, Stuart McFayden, and Adama Finn. *Global Television and Film*. New York: Oxford University Press, 1998.

Hoynes, William. "Why Media Mergers Matter." *Media Channel*, at www.mediachannel.org/ownership (accessed August 15, 2002).

Hudson, Heather E. *Communication Satellites: Their Development and Impact*. New York: Free Press, 1990.

Hugill, Peter J. *Global Communications since 1844: Geopolitics and Technology*. Baltimore: Johns Hopkins University Press, 1999.

Indian Institute of Management in Ahmedabad. "An Evaluation of Gyandoot," at www1.worldbank.org/publicsector/bnpp/Gyandoot.PDF (accessed October 17, 2005), 27.

Inskeep, Steve. "Changes Seen in al-Qaeda Structure." Morning Edition, National Public Radio, November 23, 2005.

Intelsat. "2000 and Beyond: The Future Is Now," at www.intelsat.com/about-us/history/intelsat-2000s.asp (accessed September 21, 2007).

International Crisis Group. "In Their Own Words: Reading the Iraqi Insurgency." Middle East Report No. 50, February 15, 2006, at www.crisisgroup.org/ (accessed February 2, 2006).

Internet World Stats. "Internet Usage Statistics: The Big Picture," at www.internetworldstats.com/stats.htm (accessed June 30, 2007).

———. "Usage and Population Statistics," at www.internetworldstats.com/stats.htm (accessed July 10, 2007).

Iozzi, David. "The Sustainable Coffee Activist Network," at http://depts.washington.edu/ccce/documents/David Iozzianalysis.pdf (accessed July 16, 2006).

Ishaq, Ashfaq. "On the Global Digital Divide." *Finance and Development* 38, no. 3 (September 2001), at www.imf.org/external/pubs/ft/fandd/2001/09/ishaq.htm (accessed October 9, 2005).

International Telecommunication Union (ITU). "History," at www.itu.int/aboutitu/overview/history.html (accessed July 9, 2007).

———. "ICT Statistics Database," at www.itu.int/ITU-D/icteye/Indicators/Indicators.aspx (accessed June 12, 2007).

———. "Key Global Telecom Indicators for the World Telecommunication Service Sector," at www.itu.int/ITU-D/ict/statistics/at_glance/KeyTelecom99.html (accessed October 15, 2006).

———. *Trends in Telecommunication Reform, 1999*. Geneva: Author, 1999.

———. *World Telecommunication Development Report, 1998*. Geneva: Author, 1998.

———. *World Telecommunication Development Report, 2003: Access Indicators for the Information Society*. Geneva: Author, 2003.

Jervis, Robert. *The Logic of Images in International Relations*. New York: Columbia University Press, 1989.

Johnson, Anna. "Bloggers in Mideast Transforming Political, Social Dialogue but Authorities Hitting Back." Associated Press Financial Wire, February 9, 2007.

Jonsson, Christer. "Diplomatic Signaling in the Television Age." *Harvard International Journal of Press/Politics* 1, no. 3 (Summer 1996): 24–40.

Joshi, Subash. "25 Years of Satellite Broadcasting in India," at www.orbicom.uqam.ca/ (accessed July 7, 2003).

Jouet, Josiane, and Sylvie Coudray. *New Communication Technologies: Research Trends.* Report No. 105. Paris: UNESCO, 1990.

Kalathil, Shanthi, and Taylor C. Boas. *Open Networks, Closed Regimes: The Impact of the Internet on Authoritarian Rule.* Washington, D.C.: Carnegie Endowment for International Peace, 2003.

Kanellos, Michael. "Offshoring: The Reality behind the Politics," at http://news.zdnet .com/2100-9589_22_5766212.html (accessed July 21, 2005).

Kapner, Suzanne. "U.S. TV Shows Losing Potency around the World." *New York Times,* January 2, 2003, 1.

Kazmin, Amy Louise. "Internet Access." *Financial Times,* December 2, 1998, 6.

Keck, Margaret E., and Kathryn Sikkink. *Activists beyond Borders: Advocacy Networks in International Politics.* Ithaca, N.Y.: Cornell University Press, 1998.

Keen, Andrew. *The Cult of the Amateur: How Today's Internet Is Killing Our Culture.* New York: Doubleday, 2007.

Kegley, Charles, with Eugene R. Wittkopf. *World Politics: Trends and Transformation.* 10th ed. Belmont, Calif.: Thomson Wadsworth, 2006.

Keniston, Kenneth. "Grassroots ICT Projects in India: Some Preliminary Hypotheses." 2002, at http://stuff.mit.edu/people/kken/PAPERS/ASCI_Journal_Intro_ASCI _version_.html (accessed October 18, 2005).

———. "IT for the Common Man: Lessons from India." 2002, at http://stuff.mit.edu/ people/kken/PAPERS/IT_for_the_Common_Man.html (accessed October 18, 2005).

Keniston, Kenneth, and Deepak Kumar. "The Four Digital Divides." In *IT Experience in India: Bridging the Digital Divide*, edited by Kenneth Keniston and Deepak Kumar, 11–36. New Delhi: Sage, 2004.

Keohane, Robert O., and Joseph S. Nye. "Globalization: What's New and What's Not? (And So What?)." *Foreign Policy* (Spring 2000): 104–19.

———. "Power and Interdependence in the Information Age." *Foreign Affairs* 77, no. 5 (September/October 1998): 81–94.

Kindleberger, Charles. *Manias, Panics, and Crashes: A History of Financial Crises.* New York: Basic Books, 1988.

Kinzer, Stephen. "The World: The Untold Story: Why They Don't Know Us." *New York Times,* November 11, 2001, 5(4).

Kobrin, Stephen J. "Back to the Future: Neomedievalism and the Postmodern Digital World Economy." *Journal of International Affairs* 51, no. 2 (Spring 1998): 361–86.

Krasner, Stephen D. "Sovereignty." *Foreign Policy* (January/February 2001): 20–29.

Kristof, Nicholas D. "In China It's ******* vs. Netizens." *New York Times,* June 20, 2006, 17.

Kurtz, Howard. "The Post on WMDs: An Inside Story." *Washington Post*, August 12, 2004, A1.

Lairson, Thomas D., and David Skidmore. *International Political Economy*. 3rd ed. Belmont, Calif.: Wadsworth, 2003.

Landler, Mark. "A Glut of Cable TV in India." *New York Times*, March 23, 2001, C1.

Leiner, Barry M., et al. "A Brief History of the Internet." Internet Society, 2000, at www.isoc.org/internet/history/brief.shtml (accessed October 15, 2006).

Levinson, Nanette S., and Anne-Claire Hervy. "Bridging Knowledge Gaps: Communication, Digital Divides, and Development." Paper presented at the annual meeting of the International Studies Association, Portland, Ore., February 26, 2003.

Lichbach, Mark Irving. "Global Order and Local Resistance: Structure, Culture, and Rationality in the Battle of Seattle," at http://depts.washington.edu/wtohist/Research/documents/Lichbach.pdf (accessed July 18, 2006).

Lind, William S. "The Changing Face of War: Into the Fourth Generation." *Marine Corps Gazette* (October 1989): 22–26.

Livingston, Steven. "Diplomacy in the New Information Environment." *Georgetown Journal of International Affairs* (Summer/Fall 2001): 111–16.

Livingston, Steven, and W. Lance Bennett. "Gatekeeping, Indexing, and Live-Event News: Is Technology Altering the Construction of News?" *Political Communication* 20, no. 4 (October–December 2003): 363–80.

Livingston, Steven, and Todd Eachus. "Humanitarian Crises and U.S. Foreign Policy: Somalia and the CNN Effect Reconsidered." *Political Communication* 12, no. 4 (October–December 1995): 413–29.

Lord, Kristen. "War and Peace in the Age of Transparency." *Georgetown Journal of International Affairs* 4, no. 2 (Summer/Fall 2003): 130–34.

Luft, Oliver. "BBC Global News Chief Gets Web 2.0 News via Facebook, not Beeb." *Online Journalism News*, June 5, 2007, at www.journalism.co.uk/news/story3342.shtml (accessed June 22, 2007).

Lynch, Marc. *Voices of the New Arab Public: Iraq, Al-Jazeera, and Middle East Politics Today*. New York: Columbia University Press, 2006.

MacKinnon, Rebecca. "China's Internet: Let a Thousand Filters Bloom." *YaleGlobal Online*, June 28, 2005, at http://yaleglobal.yale.edu/display.article?id=5928 (accessed August 28, 2007).

Marvasti, Akbar, and E. Ray Canterberry, "Cultural and Other Barriers to Motion Pictures Trade." *Economic Inquiry* 43, no. 1 (January 2005): 39–55.

Mathews, Jessica T. "Power Shift." *Foreign Affairs* 76, no. 1 (January/February 1997): 50–66.

Mazarr, Michael. *Global Trends 2005*. London: Palgrave, 1999.

———, ed. *Information Technology and World Politics*. New York: Palgrave/Macmillan, 2002.

McCartney, Scott. *ENIAC: The Triumph and Tragedies of the World's First Computer*. Berkeley, Calif.: Berkeley Publishing Group, 2001.

McGrew, Anthony. "The Logics of Globalization." In *Global Political Economy*, edited by John Ravenhill, 207–34. New York: Oxford University Press, 2005.

McLellan, Hilary. Summary of U.S. Institute of Peace Conference on "Virtual Diplomacy." April 2, 1997, at www.tech-head.com/diplomacy (accessed December 5, 2005).

McLuhan, Marshall. *Understanding Media*. London: Routledge and Kegan Paul, 1964.

McNulty, Timothy J. "Television's Impact on Executive Decisionmaking and Diplomacy." *Fletcher Forum of World Affairs* 17, no. 1 (Winter 1993): 67–84.

McQuail, Denis, and Karen Siune. *Media Policy: Convergence, Concentration, and Commerce*. London: Sage, 1998.

Meislin, Rich. "Blogs 101," at http://nytimes.com/ref/technology/blogs_101.html (accessed June 21, 2007).

Mermin, Jonathan. *Debating War and Peace: Media Coverage of U.S. Intervention in the Post-Vietnam Era*. Princeton, N.J.: Princeton University Press, 1999.

———. "Television News and American Intervention in Somalia: The Myth of a Media-Driven Policy." *Political Science Quarterly* 112, no. 3 (Fall 1997): 386–403.

Merritt, Richard L., and Elizabeth C. Hanson. *Science, Politics, and International Conferences: A Functional Analysis of the Moscow Political Science Congress*. Boulder, Colo.: Lynne Rienner Publishers, 1989.

Mitra, Ananda. "Creating Immigrant Identities in Cybernetic Space: Examples from a Non-Resident Indian Website." *Media, Culture, and Society* 27, no. 3 (2005): 371–90.

———. "Virtual Commonality: Looking for India on the Internet." In *Virtual Culture: Identity and Communication in Cybersociety*, edited by Steven G. Jones, 55–79. Thousand Oaks, Calif.: Sage, 1997.

Morgenthau, Hans J. *Politics among Nations*. 3rd ed. New York: Alfred A. Knopf, 1966.

M. S. Swaminathan Research Foundation. "Measures of Impact of Science and Technology in India: Agriculture and Rural Development," 2007, at www.mssrf.org/studies/measures_impact.pdf (accessed October 3, 2007).

National Intelligence Estimate. "Declassified Key Judgments of the National Intelligence Estimate," from "Trends in Global Terrorism: Implications for the United States," April 4, 2006, at www.dni.gov/press_releases/Declassified_NIE_Key_Judgments.pdf (accessed December 1, 2006).

The National Security Strategy of the United States. September 2002, at www.whitehouse.gov/nsc/nss.pdf (accessed November 25, 2005).

Negroponte, Nicholas. *Being Digital*. New York: Alfred A. Knopf, 1996.

Neuman, Joanna. *Lights, Camera, War: Is Media Technology Driving International Politics?* New York: St. Martin's Press, 1996.

"News Track." *Communications of the ACM* 48, no. 4 (April 2005): 9.

New York Times. "The Times and Iraq," May 26, 2004, A10.

———. World Briefing, May 23, 2007, A8.

Norris, Pippa. *The Digital Divide: Civic Engagement, Information Poverty, and the Internet Worldwide*. New York: Cambridge University Press, 2001.

———. *A Virtuous Circle: Political Communications in Postindustrial Societies*. New York: Cambridge University Press, 2000.

Nye, Joseph S., Jr. *The Paradox of American Power: Why the World's Only Superpower Can't Go It Alone*. New York: Oxford University Press, 2002.

———. "Soft Power." *Foreign Policy*, no. 80 (Fall 1990): 155–74.

Nyiri, J. C. "Cyberspace: A Planetary Network of People and Ideas." *UNESCO Courier* 50 (June 1997): 25–29.

Onishi, Norimitsu. "Roll Over, Godzilla: Korea Rules: Seoul's Pop Culture Takes Asia by Storm." *New York Times*, June 28, 2005, 3.

O'Reilly, Tim. "The Open Source Paradigm Shift." In *Perspectives on Free and Open Source Software*, edited by Joseph Feller, Brian Firzgerald, Scott A. Hissam, and Karim R. Lakhani, 461–81. Cambridge, Mass.: MIT Press, 2007.

———. "What Is Web 2.0: Design Patterns and Business Models for the Next Generation of Software." September 30, 2005, at www.oreillynet.com/pub/a/oreilly/tim/news/2005/09/30/what-is-web-20.html (accessed June 18, 2008).

Owens, Bill. *Lifting the Fog of War*. New York: Farrar, Straus and Giroux, 2000.

Page, David, and William Crawley. *Satellites over South Asia: Broadcasting, Culture, and the Public Interest*. New Delhi: Sage, 2001.

Panos. "Can the Internet Improve Life in Developing Countries?" *Monthly Public Opinion Surveys* 44, no. 2 (November 1998).

PBS *Frontline*. "Is Wal-Mart Good for America?" at www.pbs.org/wgbh/pages/frontline/shows/walmart (accessed August 21, 2005).

PBS *Wide Angle* documentary. "Exclusive to Al-Jazeera," July 10, 2003.

Perlez, Jane. "Satellite TV Tries to Bridge a Culture Gap." *New York Times*, February 9, 2003, 13.

———. "U.S. Courts Network It Once Described as 'All Osama.'" *New York Times*, March 20, 2003, A24.

Pew Research Center for People and the Press. "Global Opinion: The Spread of Anti-Americanism, Trends 2005," January 20, 2005, at http://pewresearch.org/trends (accessed December 4, 2005).

———. "Views of a Changing World, 2003," June 2003, at http://pewglobal.org/reports/pdf/185.pdf (accessed December 4, 2005).

Pool, Ithiel de Sola. *Technologies without Boundaries*. Cambridge, Mass.: Harvard University Press, 1990.

Potter, Evan. "The Role of Advocacy: Mass Media and the New Diplomacy." Paper presented at the International Studies Association Annual Meeting, Portland, Ore., February 26, 2003.

Pratap, Anita. "Challenge or Threat?" *Time*, October 21, 1991.

Price, Monroe E. *Media and Sovereignty: The Global Information Revolution and Its Challenge to State Power*. Cambridge, Mass.: MIT Press, 2002.

Purdum, Todd S. "After the Attacks: The White House." *New York Times*, September 17, 2001, A2.

Rai, Saritha. "Software Success Has India Worried." *New York Times*, February 3, 2003, C7.

Rampal, Kuldip R. "The Collection and Flow of World News." In *Global Journalism: Survey of International Communication*, edited by John C. Merrill, 35–51. 3rd ed. White Plains, N.Y.: Longman, 1995.

Rawnsley, Gary D. *Radio Diplomacy and Propaganda: The BBC and VOA in International Politics, 1956–64.* New York: St. Martin's Press, 1996.

Record, Jeffrey. "Why the Strong Lose." *Parameters* 35, no. 4 (Winter 2005/2006): 16–31.

Reuters. "China Expected to Have 50 Million Bloggers on the Internet by 2007." *Financial Post* (Canada), May 11, 2006.

Rheingold, Howard. *The Virtual Community: Homesteading on the Electronic Frontier.* Revised ed. Cambridge, Mass.: MIT Press, 2000.

Ricks, Thomas E. "A New Way of War." *Washington Post National Weekly Edition*, December 10–16, 2001.

Roberts, Susan. "Fictitious Capital, Fictitious Spaces: The Geography of Offshore Financial Flows." In *Money, Power, and Space*, edited by Nigel Thrift, Stuart Corbridge, and Ron Martin, chap. 5. Oxford: Blackwell, 1994.

Robertson, Roland. *Globalization: Social Theory and Global Culture.* Newbury Park, Calif.: Sage, 1992.

Rohter, Larry. "How Do You Say 'Desperate' in Spanish?" *New York Times*, August 13, 2006, 22.

Romero, Simon. "Shining Future of Fiber Optics Loses Glimmer." *New York Times*, June 18, 2001, A17.

Rosenthal, Elizabeth. "China's Mood: Real Public Rage Stoked by Propaganda Machine." *New York Times*, May 14, 1999, A13.

Rourke, John T. *International Politics on the World Stage.* 10th ed. New York: McGraw-Hill, 2005.

Rumsfeld, Donald H. Speech to Council on Foreign Relations, New York, February 17, 2006, at www.defenselink.mil/speeches/speech.aspx?speechid=27 (accessed March 9, 2006).

Saches, Susan. "Arab Media Portray War as Killing Field." *New York Times*, April 4, 2003, B1.

Sakr, Naomi. *Satellite Realms: Transnational Television, Globalization, and the Middle East.* New York: I. B. Tauris, 2001.

Salamon, Lester M. "The Rise of the Nonprofit Sector." *Foreign Affairs* 73, no. 4 (July/August 1994): 109–14.

Saxby, Stephen. *The Age of Information: The Past Development and Future Significance of Computing and Communications.* London: Macmillan, 1990.

Sayen, John. "4GW—Myth, or the Future of Warfare?" Defense and the National Interest website, at http://d-n-i.net/fcs/sayen_4gw_reply.htm (accessed February 2, 2006).

Schatz, Bruce R., and Joseph B. Hardin. "NCSA Mosaic and the World Wide Web: Global Hypermedia Protocols for the Internet." *Science* 265:895–901.

Schleifer, S. Abdallah. "An Interview with Ali Al-Hedeithy." *Transnational Broadcasting Studies*, no. 9 (Fall/Winter 2002), at www.tbsjournal.com/ (accessed August 5, 2003).

Schlesinger, James. "Quest for a Post-Cold War Foreign Policy." *Foreign Affairs* 72, no. 1 (Winter 1993): 17–28.

Schmitt, Eric. "Military Admits Planting News in Iraq." *New York Times*, December 3, 2005, 11.

———. "Smart Bombs, Dumb Map." *New York Times*, May 16, 1999, 6.

Seib, Philip. "Hegemonic No More: Western Media, the Rise of Al-Jazeera, and the Influence of Diverse Voices." *International Studies Review* 7, no. 4 (December 2005): 601–15.

Shanker, Thom, and Eric Schmitt. "Hearts and Minds: Pentagon Weighs Use of Deception in a Broad Area." *New York Times*, December 13, 2004, A1.

Shannon, Victoria. "A Compromise of Sorts on Internet control." *New York Times*, November 16, 2005, C2.

———. "U.S. Loosens Its Control over Web Address Manager." *New York Times*, September 30, 2006, C4.

Shie, Tamara Renee. "The Tangled Web: Does the Internet Offer Promise or Peril for the Chinese Communist Party?" *Journal of Contemporary China* 13, no. 4 (August 2004): 523–40.

Sigal, Leon. *Reporters and Officials: The Organization and Politics of Newsgathering.* Lexington, Mass.: D. C. Heath, 1973.

Silicon Valley Indian Professionals Association. "About," at www.sipa.org/about.php (accessed July 30, 2006).

Sims, Calvin. "New Atlantic Cable Makes More Calls Possible." *New York Times*, December 14, 1988, A1.

Sinclair, John. "Mexico, Brazil, and the Latin World." In *New Patterns in Global Television: Peripheral Vision*, edited by John Sinclair, Elizabeth Jacka, and Stuart Cunningham, 33–66. New York: Oxford University Press, 1995.

Sinclair, John, Elizabeth Jacka, and Stuart Cunningham, eds. *New Patterns in Global Television: Peripheral Vision.* New York: Oxford University Press, 1995.

Singh, J. P. "Introduction: Information Technologies and the Changing Scope of Global Power and Governance." In *Information Technologies and Global Politics: The Changing Scope of Power and Governance*, edited by James N. Rosenau and J. P. Singh, 1–38. Albany: State University of New York Press, 2002.

Singhal, Arvind, and Everett M. Rogers. *India's Information Revolution.* Newbury Park, Calif.: Sage, 1989.

Smith, Anthony, ed. *Television: An International History.* New York: Oxford University Press, 1995.

———. "Television: A Public Service Medium." In *Television: An International History*, edited by Anthony Smith, 62–91. New York: Oxford University Press, 1995.

Smith, Gordon. "The Challenge of Virtual Diplomacy." Speech at the U.S. Institute of Peace Conference on "Virtual Diplomacy," April 2, 1997, at www.usip.org/virtual diplomacy/publications/vdpresents.html (accessed December 5, 2005).

Smith, Peter J., and Elizabeth Smythe. "Globalization, Citizenship, and Information Technology: The Multilateral Agreement on Investment (MAI) Meets the Internet." In *Culture and Politics in the Information Age: A New Politics?* edited by Frank Webster, 183–206. London: Routledge, 2001.

Sood, Aditya Dev. "How to Wire Rural India: A Survey of the Problems and Possibilities of Digital Development." Center for Knowledge Societies, Bangalore, India, at www.cks.in/html/cks_pdfs/how_to_wire_rural_india.pdf (accessed October 20, 2005).

Sreberny-Mohammadi, Annabelle. "The Global and the Local in International Communications." In *Mass Media in Society*, edited by James Curran and Michael Gurevitch, 177–203. New York: Arnold, 1996.

Standage, Tom. *The Victorian Internet*. New York: Walker and Company, 1998.

Strobel, Warren P. *Late-Breaking Foreign Policy: The News Media's Influence on Peace Operations*. Washington, D.C.: U.S. Institute of Peace Press, 1997.

Tarrow, Sidney. *The New Transnational Activism*. New York: Cambridge University Press, 2005.

Technology Review. "Lessons e-Learned: We Have the Technology to Reinvent Teaching, Says MIT's Distance-Learning Guru, but Do We Have the Will?" July 31, 2001, at www.technologyreview.com/articles/01/07/wo_leo073101.asp (accessed October 22, 2005).

Technorati. "The State of the Live Web." April 2007, at http://technorati.com/weblog/2007/04/328.html (accessed September 30, 2007).

Telegeography 2002: Global Traffic Statistics and Summary. Executive summary online, at www. telegeography.com/ (accessed October 14, 2004).

Thomas, Timothy. "Al Qaeda and the Internet: The Danger of 'Cyberplanning.'" In *Through Alternative Lens: Current Debates in International Relations*, edited by Daniel J. Kaufman, Jay M. Parker, Patrick V. Howell, and Kimberly Field, 153–61. Boston: McGraw-Hill, 2004.

Thompson, Clive. "Open-Source Spying." *New York Times Magazine*, December 3, 2006, 54.

Thussu, Daya Kishan. *International Communication: Continuity and Change*. London: Arnold, 2000.

Thussu, Daya Kishan, and Des Freedman. "Introduction." In *War and the Media*, edited by Daya Kishan Thussu and Des Freedman, 1–12. Thousand Oaks, Calif.: Sage, 2003.

Truscott, Lucian K. "In This War, News Is a Weapon." *New York Times*, March 25, 2003, A17.

United Nations Charter. "Consultative Status with ESOSOC," at www.un.org/esa/coordination/ngo/about.htm (accessed July 11, 2006).

———. "Principles Governing the Nature of the Consultative Arrangements," at www.un.org/esa/coordination/ngo/Resolution_1996_31/Part_2.htm (accessed July 11, 2006).

United Nations Conference on Trade and Development (UNCTAD). *World Investment Report 1995: Transnational Corporations and Competitiveness*. New York: United Nations, 1995.

———. *World Investment Report 2001: Promoting Linkages*. New York: United Nations, 2001.

———. *World Investment Report 2004: The Shift toward Services*. New York: United Nations, 2004.

United Nations Department of Economic and Social Affairs, Population Division. *International Migration 2002*. New York: United Nations, 2002.

United Nations Development Programme (UNDP). *Human Development Report 1999*. New York: Oxford University Press, 1999.

———. *Human Development Report 2005*, at http://hdr.undp.org/reports/global/2005/pdf/HDR05_complete.pdf, 117 (accessed September 10, 2005).

United Nations Educational, Scientific and Cultural Organization (UNESCO). *International Flows of Selected Cultural Goods and Services, 1994–2003: Defining and Capturing the Flows of Global Cultural Trade*. Montreal: UNESCO Institute for Statistics, 2005.

———. *World Communication Report: The Media and the Challenge of the New Technologies*. Paris: Author, 1997.

United Nations Information and Communication Technologies Task Force. "Digital Diaspora Networks," at http://unicttaskforce.org/stakeholders/ddn.html (accessed July 29, 2006).

van Dijk, Jan A. G. *The Deepening Divide: Inequality in the Information Society*. Thousand Oaks, Calif.: Sage, 2005.

Verhovek, Sam Howe. "Bill Gates Turns Skeptical on Digital Solutions." *New York Times*, November 3, 2000, A18.

Vickers, Rhiannon. "The New Public Diplomacy: Britain and Canada Compared." *British Journal of Politics and International Relations* 6, no. 2 (2004): 182–94.

Wade, Robert Hunter. "Bridging the Digital Divide: New Route to Development or New Form of Dependence." *Global Governance* 8, no. 4 (October–December 2002): 443–67.

Waisbord, Silvio. "McTV: Understanding the Global Popularity of Television Formats." *Television and New Media* 5, no. 4 (November 2004): 359–83.

Waldman, Paul. "Why the Media Don't Call It as They See It." *Washington Post*, September 28, 2003, B4.

Wayland, Sarah. "Ethnonationalist Networks and Transnational Opportunities: The Sri Lankan Tamil Diaspora." *Review of International Studies* 30 (2004): 405–26.

Weimann, Gabriel. *Terror on the Internet*. Washington, D.C.: U.S. Institute of Peace Press, 2006.

———. "www.terror.net: How Modern Terrorism Uses the Internet." Washington, D.C.: U.S. Institute of Peace Press, 2004, at www.usip.org/pubs/specialreports/sr116.pdf (accessed March 7, 2006).

White House Office of Global Communications website, at www.whitehouse.gov/ogc/aboutogc.html (accessed December 1, 2005).

Williams, Bruce A. "The New Media Environment, Internet Chatrooms, and Public Discourse after 9/11." In *War and the Media*, edited by Daya Kishan Thussu and Des Freedman, 176–89. Thousand Oaks, Calif.: Sage, 2003.

Wolfsfeld, Gadi. *Media and Political Conflict: News from the Middle East*. Cambridge, UK: Cambridge University Press, 1997.

Wood, James. *History of International Broadcasting*. London: Peter Peregrinus, 1992.

World Bank. *World Bank Report, 2006: Equity and Development.* Washington, D.C.: World Bank Publications, 2005.

———. *World Development Indicators 2006.* Washington, D.C.: Author, 2006, at http://devdata.worldbank.org/wdi2006/contents/Section2.htm (accessed October 2, 2006).

———. *World Development Report 1998/1999: Knowledge for Development.* Washington, D.C.: Author, 1999.

World Economic Forum. "IT Access for Everyone: Global Benchmarking Study." Geneva, January 2005, at www.weforum.org/pdf/Initiatives/Global_Digital_Inclusion _Benchmarking_Study_Jan05.pdf (accessed October 10, 2005).

"World Film Production/Distribution: Global Production Total Soars as Local Films Gain Market Share." *Screen Digest* 417 (June 2006): 205. InfoTrac OneFile, Thomson Gale, University of Connecticut (accessed August 16, 2006).

World Summit on the Information Society. "Declaration of Principles: Building the Information Society: A Global Challenge in the New Millennium." December 12, 2003, at http://itu.int/wsis/docs/geneva/official/dop.html (accessed September 6, 2007).

World Trade Organization (WTO). "Recent Trends in World Trade." June 11, 2004, at www.wto.org/english/news_e/pres04pr378_e.htm (accessed July 18, 2005).

———. "World Trade 2004: Prospects for 2005." Press release, April 14, 2005, at www.wto.org/english/news_e/pres05_e/pr401_e.htm (accessed September 8, 2005).

———. *World Trade Report 2005.* Geneva: Author, 2005.

Wriston, Walter B. *The Twilight of Sovereignty: How the Information Revolution Is Transforming Our World.* New York: Charles Scribner's Sons, 1992.

Yang, Guobin. "The Internet and Civil Society in China: A Preliminary Assessment." *Journal of Contemporary China* 12, no. 36 (August 2003): 453–75.

Zee Network. Home page, at www.zeetelevision.com/ (accessed September 10, 2006).

Zheng, Yongnian, and Guoguang Wu. "Information Technology, Public Space, and Collective Action in China." *Comparative Political Studies* 38, no. 5 (June 2005): 507–36.

Index

Sesame Street in, 209–10; and
television, 37–38, 72–76
Indian Institute of Science, 151
Indian Institute of Technology, 151
Indian Telegraph Act (1885), 73
India Today (television show), 75
indigenous peoples, 195–97
individuals: and economic globalization,
155; as factor in innovation, 8, 25,
28, 55, 57, 63, 91; ICTs effect on, 2
Indonesia, 37, 82, 115, 150
information, access to, 13, 132, 184,
230, 232
information and communication
technologies (ICTs): contradictory
effects of, 7, 41, 76, 81, 162–63,
173–74, 206, 221–22, 232;
convergence of, 2, 10, 86–87;
governments and, 2–3, 172–73,
183–84, 223–25, 229; individual
lives altered by, 2; influences on, 7,
62–63, 222–23, 223; proliferation of,
1–2; revolution in, 1–3, 13–14,
39–42, 64, 86–91, 221–22, 228; use
and control issues in, 223–27; world
politics and, 3–4
information operations, 118
information technology services,
150–51
instant messaging, 86
Institute for Global Communications,
84
intelligence community, 89
Intelsat. *See* International
Telecommunications Satellite
Organization
Intelsat I satellite, 52
International Campaign for Tibet, 203
International Chamber of Commerce, 24
International Committee to Ban Land
Mines, 111–12
international criminal court, 112
International Crisis Group, 124

International Development Research
Center (Canada), 168
international finance: banking and,
148; currency trading and, 147;
deregulation and, 146–47; floating
exchange rate system and, 146;
growth of, 145, 157; information
environment for, 148–49; market
orientation and, 149–50; oil prices
and, 146; states involved in, 157;
stock trading and, 148; structural
changes in, 147–48; trade
imbalances and, 146; transactions of,
147
International Maritime Satellite
Organization (Inmarsat), 52
International Organization of Space
Communications (Intersputnik), 52
international relations: ICTs and, 3,
229; images and, 100–101; nation-
states and, 229; news availability
and, 99, 131–32; public diplomacy
and, 97; radio and, 27, 31–35;
telegraph and, 19; transnational
satellite networks and, 71. *See also*
foreign policy; public diplomacy
International Telecommunications
Satellite Organization (Intelsat),
51–53, 225
International Telecommunication
Union (ITU), 18, 67
International Telegraph Union (ITU),
18, 28
International Tibet Independence
Movement, 203
Internet, 57–64; access to, 83, 85–86,
163–65, 225–27; advantages of,
82–83; in China, 85–86, 184–89, 212,
230–31; developing countries and, 49;
development of, 57–64; distributive
effects of, 163; domain names on, 226;
and education, 170–72; and fiber-
optic cable, 49; governments and, 63,

About the Author

Elizabeth C. Hanson is professor of political science and director of the India Studies Program at the University of Connecticut. Her publications have covered a wide range of subjects in international relations, including the foreign policy beliefs of American businessmen, national policies with respect to foreign direct investment, the role of conferences in international scientific communication, and the political economy of the Internet. She has served as vice president of the International Studies Association and as chair of the Political Communication Sections of the International Studies Association, the American Political Science Association, and the International Political Science Association. She has been a research fellow at the Joan Shorenstein Center on the Press, Politics, and Public Policy at Harvard University, and she has received two Fulbright Awards to India. She received the 2004 University of Connecticut Alumni Association Excellence in Undergraduate Teaching Award.